A Gendered African Perspective on Christian Social Ethics

A Gendered African Perspective on Christian Social Ethics

Empowering Working Women in Cameroon

Joseph Loïc Mben, S.J.

LEXINGTON BOOKS/FORTRESS ACADEMIC
Lanham • Boulder • New York • London

Published by Lexington Books/Fortress Academic
Lexington Books is an imprint of The Rowman & Littlefield Publishing Group, Inc.
4501 Forbes Boulevard, Suite 200, Lanham, Maryland 20706
www.rowman.com

6 Tinworth Street, London SE11 5AL, United Kingdom

British Library Cataloguing in Publication Information Available

Library of Congress Cataloging-in-Publication Data

ISBN: 978-1-9787-0741-2 (cloth : alk. paper)
ISBN: 978-1-9787-0742-9 (electronic)

♾™ The paper used in this publication meets the minimum requirements of American National Standard for Information Sciences—Permanence of Paper for Printed Library Materials, ANSI/NISO Z39.48-1992.

Contents

Figure and Tables

FIGURE

TABLES

Acknowledgments

I would like to express my gratitude toward Professor Lisa Sowle Cahill, Ph.D., for her many precious assistance throughout the course of writing this project, especially in its conception and redaction stages. I would also like to thank Professors James Keenan, SJ, and Kenneth Himes, O.F.M., for their academic support, mentoring, and corrections.

I am especially grateful to Fr Harvey Eagan, SJ, who painstakingly proofread and reviewed my various papers and all the chapters of this project. I also want to thank my fellow Jesuit Eziokwubundu Amadi, SJ, for patiently proofreading this book and offering many useful insights.

I would like to extend my gratitude to the Society of Jesus—particularly the conference of U.S. Jesuit superiors and my Jesuit superiors—for giving me the opportunity to study and for their financial support.

I have a thought here for my mother, Hélène Mben, for her motherly care and support. Without her dedication, my academic journey would not have been possible. I would also like to acknowledge two fellow Jesuits, Fathers François-Xavier Akono, SJ, and Tang Abomo Paul-Emile, SJ, for their friendship, mutual support, and encouragement. My former parishioners at Abobo in Côte d'Ivoire (West Africa), whose life experiences have inspired part of this project, deserve my heartfelt gratitude. Thank you!

I cannot name everyone here, but I would like to thank my family and friends and my fellow Jesuits for all the support and prayers that have made the completion of this project possible.

Abbreviations and Acronyms

AIC	African Independent/Initiated/Instituted Churches
ANARELA	African Network of Religious Living with AIDS
CA	*Centesimus Annus*
CDF	Congregation for the Doctrine of the Faith
CEDAW	The Convention for the Elimination of all forms of Discrimination Against Women
CST	Catholic Social Teaching
CV	*Caritas in Veritate*
EHAIA	Ecumenical HIV and AIDS Initiative in Africa
GASE	Gendered African Social Ethics
GDP	Gross Domestic Product
HIPC	High Impoverished Poor Country
ILO	the International Labor Organization
IMF	International Monetary Fund
J2K	Jubilee 2000
JiM	*Justitia in Mundo*
LE	*Laborem Exercens*
LG	*Lumen Gentium*
LS	*Laudato Si'*
MWDA	Mbonweh's Women Development Association
NGO	Nongovernmental Organization
NT	New Testament
OA	*Octogesima Adveniens*
PP	*Populorum Progressio*
SRS	*Sollicitudo Rei Socialis*

STF	Socializing the Feminine
UNO	United Nations Organization
WCC	World Council of Churches
WID	Women in Development
WTO	World Trade Organization

General Introduction

Two groups of people have inspired this work. My mother, who singlehandedly raised my siblings and me when my father passed away, personifies the first group. Through her hard work, she took care of our education by ensuring that we attend the best schools in order for us to succeed. I come from a family of strong women who have been able to hold the family together through their leadership and care. The second group consists of the women of Abobo in Côte d'Ivoire, where I served as pastor for three years between 2010 and 2013. I would like to stop on one image: the image of women fetching water at odd hours (10:00 p.m. or 1:00 or 2:00 a.m.) because of the water problem that our parish neighborhood experienced. You could see them carrying big and heavy containers of water on their heads. The water was not primarily meant for themselves, rather for their families. Both groups of women have inspired me to reflect on working women in Africa, especially in my home country, Cameroun.

SCOPE, THESIS, AND ARGUMENT

I want to elaborate a contextual African social ethics that builds on but also addresses the limits of Catholic Social Teaching (CST) and of African liberation theology on work and economics to address the ethics of women's work in Africa from a Christian perspective. In Cameroon and elsewhere, women's work is overexploited and undervalued. I have chosen Cameroon as my case study partly because I am originally from the country and partly because I have a good knowledge of the country. Despite the existence of a rich tradition of CST that upholds workers' rights (*Laborem Exercens*), asserts the right of women to equal pay and rights (*Familiaris Consortio* §§ 22–24), and exalts the contributions of working women (Pope John Paul II's 1995 *Letter to women*), the Catholic Church in Africa has done little, either at the theological or at the practical level, to secure justice for women in the areas of labor and employment.

My thesis is that, to meet this goal, it is necessary to adapt CST to the realities of the African context, introduce a feminist hermeneutic, including the writings of African women theologians; expand their economic analysis with the tools of the social sciences; and propose specific theological, pastoral, and political strategies that can begin to change social attitudes and practices toward women.

I retain the idea shared by CST and feminist theology that human beings are relational and social beings. I subscribe to a liberationist perspective, which emphasizes a preferential option for the marginalized, and a transformative approach. From feminist ethics, I take the denunciation and annunciation discourse, which is well articulated by the following goals: "First, to articulate moral critiques of actions and practices that perpetuate women's subordination; second, to prescribe morally justifiable ways of resisting such actions and practices; and, third, to envision morally desirable alternatives that will promote women's emancipation."[1]

CONTRIBUTION TO WORK IN THE FIELD

I want to bring together fields of thought, namely CST, African theology, and feminist/women's theology, that have not yet been put together in the way I am proposing. I will expand their contributions to meet the need for economic justice for African women that none of these other categories of scholarship have yet accomplished. Concretely, I want to enrich CST with feminist and African theology. I want to open African liberation theology to a gender perspective. Finally, I wish to expand African feminist/women's theology with the use of social sciences.

METHODOLOGY

I will use in the book narratives[2] from my personal experience, social sciences, feminist/women's theology, CST, liberation, and African theology. In the social sciences, I will rely on the works of feminist/female economists, such as Drucilla K. Barker and Susan F. Feiner,[3] and of the African social scientists such as Ayesha Iman, Fatou Sow, and other[4] who look at the way a gender-biased approach of economics and social sciences, in general, affect their analysis of social phenomena. Claude Barbier's study on Cameroonian women[5] and the works of Severin Cecile Abega,[6] Lotsmart Fonjong[7] and others[8] that have looked more recently at the conditions of Cameroonian working women are also explored. Studies and statistics on gender and macroeconomics[9] by the World Bank, the International Labor Organization (ILO), and the National Institute of Statistics of Cameroon are useful materials for this project.

Overall, the social sciences help to clarify the nature and scope of labor and provide the analytical tools to properly assess gender division of labor as well as gender disparities in the workplace. The surveys and data from social sciences provide precious material from which social ethics can glean useful information and insights.

Furthermore, I use African liberation theology from Jean-Marc Ela and Engelbert Mveng, which allows a grounding of the reflection from an African perspective, and highlights the pervasive context of oppression and suffering in Africa.

Female theologians from Africa and beyond offer an alternative vision that highlights the impact and importance of gender in labor and economics. I will rely on works from Christine Hinze,[10] Patricia Lamoureux,[11] Christine Gudorf,[12] Mercy Amba Oduyoye,[13] and Musa Dube.[14] In addition to these, I will make use of many other valuable contributions from female theologians from Africa and non-African origins.[15]

African liberation theology and African female theologians are useful in the sense that they offer, among other things, an African perspective and contextualization of realities. The African perspective is virtually absent from CST, yet it is important because it offers the theological views from the dominated, oppressed, and resilient people. It differs from the dominant discourse of the rich and powerful, which, erroneously, arrogates to itself the prerogative to determine what ought to be called objective and what ought not to be called such and a certain neutrality. African liberation theology puts the plight of the oppressed forward in virtue of the gospel. In this sense, contextualization draws attention to the postcolonial condition of African societies, which signals the historical, unbalanced, and unfair relationships between rich and poor nations. The postcolonial reality affects every African in various dimensions of their lives. To that respect, African female theologians nuance the tendencies of African male theologians to amalgamate and generalize the conditions of all Africans. Obviously, both genders are affected by political and economic oppression, but women suffer differently than men. Moreover, African female theologians are more critical of African social institutions than their male counterparts.

In addition, African liberation theology has different emphases. First, Christian revelation is at the center of its reflection. There is a different use here of revelation compared with that of CST. In CST, revelation provides the grounding and the inspiration as in African liberation theology. However, in CST, revelation includes the tradition, while in African theology, it centers on the Bible with a special focus on Jesus and on the Exodus event. Moreover, African liberation theology also believes that the Word of God is performative and its effects must be felt here and now.

The second emphasis is on the Church's witness. The Church is not immune from criticism, and it is called to live by the values which it proudly proclaims. There are other emphases that are peculiar to African female theologians. First, there is the need for a more comprehensive analysis that integrates gender. Second, one must be attentive to particularities among women, which calls for the following dispositions: avoiding generalization, being more inclusive, and paying attention to those who are left out of the "main" picture.

DEFINITIONS OF THE KEY NOTIONS

Before moving forward, it is vital to define the key notions that will be used in the book, namely, work/labor, empowerment, and African gendered social ethics.

Work/Labor: My understanding of work follows that of the ILO that views work as "all productive activities," even unpaid household services and volunteers as work.[16]

Employment is distinguished from unpaid work as "work for pay or profit."[17] This idea of employment allows the inclusion of informal activities like rural farming in which people contribute to their own family shop or farm without getting a remuneration. My focus is on women from working and poor classes, whether they live in urban or rural areas. Instead of using the traditional division of labor as primary (agriculture), secondary (industrial), and tertiary (services), which ignores reproductive labor, I shall look at Cameroonian working women in reproductive labor and the informal and formal sectors.

Empowerment: It "refers to the expansion in people's ability to make strategic life choices in a context where this ability was previously denied to them."[18] Hence, empowerment assumes a context of disempowerment and is closely associated with the latter. Moreover, empowerment is made of processes of change,[19] which indicates that it takes time to be achieved, and it entails the transformation of society. As I will point out in the following pages, although the word "empowerment" is rarely used by CST, its reality remains the primary concern of CST.

Looking at "gendered African social ethics," I will separate the phrase into three, namely, African, gender, and "social ethics." This social ethics is Christian, and it is particularly grounded within the Catholic tradition although it borrows elements from thinkers from other Christian denominations. By African, I limit my scope to Sub-Saharan Africa.

Gender refers to "the nature of our experience as women and men, female and male, feminine and masculine: the origins and attributions of these categories, and their implications for all aspects of individual and corporate life."[20] In addition, "it is a primary characteristic by which we structure intimate relationships, divide labor, assign social value, and grant privilege."[21] As such, gender is "a fundamental form of social organization."[22] Usually gender is distinguished from sex. While the latter is perceived as natural and biological, the former, gender, is viewed as the social and cultural aspect. Gender is the social construction and organization of sexual difference.[23] Furthermore, a gendered ethics gives peculiar attention to the categories of women and men, male and female in its reflection, and tries to avoid gender amalgamation and gender neutrality.

To understand the term "social ethics," it is necessary, before anything else, to clarify what ethics is about. Simply put, ethics can be understood as "the reflection about rules and norms, virtues and role models that give orientation to human decision."[24] To put it in a more detailed way, ethics is concerned with "the study of moral character (virtue and vice), action (right and wrong), and the ultimate end (good and evil, happiness and unhappiness)."[25] Social ethics, therefore, is a reflection on social laws and institutions "with regard of their being just or unjust."[26] Christian social ethics in particular uses the Bible, Tradition, human sciences, philosophy, and human experience as foundations for its reflection.

In a nutshell, a gendered African social ethics (GASE) in the context of Sub-Saharan Africa is one which takes the social construction and organization of sexual differences into account and which is a reflection on social institutions grounded on the Christian revelation and its implications. The novelty of this framework is to bring together CST, African liberation theology, and African women's theologies under the same roof. In addition, this moral framework does not separate theory from practice.

Overview of the Argument

Part I, which consists of chapters 1–4, reviews the strengths and limits of CST's approach to the empowerment of the working woman. Chapter 1 offers a brief presentation of what CST is and enunciates some of its key themes and principles, namely, human dignity (and human rights), solidarity, common good, and participation. Chapter 2 focuses on post-conciliar magisterial teaching as discussed, in particular, in the encyclicals *Populorum Progressio* (1967) of Pope Paul VI and *Laborem Exercens* (1981) of Pope John Paul II.

With these documents, this chapter explores the themes of integral development and the primacy of human labor over capital. CST does not use the word "empowerment," but, through its holistic approach, addresses the issue in terms of worker justice. This chapter also explores, in a special way, magisterial discourse on women. Chapter 3 explores the contributions of the African Catholic bishops. In their declarations and pastoral letters, these bishops draw attention both to the terrible condition of the African workers and the neocolonial reality that hamper African countries. However, the subject of working women is treated as a side issue. This is true of Cameroonian bishops upon whom I specifically focus at the end of the chapter. Chapter 4 is dedicated to an evaluation of CST on the issue of the empowerment of (working) women. Other issues that this chapter discusses include the use of the Bible as a foundational resource, the dignity of the worker as the defining element of any economic system, the emphasis on the social nature of human beings, the indirect employer's responsibility, the option for the poor, social sin and a certain attention to gender. There are limits in the form and content of CST's argument. In terms of the form, there are the broad definition of labor, the lack of nuance in the interaction between labor and capital and the use of the Bible. In terms of content, the Western and patriarchal views of the role of women and the inadequate vision of development appear as clear limits.

As a response to some of the limits pointed in part I, part II, which consists of chapters 5–7, presents the concrete experience of working women in Africa, especially those from Cameroon. It does so with the help of statistics and social sciences' studies. The second part of the book has three chapters. Chapter 5 offers a feminist criticism against the dominant paradigm of economics used by international institutions, namely, neoclassical economics. The criticism is located at four levels: the fundamental level, the rational economic man/subject level, macroeconomics versus microeconomics level, and the predominance of money level. What emerges is the conviction of the inability of neoclassical economics to give a fair and thorough account of women's work and working women.

Chapter 6 presents the general characteristics of women's work. Women are found in reproductive labor, which is undervalued. In addition, they are victims of occupational segregation whereby they are given or they take on jobs and positions that are less advantageous than those of men. Even in the informal sector, which is characterized by cheap labor, women are found in the most vulnerable positions. To complete the picture, they work in an unfriendly environment, and practices such as customary land tenure law do not work to their advantage. This chapter closes by looking at the limits of the usual solutions (access to paid work, education, legislative change).

Chapter 7 looks at the reality of women's work in Cameroon and focuses on more concrete examples that illustrate how difficult the task of working women is. The case of Cameroon confirms the features seen in the previous chapter. I look at how concretely unpaid reproductive labor plays out in Cameroon in terms of time spent and tasks carried out. I then look at two aspects of informal employment, agriculture through women farmers and non-agricultural jobs with petty traders. I end the chapter with the negative attitudes toward the autonomous woman in an African environment.

Part III presents the theological elements that make up the core of a GASE. This part has chapters 8 and 9. Chapter 8 discusses African liberation theology as general orientation of this social ethics. I use the works of Engelbert Mveng, Jean-Marc Ela, and Amba Oduyoye. These African thinkers offer a theological perspective to the African situation within the context of oppression of Africa. This reading takes into account the cultural, the politico-economic and gender dimension of Africa's oppression. The African liberation theologians Mveng and Ela look at the economic injustice as part of a global structure of the oppression of African people, and consider liberation especially as freedom from the shackles of inhumanity. On her own part, Oduyoye decries the patriarchal character of African societies that make women second-class citizens. The theological images that they promote are those of a liberating God/Jesus Christ who side with the oppressed as well as with the marginalized. For these African authors, the credibility of the Church lies in its capacity to emulate the God of the Bible.

In chapter 9, I present the core elements of the GASE; these are preferential option for the poor (working) women, the disempowerment of working women as social sin and the communal approach to empowerment. The preferential option for the working woman is grounded on faith in a liberating God who sides with the oppressed and the marginalized. It has two aspects, namely, the option of the working woman for herself and her option for others. Moreover, social sin regarding women reveals the social sinful structures that feed and reinforce the marginalization of working women. There are two: kyriarchy and colonialism. Social sin calls for social conversion. The following areas are critical means toward social conversion: the Kingdom of God, breaking the silence, alternative paradigms of economics and labor, and the integration of caring labor into the economy. The communal approach to empowerment has two aspects: intersectionality and the institutional approach. Intersectionality reinforces the insights of social sin by highlighting the multilayered dimension of marginalization in the lives of working women. The notion of intersectionality pays attention to power dynamics and how these coalesce to negatively impact working women. The institutional approach is at the level of social policy engagement where one engages various actors and institutions at the local and global levels. It also points to the necessity of praxis in social ethics. The institutional approach is enlightened and guided by CST's principles such as the common good, subsidiarity, participation, and solidarity.

The fourth part of the book addresses the specific issue of the empowerment of working women and looks at concrete practices destined to result in the desired condition for women. The content of this part of the book is spread over two chapters, 10 and 11. Chapter 10 offers and discusses the notion of empowerment by secular disciplines (social sciences and political philosophy) and by theologians. The understanding of empowerment cannot be dissociated from that of power, and empowerment is only relevant within society. Here, I use Naila Kabeer's understanding of development and Martha Nussbaum's capabilities approach along with biblical theologians and African female theologians. Kabeer and Nussbaum offer an understanding of empowerment that pays attention to power and the way it is distributed in the social arena. Biblical theologians and African female theologians provide alternative understandings of power by looking at Jesus's teachings and actions, and African women's ideas of power.

Chapter 11 looks at four concrete practices that the Church can use to challenge the status quo and foster the empowerment of working women. They are socializing the feminine, the Church's conversion, biblical storytelling, and collaborating with other institutions. Socializing the feminine targets deep-rooted social perceptions and behaviors in order to change people's attitudes toward the so-called feminine jobs. Church's conversion acknowledges that she needs to put her own house to be credible. This means acknowledging its wrongdoings against working women and making concerted efforts to amend its conduct at all levels of ecclesiastical institutions. Biblical storytelling is centered on the working woman, and helps in shaping women's imagination and self-understanding. Finally, the Church needs to partner at the local and global level with other non-ecclesiastical institutions to effect a more sustained and greater change. At the local level, I take the example of Mbonweh Women's Development Association (MWDA), which works to improve the condition of female farmers in rural Cameroon. At the global level, the 2000 Jubilee Campaign for the Cancellation of Debt is used as a template for activism for the course of women workers.

Eventually, GASE should be theoretical and practical. On the theoretical side, it takes the best insights of CST and of social sciences. It adds to these a liberationist orientation and preferential option for the underprivileged and oppressed; it is transformative as it identifies and exposes social sinful structures, and it applies a communal approach with intersectionality and an institutional approach. On the practical side, GASE looks at what and how the Church needs to act to challenge and reconstruct the social frames of reference, change its own ways of treating working women, and collaborate with other groups and structures to effect change. One of the particularities of GASE is that it is not just a task for academics. If the theoretical level of GASE is the prerogative of academics, its practical level demands the involvement of living Christian communities. This framework assumes a collaboration between Christian theologians and local Christian communities. Furthermore, GASE makes it clear that the individual cannot be comprehended outside of social structures, which shape and influence him or her.

The empowerment of working women illustrates well the way how GASE operates. GASE insists that empowerment does not occur outside of a social context. Hence, taking the latter into account is essential to durably transform women's condition. As such, individuals must be empowered, but empowerment is not the issue of an individual; it is rather the task of the whole society. Since power is conceived and distributed within social institutions, empowerment requires a reconceptualization of power, in which mutuality than hierarchy is primed. GASE, furthermore, offers this through its use of biblical theology and social sciences. In the same vein, a thorough appraisal of labor and ways in which society determines its worth is critical for empowerment. The GASE builds on CST and social sciences and takes a liberationist orientation, which allows for a holistic understanding of the person that takes seriously the embodied and historical experience of the working woman as African and as a member of postcolonial African societies. The empowerment of the working woman means the transformation of society through the identification of the specific sinful social structures; the challenge of social ideologies that perpetuate women's marginalization; hearing working women's voices and letting them create their own space; and finally, engaging and changing social institutions and actors involved in labor.

NOTES

1. Jagger quoted in Christine Firer Hinze, *Glass Ceilings and Dirt Floors: Women, Work, and the Global Economy*, 2014 Madeleva Lecture in Spirituality (New York: Paulist Press, 2015), 42.

2. On the use of narratives see, John W. Creswell, *Qualitative Inquiry and Research Design: Choosing among Five Approaches*, 3rd ed. (Los Angeles: SAGE Publications, 2013), 55–84.

3. Drucilla K. Barker and Susan Feiner, *Liberating Economics: Feminist Perspectives on Families, Work, and Globalization* (Ann Arbor: The University of Michigan Press, 2004).

4. Their works are published in the collective book Ayesha Imam et al., eds., *Engendering African Social Sciences*, Codesria Book Series (Dakar, Senegal: Codesria, 1997).

5. J. C. Barbier, ed., *Femmes du Cameroun: mères pacifiques, femmes rebelles*, Hommes et sociétés (Bondy [France]: Paris: Orstom ; Karthala, 1985). Although this

book was published three decades ago, it still contains valuable information on the condition of Cameroonian women today.

6. Séverin Cécile Abéga, *Les violences sexuelles et l'État au Cameroun*, Les terrains du siècle (Paris: Karthala, 2007).

7. Lotsmart N. Fonjong, "Challenges and Coping Strategies of Women Food Crops Entrepreneurs in Fako Division, Cameroon," *Journal of International Women's Studies* 5, no. 5 (2004): 1–17; Lotsmart N. Fonjong, ed., *Issues in Women's Land Rights in Cameroon* (Mankon, Bamenda: Langaa Research & Publishing CIG, 2012); L. Fonjong, Lawrence Fombe, and Irene Sama-Lang, "The Paradox of Gender Discrimination in Land Ownership and Women's Contribution to Poverty Reduction in Anglophone Cameroon," *GeoJournal* 78, no. 3 (June 2013): 575–89, doi:10.1007/s10708-012-9452-z.

8. Ivo Ngome and Dick Foeken, "'My Garden Is a Great Help': Gender and Urban Gardening in Buea, Cameroon," *GeoJournal* 77, no. 1 (February 2012): 103–18, doi:10.1007/s10708-010-9389-z; Stella Nana-Fabu, "An Analysis of the Economic Status of Women in Cameroon," *Journal of International Women's Studies* 8, no. 1 (November 2006): 153–67; Billa Robert Nanche, "Gender Difference and Poverty in the City of Douala," *Journal of International Women's Studies* 15, no. 2 (July 2014): 227–40; Henry Kam Kah, "Husbands in Wives' Shoes: Changing Social Roles in Child Care among Cameroon's Urban Residents," *Africa Development* XXXVII, no. 3 (2012): 101–14.

9. Raj Nallari and Breda Griffith, *Gender and Macroeconomic Policy* (Washington, DC: World Bank, 2011).

10. Hinze, *Glass Ceilings and Dirt Floors*; Christine Firer Hinze, "Bridge Discourse on Wage Justice: Roman Catholic and Feminist Perspectives on the Family Living Wage," in *Feminist Ethics and the Catholic Moral Tradition*, ed. Charles E. Curran, Margaret A. Farley, and Richard A. McCormick, Readings in Moral Theology 9 (New York/Mahwah, NJ: Paulist Press, 1996), 511–40.

11. Patricia A. Lamoureux, "Commentary on *Laborem Exercens* (on Human Work)," in *Modern Catholic Social Teaching, Commentaries & Interpretations*, ed. Kenneth R. Himes O.f.M. et al. (Washington, DC: Georgetown University Press, 2005), 389–414.

12. Christine E. Gudorf, "Encountering the Other: The Modern Papacy on Women," in *Feminist Ethics and the Catholic Moral Tradition*, ed. Charles E. Curran, Margaret A. Farley, and Richard A. McCormick, Readings in Moral Theology, No. 9 (New York/Mahwah, NJ: Paulist Press, 1996), 66–89; Christine E. Gudorf, "Western Religion and the Patriarchal Family," in *Feminist Ethics and the Catholic Moral Tradition*, ed. Charles E. Curran, Margaret A. Farley, and Richard A. McCormick, Readings in Moral Theology, No. 9 (New York/Mahwah, NJ: Paulist Press, 1996), 251–77.

13. Mercy Amba Oduyoye, *Daughters of Anowa: African Women and Patriarchy* (Maryknoll, NY: Orbis Books, 1995); Mercy Amba Oduyoye and Rachel Angogo Kanyoro, eds., *The Will to Arise: Women, Tradition, and the Church in Africa* (Maryknoll: Orbis Books, 1992); Mercy Amba Oduyoye, "Transforming Power: Paradigms from the Novels of Buchi Emecheta," in *Talitha Cum!: Theologies of*

African Women, ed. Nyambura J. Njoroge and Musa W. Dube (Pietermatritzburg: Cluster Publications, 2001), 222–43.

14. Nyambura J. Njoroge and Musa W. Dube Shomanah, eds., *Talitha Cum!: Theologies of African Women* (Pietermaritzburg: Cluster Publications, 2001).

15. I have in mind, Anne Arabome, Teresia Hinga, and Musimbi Kanyoro.

16. United Nations, *The World's Women 2015: Trends and Statistics* (New York: United Nations, Department of Economic and Social Affairs, Statistics Division, 2015), 95.

17. Ibid.

18. Naila Kabeer, "Resources, Agency, Achievements: Reflections on the Measurement of Women's Empowerment," *Institute of Social Studies* 30 (1999): 437.

19. Ibid.

20. Elaine Graham, "Gender," In *An A to Z of Feminist Theology,* ed. Lisa Isherwood and Dorothea McEwan (Sheffield: Sheffield Academic Press, 1996), 78.

21. Laura L. O'Toole, Jessica R. Schiffman, and Margie L. Kiter Edwards, "Preface: Conceptualizing Gender Violence," in *Gender Violence: Interdisciplinary Perspectives*, ed. Laura L. O'Toole, Jessica R. Schiffman, and Margie L. Kiter Edwards, second edition (New York/London: New York University Press, 2007), xii.

22. Graham, "Gender," 79.

23. Barker and Feiner, *Liberating Economics*, 7.

24. Gabriel Ingeborg, "Where Difference Matters: Social Ethics in the Contemporary World," *Journal of Ecumenical Studies* 48, no. 97–106 (Winter 2013): 98.

25. Philip Blosser, "Ethics," In *Encyclopedia of Catholic Social Thought, Social Science, and Social Policy,* ed. Michael L. Coulter et al. (Lanham, MD; Toronto; Plymouth: The Scarecrow Press, 2007), 369.

26. Ingeborg, "Where Difference Matters," 98.

Part I

CATHOLIC SOCIAL TEACHING (CST) AND THE EMPOWERMENT OF THE (FEMALE) WORKER

This part contains four chapters. Chapter 1 offers an overview of CST by outlining its key features and how it addresses the condition of workers in general and of working women in particular. The dignity of the person and the common good are at the heart of the economic system and inform the discourse of CST on labor and workers' empowerment.

Chapter 2 focuses on specific encyclicals since the Second Vatican Council, namely *Populorum Progressio* and *Laborem Exercens*. Pope Paul VI's *Populorum Progressio* (1967) is a turning point in the awareness of both the impact of international/colonial relations at the local level and the need for a global approach, the imbalanced relationships between poor and rich countries, and the growing interconnection and interdependence between peoples generated as a result. It also introduces a theological understanding of development later used by African bishops. Pope John Paul II's *Laborem Exercens* (1981) offers an updated theology of human work that integrates the local into the global picture. It upholds the priority of human labor (the worker) over capital (the means of production).[1] I will briefly look at the ways in which *Octogesima Adveniens* (1971), *Justitia in Mundo* (1971), *Sollicitudo Rei Socialis* (1987), *Centesimus Annus* (1991), and *Caritas in Veritate* (2007) expand *Populorum Progressio* and *Laborem Exercens*.

An important concept in the developing tradition is social or structural sin, a relevant and necessary concept in appreciating how cultural norms, practices, and institutions reinforce the economic exploitation of women. Other papal writings such as *Familiaris Consortio* (1981), *Mulieris Dignitatem* (1988), and the 1995 *Letter to Women*, which address the situation of working women, are also included in the discussion.

In chapter 3, I look at how African and Cameroonian Catholic bishops have addressed the question of worker empowerment, since as Paul VI points out

13

in *Octogesima Adveniens*, the Magisterium cannot put forward solutions to contextual problems that have universal validity.[2] African bishops address the issue of human work usually within the general economic context and, sometimes, as a specific topic.[3] The bishops also routinely denounce poor working conditions, bad working habits, unemployment, underemployment, and the casualization[4] of workers. Except for the sparse mention of work in the social, economic, and political context of the country, Cameroonian bishops have not issued a single pastoral letter on the issue of labor.[5]

Chapter 4 looks at the strengths and limits of CST from the standpoint of African theological ethics and feminist ethics. The noteworthy strengths are its biblical grounding, the emphasis on the dignity of the worker, the social responsibility of the (direct and indirect) employer, the option for the vulnerable, the recognition of social sin, and the attention to the general economic framework.

Among the weaknesses of CST, one can note the inadequate notion of "development" and a Westernized and patriarchal view of the role of women in the family. African bishops, for their part, lament how international terms of trade are conducted at the expense of African countries. However, they fail to go beyond this criticism and do not question the international economic system inherited from colonization that makes African countries a stock of raw materials for industrialized nations. In addition, although African bishops show a genuine concern for gender-related issues, they rarely offer a thorough reflection on gender and work, and concrete solutions.

NOTES

1. John Paul II, *On Human Work, Encyclical* Laborem Exercens (Rome: Libreria Editrice Vaticana, 1981), 12, http://w2.vatican.va/content/john-paul-ii/en/encyclicals/documents/hf_jp-ii_enc_14091981_laborem-exercens.html.

2. Paul VI, *On the Occasion of the Eightieth Anniversary of the Encyclical "Rerum Novarum" Apostolic Letter* Octogesima Adveniens (Libreria Editrice Vaticana, 1971), 4, http://w2.vatican.va/content/paul-vi/en/apost_letters/documents/hf_p-vi_apl_1971 0514_octogesima-adveniens.html.

3. This is particularly the case of the bishops of North Africa, Senegal, Nigeria, and South Africa; see Maurice Cheza, Henri Derroitte, and René Luneau, eds, *Les évêques d'Afrique parlent, 1969–1991: documents pour le Synode africain*, Les Dossiers de la Documentation Catholique (Paris: Centurion, 1992), 311–18, 341–42, 348–54, 386–95. The bishops of North Africa (Algeria especially) are mostly Europeans who address the reality of work in their country of ministry in one document, and are mostly concerned with the condition of migrant workers in France.

4. Casualization refers to the growing precariousness of modern workers; the dictionary of my Apple computer defines it as "the transformation of a workforce from

one employed chiefly on permanent contracts to one engaged in a short-term tempo-rary basis." In some quarters, the neologism for this situation is a new class called the precariat, see Guy Standing, *The Precariat: The New Dangerous Class* (London; New York, NY: Bloomsbury, 2014).

    5. Conférence Episcopale du Cameroun, ed., *L'enseignement social des évêques du Cameroun 1955–2005: lettres pastorales et messages, communiqués et déclara-tions, approche analytique* (Yaoundé: AMA-CENC, 2005), 149–69, 199–204.

Chapter 1

An Overview of Catholic Social Teaching

Catholic social teaching (CST) refers to a vast body of literature produced by popes, bishops, and other Church leaders that addresses social issues and challenges from a Christian faith perspective. CST seeks to offer ways in which Catholics and other people of goodwill should tackle those challenges by laying down principles rooted or compatible with the Christian tradition that should inform social practice and way of life.

The encyclical letter *Rerum Novarum* (1891) by Pope Leo XIII marks the official birth of modern CST, although it was preceded by a century of development in Catholic social thoughts.[1] Since 1891, thirteen magisterial documents (eleven from papal sources, one conciliar constitution, and one post-synodal document from the Synod of Bishops) have been published and constitute the core of CST.[2] As Peter J. Henriot and others observe, "the body of Catholic social teaching is by no means a fixed set of tightly developed doctrine. Rather, it is a collection of key themes which has evolved in response to the challenges of the day."[3] In fact, "rooted in biblical orientations and reflections on Christian tradition, the social teaching shows a lively evolution marked by shifts both in *attitude* and *methodology*."[4] CST is inherently dynamic; however, "while new times surely call for creative solutions that adjust to changing realities, there is also a set of core principles regarding social justice and moral obligations that should shape human activity in every age."[5] This underscores the fact that within the apparent discontinuity between documents, there is evidence of continuity, which is displayed by the tendency of the popes to refer to the work of their predecessors, even when their thought goes beyond.

Two of the most essential concepts of CST are the dignity of the person and the common good, as is captured in the title of the classic work of Jacques Maritain, *The Person and the Common Good*.[6] The person and the community are interdependent. As John Coleman expresses this relationship, "The dignity of persons can be realized only in community, and genuine community, in its turn, can only exist where the substantial freedom and the dignity of the human person are secured."[7] Although the realization of freedom and dignity in community will and should take different forms in different contexts,[8] there are some basic values and principles that have validity across cultures. These can be formulated differently, but Thomas Massaro identifies nine key themes in a representative way. These are: (1) dignity of every person and human rights; (2) solidarity, common good, and participation; (3) family life; (4) subsidiarity and the proper role of government; (5) property ownership in modern society; (6) dignity of work, rights of workers, and support for labor unions; (7) colonialism and economic development; (8) peace and disarmament; and (9) option for the poor and vulnerable.[9] For the sake of concision and space, I will only address the first two themes in this subsection that are central to CST. The themes relevant to the question of labor and workers are treated in subsequent sections. Other themes such as peace and disarmament are left out because they are not immediately relevant to the objective of this book.

HUMAN DIGNITY AND HUMAN RIGHTS

The well-being of the human person is at the heart of CST. In the Christian tradition, human dignity, that is, the inestimable worth of the human person, is rooted as *imago Dei* in the first creation story (Gen 1:26): "Then God said: 'let us make man in our image, after our likeness' . . . God created man in his image; in the divine image he created him; male and female he created them." For centuries, Jewish and Christian thinkers have tried to grasp what is precisely the image of God in human beings, and such a debate is beyond the scope of the present book. However, I will try to engage the social implications of the *imago Dei*. *Imago Dei* speaks of a special status of human beings within God's creation. There are two main understanding of the *imago Dei*, namely, ontological and relational.[10] The ontological version emphasizes human capacities and natural powers such as reason and free will, and the fact of developing one's natural abilities to achieve one's full potential. The relational trend insists on the fact that the *imago Dei* comes as a result of humans being invited into a relationship with God. Indeed, "the meaning and value of human life does not depend on our capacities to function . . . but on the belief that the divine image reflects the relationship with God."[11] In this perspective, the life of the Trinity and the person of Christ mirror what the image of God looks like. What is particular to humans is "their capacity for subject-subject relationships."[12] In that respect, the "Trinity provides insights not only for understanding the human person but from which to engage in social critique of communities of persons."[13]

This special status entails a particular anthropology that sets human beings apart from the rest of creation and demands that they should be treated in a certain way. For instance, the shedding of human blood is prohibited because human beings are made according to God's image (Gen 9:6).[14] God's commandments that demand respect of other's property, of one's parents, of the poor, and of those who are socially disadvantaged, are some of the implicit implications of the *imago Dei* (see Ex 34; Lv 19). As a consequence of being God's image, human beings ought to be treated with respect no matter what they do. In fact, "there is nothing a person can do or undergo to forfeit this lofty status."[15] If one can lose God's grace, one cannot lose his/her human character. Inspired by the biblical tradition, CST affirms the sanctity of human life from natural conception to the very moment of natural death, and denounces the various threats and abuses against it (capital punishment, abortion, euthanasia, slavery, sex trafficking, and exploitation).[16] In harmony with the ontological interpretation of *imago Dei*, CST singles out human conscience and freedom as signs and conditions of human dignity.[17] Recent evolution of CST integrates the nonhuman world in the opposition to threats to life. This comes as a result of the growing awareness of the interdependence of all forms of life, and also the recognition of the intrinsic value of nonhuman creation. Human beings thrive within creation not outside of it, and they are a part of creation not apart from it. As creatures, human beings cannot sustain themselves without the rest of creation. And as the ecological crisis suffered in parts of Africa illustrates, threats against the environment are threats against life, especially human life.

Since the encyclical *Pacem in Terris* (1963) of Pope John XXIII, the language of human rights has entered CST and serves to articulate the concept of human dignity to a broader audience. However, the Catholic version of human rights offers some nuances.[18] First, it is centered on God, and views God as the ultimate source of rights. Second, rights are always located within actual and existing human societies. Third, rights are always linked with corresponding obligations.

The human rights language, which originates from the Western liberal and democratic tradition, pairs, in a particular way, human dignity and equality. Dignity and equality carry different emphasis and are not synonymous. Dignity basically refers to status and may be attributed of persons or institutions.[19] Human dignity "is connected, variously, to ideas of sanctity, autonomy, personhood, flourishing, and self-respect."[20] Dignity does not necessarily imply that persons must be treated equally, since it might be argued that, although all human beings have dignity, their status and treatment differ according to age, gender, race, ethnicity, and social class. Equality originally refers to standards, and touches on relationships. In particular, equality implies that all human beings should be treated equally in regard to basic needs and opportunities. Dignity carries with it the idea of propriety and respect, while equality refers to what is right and is concerned with justice.

Although human dignity carries different meanings in various contexts, there are three basic elements that are always attached to it: the ontological (intrinsic worth of the human person), relational (recognition and respect of that intrinsic worth by others), and the limits to the claims of the state (the state at the service of the individual).[21] The first two basic elements are similar to the ontological and relational understanding of the *imago Dei*—if one removes any reference to God or religion. And the last element reminds one of Pius XI's principle of subsidiarity and Maritain's distinction between the body politic and the state.[22] In the Catholic perspective, human dignity comes from God, and it entails basic equality that has to be recognized and upheld at the social level by the political community prior to any social convention.

There are many types of equality, but for the sake of my argument I will only consider the social dimension of equality within the idea of "complex equality."[23] Following John Baker and others, I only consider three aspects: basic equality, liberal egalitarian equality, and equality of condition. According to Baker, "Basic equality is the idea that every human being deserves some basic minimum of concern and respect, placing at least some limits on what it is to treat someone as human being."[24] The minimum standard expectations include the respect of the physical integrity of a person, prohibition of inhuman and degrading treatment, and the fulfillment of some basic needs.

Liberal egalitarianism builds on basic equality and moves beyond it.[25] It acknowledges the existence of social inequalities, and uses the idea of equality "to provide a fair basis for managing these inequalities, by strengthening the minimum to which everyone is entitled and by using equality of opportunity to regulate the competition for advantage."[26] Liberal equality emphasizes individual choices over structures. A qualification from CST, one important in the global South, is that individual identity and choice can exist only within social relationships and structures, and interdependent with "the common good."

Equality of condition aims at eliminating "major inequalities, or at least massively reduce the current scale of inequality."[27] The latter is essentially rooted in social structures that can be changed and transformed. This point introduces the social nature of the person so key to CST. Capitalism, patriarchy, racism, and other structures of oppression perpetuate the cycle of inequality. Moreover, "equality of condition is about opportunities . . . about enabling and empowering people to exercise what might be called real choices among real options."[28]

I do not affirm without qualification the modern Western (North Atlantic) concept of political liberalism as centered on individual freedom and choice. Perhaps a better term or approach, and one that is more consistent with CST, especially from a global perspective, is "communitarian liberalism."[29] However, with liberalism, I do affirm the empowerment of all, that is, that all have "real options" that further individual and social well-being. We may consider five dimensions: (1) recognition and respect, (2) resources, (3) love, care, and solidarity, (4) power, and (5) working and learning.[30] All these key dimensions are closely intertwined. For instance, imbalances in working and learning affect the access to resources, which, in turn, play negatively on recognition and power. David Hollenbach reminds us that individual moral claims, sometimes termed "human rights," are claims of persons "to be treated, by virtue of their humanity, as participants in the shared life of the community." Thus, "the protection of human rights is part of the common good, not an individualistic alternative to the common good."[31]

The language of human rights gives substance to the notions of dignity and equality in contemporary discourse. Indeed, "human rights give specificity to the language of human dignity; they articulate the freedoms, the goods, and the relationships that are expressive of a person's dignity."[32] Article I of the Universal Declaration of Human Rights (1948) clearly states that "all human beings are born free and equal in dignity and rights."[33] In contemporary discourse, human dignity affirms that all persons are equal. Equality is based on the assumption of the worth of every human being, and the aspiration to equality is one of the two forms of the person's dignity and freedom.[34] "When [CST] calls for a more equal sharing and political power, social status, and economic resources, it is merely extending the Christian theological doctrine of equal human dignity to the concrete realm of social existence."[35] Dignity and equality bear many similarities. Both dignity and equality are relational notions. They can be used at the individual as well as the collective level. In CST, equal dignity gives more substance to other themes (subsidiarity, solidarity, participation, and the common good).

The "equal in dignity" phrase gains traction in magisterial teaching particularly in gender-related issues. *Gaudium et Spes* 49 asserts "the equal personal dignity of wife and husband."[36] Subsequent magisterial documents will repeat this point. *Mulieris Dignitatem* takes a more general perspective, which includes other dimensions than marriage. In virtue of creation and redemption, men and women are human beings to an "equal degree," and there is an "essential" or "fundamental" equality between the two.[37] The *Letter to Women* acknowledges the necessity to achieve concrete equality for women in every area, especially in labor and in marriage/family life.[38] This document reminds that the equality between husband and wife is not static or undifferentiated, although John Paul II does not elaborate on this last aspect.[39]

The pervasive existence of social inequalities illustrates the gap between the proclamation of principles and their actual realization. This explains why Pope Francis laments women's lack of equal access to dignified work and role of decision-making.[40]

SOLIDARITY, COMMON GOOD AND PARTICIPATION

Solidarity

The second theme is based on the assumption of the social nature of human beings. Since the human person is CST's primary concern, it comes as no surprise that the human community receives critical attention. Solidarity is grounded in the conviction of the interconnection and interdependence of human beings. Solidarity, Pope John Paul writes,

> is not a feeling of vague compassion or shallow distress at the misfortunes of so many people, both near and far. On the contrary, it is a firm and persevering determination to commit oneself to the common good; that is to say to the good of all and of each individual, because we are all really responsible for all.[41]

Pope Francis suggests that "solidarity is a spontaneous reaction by those who recognize that the social function of property and the universal destination of goods are realities which come before private property."[42] Following Pope Benedict XVI, he emphasizes that solidarity needs to be closely linked to subsidiarity, because subsidiarity without solidarity becomes "social privatism," and solidarity without subsidiarity turns into "paternalistic social assistance."[43] He explains that subsidiarity

> is first and foremost a form of assistance to the human person via the autonomy of intermediate bodies. Such assistance is offered when individuals or groups are unable to accomplish something on their own, and it is always designed to achieve their emancipation, because it fosters freedom and participation through assumption of responsibility. Subsidiarity respects personal dignity by recognizing in the person a subject who is always capable of giving something to others.[44]

Participation

The aspiration to participation is one of the two forms of the person's dignity and freedom according to Paul VI.[45] Participation is the practical application of the principle of the equal dignity of human beings.

Every person has at once a right and a duty to participate in the full range of activities and institutions of social life. To be excluded from playing a significant role in the life of society is a serious injustice, for it frustrates the legitimate aspirations of all people to express their human freedom.[46]

This means that "anything that blocks full political participation . . . or economic participation . . . counts as a serious offense against human rights."[47] Participation in the common good strengthens the individual's freedom, and it is closely associated with personal agency.[48] Participation in that instance is the result of subsidiarity, which "fosters freedom and participation through the assumption of responsibility."[49] Since Benedict XVI, there is the addition of the adjective "active" to participation,[50] which calls for the effective inclusion of all actors, especially the more disadvantaged.[51] The active participation of the poor and marginalized becomes the criteria through which initiatives are assessed.[52]

Moreover, participation is at the service of the common good.[53] It is closely linked to solidarity as its ultimate goal.[54] Participation in CST has evolved from being exclusively political to a more holistic notion that encompasses the social and economic realms.

Since 1971, participation has become a key concept in CST with the recognition that with equality it is one of the fundamental aspirations of people today. Participation seeks to promote a democratic society, which appears as the contemporary political paradigm.[55] Likewise, "the free and responsible participation of all citizens" is a sign of the good health of a political community.[56] Hence, "the creation of structures of participation and shared responsibility" foster the growth of the individual as well as the community.[57] The possibility of democratic participation in social life is one of the elements that prevent work from becoming a mere commodity and guaranty its dignity.[58] Participation applies to individuals as well as groups. As Meghan Clark asserts "participation in Catholic social thought offers a necessary critique of global structures that fail to have a strong determinative voice for developing peoples."[59] Participation is also regularly associated with responsibility, and in that respect a wider participation is encouraged.[60] As Kenneth Himes opines:

> Economic participation means contributing to the material well-being of oneself and others and sharing in the benefits of economic prosperity. Social participation indicates that decision making cannot be in the hands of elites who act for the masses but the grassroots must have a say in determining the process and goals of a nation's development.[61]

The "active contribution to the common good of humanity" is anterior to the logic of market and is a fundamental social need of a person.[62] Hence, the participation of the subjective dimension of labor (the worker) in the whole process of production should be effective.[63] Trade unions and various workers' organizations in their defense and protection of workers' rights help them "participate more fully and more honorably in the life of their nations."[64] A business is primarily a society of persons—not an impersonal entity—"in which people participate in different ways and with specific responsibilities."[65] Furthermore, participation concerns everyone and as such it precludes discrimination. The disabled must be allowed to participate fully in social life "in all its aspects and at the levels accessible to their capacities."[66] In addition, denying the disabled the possibility of working is "unworthy" of humanity and a denial of "our common humanity."[67] Through his/her work, the person participates in God's creative work.[68]

Participation is expressed in terms of employee participation or involvement within the context of an enterprise. Employee participation is concerned with sharing the fruits/products of labor, the incorporation of workers at the level of decision and in the administration of the enterprise, and the ownership rights of the means of production.[69] Employee participation recognizes the worker as a person with dignity capable of growth and responsible.[70] In this perspective, the corporation is like a laboring community, "where the employers still have obligations to the employees other than those which merely flow forth from a labor contract."[71] One reservation against employee

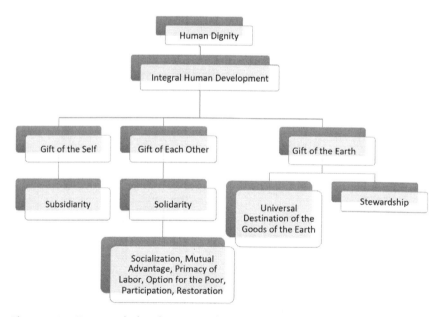

Figure 1.1. Framework for the Economic Common Good. *Source*: Albino Barrera (2010).

participation would be the narrowness of its scope, which does not integrate the perspective of self-employment that characterizes the vast majority of workers in the developing world.

The Common Good

The common good is "the sum total of those conditions of social living whereby [human beings] are enabled more fully and more readily to achieve their own perfections."[72]Albino Barrera has explicated the notion of common good that he addresses from an economic perspective. He suggests the framework displayed in figure 1.1 for the economic common good.[73]

This framework shows that the common good is a comprehensive notion that encompasses all the other notions such as human dignity, participation, and solidarity. In CST, the government or the state is "the privileged agent of the common good."[74] However, the state's action is analyzed on the basis of subsidiarity and the promotion of basic human rights.

NOTES

1. Thomas Massaro, *Living Justice: Catholic Social Teaching in Action*, Third Classroom Edition (Lanham: Rowman & Littlefield, 2015), 45–48.

2. The eleven documents from papal sources are *Rerum Novarum* (1891), *Quadragesimo Anno* (1931), *Mater et Magistra* (1961), *Pacem in Terris* (1963), *Populorum Progressio* (1967), *Octogesima adveniens* (1971), *Laborem Exercens* (1981), *Sollicitudo Rei Socialis* (1987), *Centesimus Annus* (1991), *Caritas in Veritate* (2009), and *Laudato Si!* (2015). *Gaudium et Spes* (1965) is the conciliar constitution and *Justitia in Mundo* (1971) is the statement by the bishops.

3. Peter J. Henriot, Edward P. DeBerri, and Michael J. Schultheis, *Catholic Social Teaching: Our Best Kept Secret*, Centenary ed. (Maryknoll, NY; Washington, DC: Orbis Books; Center of Concern, 1992), 17.

4. Ibid.

5. Massaro, *Living Justice*, 50.

6. Jacques Maritain, *The Person and the Common Good*, trans. John J. Fitzgerald (New York: Charles Scribner's Sons, 1947).

7. John A. Coleman S.J., "The Future of Catholic Social Thought," in *Modern Catholic Social Teaching: Commentaries & Interpretations*, ed. Kenneth R. Himes O.f.M. et al. (Washington, DC: Georgetown University Press, 2005), 522; Brian Stiltner, *Religion and the Common Good: Catholic Contributions to Building Community in a Liberal Society* (Lanham, MD: Rowman & Littlefield, 1999).

8. For an African perspective on the Western origins of CST and the need for global adaptations of its central expressions, see David Kaulemu, "Building Solidarity for Social Transformation through the Church's Social Teaching," in *Catholic Social Teaching in Global Perspective*, ed. Daniel McDonald, Gregorian

University Studies in Catholic Social Teaching (Maryknoll, NY: Orbis Books, 2010), 36–80; David Kaulemu, "The African Synod for Those of Us Who Stayed at Home," in *Reconciliation, Justice, and Peace: The Second African Synod*, ed. Agbonkhianmeghe E. Orobator (Maryknoll, NY: Orbis Books, 2011), 143–54.

9. Massaro, *Living Justice*, 83; For further discussion of the content and future of Catholic social teaching, see Jonathan Boswell, Francis P. McHugh, and Johan Verstraeten, eds., *Catholic Social Thought: Twilight or Renaissance?* Bibliotheca Ephemeridum Theologicarum Lovaniensium 157 (Leuven: University Press : Uitgeverij Peeters, 2000); Daniel McDonald, ed., *Catholic Social Teaching in Global Perspective*, Gregorian University Studies in Catholic Social Teaching (Maryknoll, NY: Orbis Books, 2010).

10. Johannes S. Reinders, "*Imago Dei* as a Basic Concept in Christian Ethics," in *Holy Scriptures in Judaism, Christianity and Islam: Hermeneutics, Values and Society*, ed. Hendrik M. Vroom and Jerald D. Gort, vol. 12, Currents of Encounter: Studies on the Contact Between Christianity and Other Religions, Beliefs, and Cultures (Amsterdam-Atlanta, GA: RODOPI, 1997), 188; Although traditionally the ontological trend is characteristically Catholic and the relational one, Protestant, contemporary Catholic teaching has tried to integrate both visions. see Russel F. Hittinger, "Toward an Adequate Anthropology: Social Aspects of Imago Dei in Catholic Theology," in *Imago Dei: Human Dignity in Ecumenical Perspective*, ed. Thomas Albert Howard (Washington, DC: Catholic University of America Press, 2013), 44, www.jstor-org/stable/j.ctt3fgphw.1.

11. Reinders, "*Imago Dei* in Christian Ethics," 188.

12. Rosemary Radford Ruether, "*Imago Dei*, Christian Tradition and Feminist Hermeneutics," in *Image of God and Gender Models in Judaeo-Christian Tradition*, ed. Kari Elisabeth Børresen (Oslo: Solum Forlag, 1991), 271.

13. Meghan J. Clark, *The Vision of Catholic Social Thought: The Virtue of Solidarity and the Praxis of Human Rights* (Minneapolis, MN: Fortress Press, 2014), 57.

14. Reinders, "*Imago Dei* in Christian Ethics," 193.

15. Massaro, *Living Justice*, 83.

16. From here onward see Ibid., 83–87.

17. *Gaudium et Spes* 16–17 quoted in John T. Richardson CM, ed., *Readings in Catholic Social Teaching: Selected Documents of the Universal Church 1891–2011* (Eugene, OR: Wipf & Stock Publishers, 2015), 5–6.

18. For the next lines see Massaro, *Living Justice*, 86.

19. Christopher McCrudden, "Human Dignity and Judicial Interpretation of Human Rights," *European Journal of International Law* 19, no. 4 (September 1, 2008): 656, doi:10.1093/ejil/chn043.

20. Stephen Riley and Gerhard Bos, "Human Dignity," *Internet Encyclopedia of Philosophy: A Peer-Reviewed Academic Resource*, accessed December 13, 2016, http://www.iep.utm.edu/hum-dign/.

21. McCrudden, "Human Dignity and Judicial Interpretation of Human Rights," 679–80; Christopher McCrudden, ed., *Understanding Human Dignity*, First edition, Proceedings of the British Academy 192 (Oxford: Published for the British Academy by Oxford University Press, 2013).

22. Jacques Maritain, *Man and the State* (Chicago, IL: The University of Chicago Press, 1951), 9–13. Indeed, "the Body Politic or the Political Society is the whole. The state is a part—the topmost part—of this whole" (p.10), and "the State is inferior to the Body Politic as a whole, and is at the service of the Body Politic as a whole" (p. 13).

23. Michael Walzer, *Spheres of Justice: A Defense of Pluralism and Equality* (New York: Basic Books, 1983), 13–20. Walzer opposes complex equality to simple equality where a single set of good enjoys dominance and monopoly in the whole of social spheres. He argues for the autonomy of social spheres and the non-convertibility of goods between the spheres. He argues for complex equality, which means that "no citizen's standing in one sphere or with regard to one social good can be undercut by his standing in some other sphere, with regard to some other good" (p. 19). I use complex equality, which allows for various rules and principles to be applied according to different spheres. Unlike Walzer, I argue for the interconnectedness of social spheres not their autonomy.

24. John Baker et al., *Equality: From Theory to Action* (Houndmills, Basingstoke, Hampshire ; New York: Palgrave Macmillan, 2004), 23.

25. Ibid., 24.

26. Ibid., 25.

27. Ibid., 33.

28. Ibid., 34.

29. This is the term proposed by Coleman, "The Future of Catholic Social Thought," 527.

30. Baker et al., *Equality*, 24.

31. David Hollenbach, *The Common Good and Christian Ethics*, New Studies in Christian Ethics 22 (Cambridge; New York: Cambridge University Press, 2002).

32. Kenneth R. Himes O.f.M., "Commentary on *Justitia in Mundo* (Justice in the World)," in *Modern Catholic Social Teaching: Commentaries & Interpretations*, ed. Kenneth R. Himes O.f.M. et al. (Washington, DC: Georgetown University Press, 2005), 343.

33. "The Universal Declaration of Human Rights" (1948), 1, http://www.un.org/en/documents/udhr/.

34. Paul VI, *Octogesima Adveniens*, 22.

35. Massaro, *Living Justice*, 85.

36. Vatican II Council, *On the Church in the Modern World, Pastoral Constitution* Gaudium et Spes, 1965, http://www.vatican.va/archive/hist_councils/ii_vatican_council/documents/vat-ii_cons_19651207_gaudium-et-spes_en.html.

37. John Paul II, *On the Dignity and Vocation of Women on the Occasion of the Marian Year, Apostolic Letter* Mulieris Dignitatem (Rome: Libreria Editrice Vaticana, 1988), 6,7, 10, http://www.vatican.va/holy_father/john_paul_ii/apost_letters/documents/hf_jp-ii_apl_15081988_mulieris-dignitatem_en.html.

38. John Paul II, "Letter to Women" (Libreria Editrice Vaticana, June 29, 1995), 4, https://w2.vatican.va/content/john-paul-ii/en/letters/1995/documents/hf_jp-ii_let_29061995_women.html.

39. Ibid., 8.

40. Francis, *On Love in the Family, Post-Synodal Apostolic Exhortation* Amoris Laetitia (Rome: Libreria Editrice Vaticana, 2016), 54, https://w2.vatican.va/con tent/dam/francesco/pdf/apost_exhortations/documents/papa-francesco_esortazione-a p_20160319_amoris-laetitia_en.pdf.

41. John Paul II, *The Social Concern of the Church, Encyclical* Sollicitudo Rei Socialis (Rome: Libreria Editrice Vaticana, 1987), 38, http://w2.vatican.va/content /john-paul-ii/en/encyclicals/documents/hf_jp-ii_enc_30121987_sollicitudo-rei-socia lis.html.

42. Francis, *On the Proclamation of the Gospel in Today's World, Apostolic Exhortation* Evangelii Gaudium (Rome: Libreria Editrice Vaticana, 2013), 189, http: //w2.vatican.va/content/francesco/en/apost_exhortations/documents/papa-francesco _esortazione-ap_20131124_evangelii-gaudium.html.

43. Benedict XVI, *On Integral Human Development in Charity and Truth, Encyclical* Caritas in Veritate (Rome: Libreria Editrice Vaticana, 2009), 58, http:/ /w2.vatican.va/content/benedict-xvi/en/encyclicals/documents/hf_ben-xvi_enc_200 90629_caritas-in-veritate.html.

44. Ibid., 57.

45. Paul VI, *Octogesima Adveniens*, 22.

46. Massaro, *Living Justice*, 90.

47. Ibid.

48. Séverine Deneulin, "Amartya Sen's Capability Approach to Development and *Gaudium et Spes*: On Political Participation and Structural Solidarity," ed. Cheryl Handel and Kathleen Shields, *Journal of Catholic Social Thought* 3, no. 2 (2006): 366, doi:10.5840/jcathsoc20063228.

49. Benedict XVI, *Caritas in Veritate*, 57.

50. Ibid., 21, 60.

51. Francis, *On Care of Our Common Home, Encyclical Letter* Laudato Si (Rome: Libreria Editrice Vaticana, 2015), 144, http://w2.vatican.va/content/francesco/en/enc yclicals/documents/papa-francesco_20150524_enciclica-laudato-si.html.

52. Benedict XVI, *Caritas in Veritate*, 57, 58.

53. Clark, *The Vision of Catholic Social Thought*, 26.

54. Ibid., 112.

55. Paul VI, *Octogesima Adveniens*, 24.

56. John Paul II, *Sollicitudo Rei Socialis*, 44.

57. John Paul II, *On the Hundreth Anniversary of* Rerum Novarum*, Encyclical* Centesimus Annus (Rome: Libreria Editrice Vaticana, 1991), 46, http://w2.vatican.va /content/john-paul-ii/en/encyclicals/documents/hf_jp-ii_enc_01051991_centesimus-annus.html.

58. Ibid., 19.

59. Clark, *The Vision of Catholic Social Thought*, 135.

60. Paul VI, *Octogesima Adveniens*, 41, 47.

61. Himes, "Commentary on *Justitia in Mundo*," 343–44.

62. John Paul II, *Centesimus Annus*, 34.

63. John Paul II, *Laborem Exercens*, 13.

64. John Paul II, *Centesimus Annus*, 35.

65. Ibid., 43.

66. John Paul II, *Laborem Exercens*, 22.

67. Ibid.

68. Ibid., 25.

69. Dr. E. De Jonghe, "Participation in Historical Perspective," in *Principles of Catholic Social Teaching*, ed. David A. Boileau, Marquette Studies in Theology 14 (Milwaukee: Marquette University Press, 1998), 153–55.

70. Ibid., 157.

71. Ibid., 161.

72. John XXIII, *On Christianity and Social Progress, Encyclical* Mater et Magistra (Rome: Libreria Editrice Vaticana, 1961), 65, http://w2.vatican.va/content/j ohn-xxiii/en/encyclicals/documents/hf_j-xxiii_enc_15051961_mater.html.

73. Albino Barrera O.P., "What Does Catholic Social Thought Recommend for the Economy? The Economic Common Good as a Path for True Prosperity," in *The True Wealth of Nations: Catholic Social Thought and Economic Life*, ed. Daniel K. Finn (Oxford: Oxford University Press, 2010), 23.

74. Massaro, *Living Justice*, 90.

Chapter 2

Populorum Progressio, Laborem Exercens, and the Evolution of Catholic Social Teaching

After looking broadly at some of the key themes and focus of CST, I shall now explore the question of labor by using post-conciliar encyclicals. It is important to note that the theme of the condition of workers was the starting point of CST in 1891, and has since expanded in many directions. To deal with the specific question of labor I have chosen *Populorum Progressio* (PP) and *Laborem Exercens* (LE) for the following reasons. First, the latter offers an updated discourse on the condition of workers. Second, they locate—*PP* in a special way—economic- and work-related issues in a global context that takes into account the unbalanced relationships between nations. *PP*'s articulate understanding of development makes it relevant in the African context, and would serve as inspiration for subsequent documents on economic questions by national episcopal conferences in Africa.

In this section and the next, I will be presenting the various points of views of the magisterium and African bishops. I will offer my evaluation in the final section of the chapter.

POPULORUM PROGRESSIO (1967)

The growing disparities between individuals and nations worldwide that prompt Paul VI's reflection on development is the primary focus of *PP*, not labor as such. Disparities are perceived in terms of enjoyment of possessions and in the exercise of power.[1] When one addresses the question of labor from an African perspective, development is not a side issue. Indeed, development and labor are closely related. According to *PP*, "full, integral human development involves freedom from misery and provision for subsistence, health, and fixed employment."[2]

A particular development model directly influences economic policies and the way labor is organized. Development models are generally formulated and influenced by international institutions for less developed nations. For instance, recent trade agreements are constructed under a neoliberal framework that advocates for limited government intervention and for the deregulation of the labor market. These agreements put more emphasis on multinational corporations and profits and less on the workers. Under the World Trade Organization (WTO), a government cannot subsidize a particular sector, and the WTO has the power "to dismantle national standards regarding"[3] health, safety, workers' rights, and the environment. In addition, the concept of development gives a perspective on what a mature and free person, group, or society should be like. Since the word empowerment is barely used in magisterial texts, this provides us with an entry door into that idea.

Although Pope Paul VI's *PP* marks a turning point, it is not the first encyclical to address the issue of economic disparities on the global stage. Pope John XXIII, in *Mater et Magistra* (1961)[4] and in *Pacem in Terris* (1963),[5] pointed out the disparities between rich and poor nations and the necessity for rich nations to come to the help of the poor ones. In addition, *Mater et Magistra* was the first to include "the problem of rural dwellers, of farmers and people who live in non-industrial nations."[6] Concerning *PP*, its particularity lies in the fact that Paul VI acknowledges the colonial heritage as a contributing factor to the disparity. He simultaneously recognizes the bad and the good effects of colonization on newly independent states.[7] For instance, the one-crop agricultural policy of the colonial period had long-lasting impact on many African states. It is understandable that Paul VI sees a threefold obligation of wealthier nations toward the poorer ones:

> 1) mutual solidarity—the aid that the richer nations must give to developing nations; 2) social justice—the rectification of trade relations between strong and weak nations; 3) universal charity—the effort to build a more humane world community, where all can give and receive, and where the progress of some is not bought at the expense of others.[8]

The complexity of issues demands a global and concerted approach to solve them: "The world situation requires the concerted effort of everyone, a thorough examination of every facet of the problem—social, economic, cultural and spiritual."[9] It is under this holistic framework that he analyzes labor, which is first and foremost "something willed and approved by God."[10] Human work is in continuity with divine work, and makes every worker a creator.[11] Work done in common creates a sense of belonging among humans.[12] True work preserves a person's freedom and intellect. However, the concrete reality of work is not rosy. Work "can threaten man's dignity and enslave him."[13] Indeed, among the lesser human conditions, one can distinguish "oppressive political structures resulting from the abuse of ownership or the improper exercise of power, from the exploitation of the worker or unjust transactions."[14]

Faced with the flagrant inequalities between individuals and nations, and the limits of a model of development based only on economics, Paul VI posits a holistic model of development: "The development We speak of here cannot be restricted to economic growth alone. To be authentic, it must be well rounded; it must foster the development of each [person] and of the whole [person]."[15] The goal is not simply the elimination of social injustices; integral development works for the advent of a new and better community: "It involves building a human community where [people] can live truly human lives, free from discrimination on account of race, religion or nationality, free from servitude to other [people] or to natural forces which they cannot yet control satisfactorily."[16]

LABOREM EXERCENS (1981)

If *PP* touches socioeconomic life in general, John Paul II's *LE* specifically reflects on the reality of labor and the condition of workers. John Paul II starts and grounds his reflection on labor in biblical references.[17] *LE* broadly defines work as "any human activity that can and must be recognized as work."[18] Labor is a human function. It distinguishes human beings from the rest of creatures. Human beings at the time of creation received a divine mandate to work (Gen 1:28; 2:15). Hence, "work is viewed . . . positively as a participation in God's continual creative activity."[19] Additionally, work is essential to human existence for "man's life is built up every day from work, from work it derives its specific dignity."[20] Hence, "human work is *a key,* probably *the essential key,* to the whole social question."[21] John Paul II recognizes that toil, either manual or intellectual, is something closely associated with labor.[22]

LE distinguishes work as an objective reality (what is done and produced) and as a subjective reality (the human person who performs it), and reasserts the primacy of the latter over the former.[23] Indeed, this shows that human work has an ethical value.[24] *LE* rejects the mere commodification of labor that characterizes the "economicist" argument that only considers the materialist dimension of human labor.[25] Hence, *LE* affirms the priority of labor over capital, and these dimensions cannot be separated or opposed.[26]

What has been said before provides the general framework for labor, but *LE* goes further and tackles the condition of workers. The relationship between employer and employee is critical in fulfilling the rights of workers and the obligation to work.[27] The employer can be a direct one, that is, "the person or institution with whom the workers enters directly into a work contract in accordance with definite conditions."[28] The employer can also be an indirect one, that is, the "many different factors . . . that exercise a determining influence on the shaping both of the work contract and, consequently, of just or unjust relationships in the field of human [labor]."[29] *LE* underlines the responsibility of the indirect employer in shaping the labor market, and this notion is applicable to the State that has the responsibility of conducting "a just [labor] policy."[30] However, in the interstate relationships, multinational corporations, international institutions, financial markets, and other State and non-State actors are also part of the indirect employer since they define and shape labor policies. This notion of indirect employer "implies that responsibility for the injustices that mark our world cannot be evaded because there are numerous bodies that have some degree of complicity in these injustices."[31] Respecting the objective rights of the worker is the criterion for a correct labor policy and the adequate and fundamental criterion shaping the economy both locally and internationally.[32] "The first and basic right of workers is the right to work."[33] Unemployment and underemployment hinder the individual's fulfillment and prevent his or her contribution to the common good. *LE* reasserts the importance of labor unions in securing the rights of workers.[34]

LE reaffirms the just wage as the concrete way of checking the justice of the socioeconomic system.[35] The just wage can take the form of a family wage, which allows the head of the family to take care of family needs, or of social measures, such as family allowances or grants given to stay-at-home mothers.

LE also emphasizes solidarity of and with the workers as a concrete way to advance social justice. Solidarity should be present whenever workers are exploited.[36] *LE* borrows the expression "Church of the Poor" from Latin American theology to affirm the commitment of the Church to exploited and oppressed workers. The text states that[37]

> the "poor" . . . appear as a *result of the violation of the dignity of human work:* either because the opportunities for human work are limited as a result of the scourge of unemployment, or because a low value is put on work and the rights that flow from it, especially the right to a just wage and to the personal security of the worker and his or her family.[38]

One clear case of that situation is agriculture where millions of farmers make a precarious living despite the fact that they work hard, performing physically strenuous tasks every day. They receive miserable wages—that is, when they are paid—and lack forms of legal protection as well as safety nets.[39] In addition, many farmers "are forced to cultivate the land belonging to others and are exploited by the big landowners, without any hope of ever being able to gain possession of even a small piece of land of their own."[40]

Concerning women, John Paul II recognizes that women's toil and contribution often go unnoticed or receive little acknowledgment from society,[41] although women play a critical role through reproductive labor.[42] *LE* is one of the first magisterial documents that recognizes the economic value of reproductive labor, which demands a social reevaluation of the mothers' role.[43] As Christine Hinze rightfully notices "Pope John Paul II treats family work as a crucial form of human work having the same object and subjective, necessary and personal dimensions, and same status and dignity, as work performed in the paid workforce."[44] *LE* simultaneously states that women can work outside the home and that everything should be done so that they do not have to abandon their duty as mothers.[45] Women should be performing a paid work suitable to their own nature, but paid work should be organized in such a way that they can fulfill their domestic duties. In addition, grants should be given so that mothers do not feel the need to work outside the home. Hinze adds that "this is not a 'send all women back to the home' agenda. It is, however, a gender-keyed interpretation that sees women as especially suited, and also having a distinct, feminine contribution to make to culture and society."[46]

SUBSEQUENT MAGISTERIAL EXPANSIONS ON THE IDEA OF WORKERS EMPOWERMENT IN *POPULORUM PROGRESSIO* AND *LABOREM EXERCENS*

Other magisterial documents have attempted to correct or expand *PP* and *LE*. This section specifically looks at what pertain to work and workers.

In *Octogesima adveniens* (OA), Paul VI asserts the necessity of economic activity, which is the occasion of dignity affirmed in work.[47] *OA* reaffirms the right to work, a just wage, social security, and acknowledges the role of labor unions.[48] *OA* rightfully predicted that demographic growth, and unemployment would rise in the years following 1971.[49] The novelty of *OA* lies elsewhere. *OA* sees gender as one of the new social challenges. It recognizes gender as one of the situations of injustice and denounces discriminations against women.[50] *OA* calls for legislation that simultaneously protects the "proper" role of women, and at the same time affirms their independence as persons and their "equal rights to participate in social, economic, cultural and political life."[51] *OA* rejects a "false equality" that does not acknowledge women "proper role" in the family as well as in the society.[52] By proper role, *OA* probably means the contribution of women in reproductive labor. It is worth noting how *LE*, written ten years after *OA*, follows the latter on women's reproductive labor.

Another shift is the use, for the first time in a magisterial document, of the expression "preferential respect due to the poor."[53] Earlier in the document, new forms of poverty are listed, such as "groups of those on the fringe of society" among whom are those considered to be discriminated by law, for instance, due to their gender, origin, and race.[54] *OA* affirms the right of the Church to defend the place and dignity of these new poor in a society that values competition and success. Christine Gudorf captures better the difference between *PP* and *OA*:

> While *Populorum Progressio* laid out the needs of the poor around the world and called upon the rich to cooperate in alleviating those needs, OA insists that the task of creating a just social order including the poor themselves, who cannot be—and will not be—merely the recipients of justice, but must instead be agents of justice.[55]

Indeed, not only does *OA* recognize the variety of contexts, but also it marks "the beginning of a contextualization within Catholic social Teaching."[56] As I mentioned earlier, *OA* emphasizes both participation and equality as the two forms of people's dignity and freedom.[57]

Justice in the World (1971) was a statement issued by the Synod of Bishops the same year that *OA* was promulgated. The key input of *Justice in the World* is the blending of the question of social justice and the spread of the Gospel: "Action on behalf of justice and participation in the transformation of the world fully appear to us as a constitutive dimension of the preaching of the Gospel."[58] Indeed, "Christian love of neighbor and justice cannot be separated. For love implies an absolute demand for justice, namely, a recognition of the dignity and rights of one's neighbor."[59] *Justice in the World* (henceforth JiM from *Justitia in Mundo* the original Latin title) states that global justice can only be achieved through development, and speaks of a "right to development."[60] *JiM* observes that despite the economic growth enjoyed at the time many are left unemployed, and that the number of marginalized, such as those "deprived of political power as well as of the suitable means of acquiring responsibility and moral dignity," is increasing.[61]

Furthermore, "Economic injustice and lack of social participation keep people from attaining their basic human and civil rights."[62] Participation is a right in economic as well as political life, and without it there cannot be true progress.[63] *JiM* in a more acute way than *PP* recognizes the structural dimension of the problem. It speaks of "systematic barriers and vicious circles" in which people are deprived of fair remuneration and from getting access to opportunities and collective services.[64] Following *PP*, *JiM* singles out neocolonialism as one of the structures that could turn developing nations into "victims of the interplay of economic forces."[65]

A key element in *JiM*, probably inspired by liberation theology, is the strong emphasis on the fact that the Church needs to witness to the values that she teaches. This concretely means that "within the Church rights must be preserved."[66] As far as labor is concerned those who are in service of the Church should receive a "sufficient livelihood" and social security in the case of priests and religious, and "fair wages and a system of promotion" for laypeople.[67] Concerning women, they "should have their own share of responsibility and participation in the community life of society and likewise of the Church."[68] Although this is the only mention of gender, what has been said before about rights and economic marginalization could easily be applied to women.

The encyclical, *Sollicitudo rei socialis* (1987), revisits *PP* and its concepts of authentic development. John Paul II gives a theological grounding to the notion of development in Scripture and in the tradition of the Church.[69] Development is more than a socioeconomic notion. Development is rooted in an anthropology, which sees human beings as *imago Dei*, and development is an essential dimension of a person's vocation.[70] Hence, genuine development must be grounded in "the love of God and neighbor, and must help to promote the relationships between individuals and society,"[71] and it integrates our relationship with the nonhuman world.[72] In addition, true development is only "achieved within the framework of solidarity and freedom."[73]

However, structures of sin frustrate the march toward development and liberation, which are closely intertwined. Sin is the principal obstacle to liberation.[74] Likewise, restricting development to its economic dimension can only enslave the person.[75] Structures of sin can only be overcome by a commitment to the good of one's neighbor.[76] Thus, solidarity is seen as the response to this situation. Economic oppression and every form of discrimination are negative indices.[77] Unemployment and underemployment appear as new forms of underdevelopment.[78] On the contrary, justice in employment relationships is perceived as a sign of development.[79]

John Paul II endorses the option or preference for the poor. The deprivation of the right to freedom of economic initiative is seen as a special form of poverty,[80] since it destroys the creative subjectivity of the individual person or the subjectivity of a nation.[81] This option for the poor is not simply theoretical. It "must be translated at all into concrete actions, until it decisively attains a series of necessary reforms."[82] At the international level, the way to redress is to address the international imbalance by reforming the international trade system, the world monetary and financial system, international organizations, and reviewing the issue of transfer of technology.[83] The international trade system affects the way labor is organized in developing countries. As John Paul II contends, there is a kind of international division of labor, whereby the low-cost products of certain countries which lack effective labor laws or which are too weak to apply them are sold in other parts of the world at considerable profit for the companies engaged in this form of production.[84]

The encyclical, *Centesimus Annus* (1991), reexamines the question of work in a post–Cold War world. It sees a growing awareness of the natural interconnection between a person's work and the works of others; "work is work with others and work for others."[85] In addition, in today's world, technology and skill are more valuable than land.[86] Unfortunately, many in the Third World who do not possess and cannot acquire either tool find themselves on the margins of society.[87]

The preferential option for the poor is reasserted in *CA*.[88] It is a condition for the credibility of the Church's social message, which lies on "the witness of actions."[89] Even within a free economy, the state's responsibility lies in shaping the juridical framework and on intervening in the economy directly by solidarity to defend the weakest and most vulnerable by putting limits on those who determine working conditions and on making provisions for the unemployed.[90]

Elements such as the "abundance of work opportunities, a solid system of social security and professional training, the freedom to join trade unions and the effective action of unions, the assistance provided in cases of unemployment, the opportunities for democratic participation in the life of society"[91] guarantee the dignity of human work. John Paul II calls for "a society of free work, of enterprise and of participation" where the basic needs of the entire society are met through an appropriate control of the market by the "forces of society and by the State."[92]

Development is a question "of building up a more decent life through united [labor], of concretely enhancing every individual's dignity and creativity, as well as his capacity to respond to his personal vocation, and thus to God's call."[93]

In the encyclical, *Caritas in Veritate* (2009), published by Pope Benedict XVI at a time of global economic downturn, looked afresh at *PP* and the issue of human development. Benedict XVI borrows from his predecessor the phrase "decent work," which he defines as "work that expresses the essential dignity of every man and woman in the context of their particular society."[94] Benedict XVI then expands the definition by stating that decent work is

work that is freely chosen, effectively associating workers, both men and women, with the development of their community; work that enables the worker to be respected and free from any form of discrimination; work that makes it possible for families to meet their needs and providing schooling for their children, without the children themselves being forced into [labor]; work that permits the workers to organize themselves freely, and to make their voices heard; work that leaves enough room for discovering one's roots at a personal, familial and spiritual level; work that guarantees those who have retired a decent standard of living.[95]

Two things stand out in this statement: its inclusive character and the fact that freedom occurs at least three times. There are three levels of freedom: in the choice of activity, from any form of discrimination, and on joining labor unions. Moreover, Benedict XVI calls for an expansion of labor unions, which "should turn their attention to those outside their membership, and in particular to workers in developing countries where social rights are often violated."[96] He sees full employment as an imperative.[97] Benedict XVI denounces the growing casualization of workers. The downsizing of social security systems through the deregulation of labor and other incentives to stimulate competition has weakened the legal protection of workers as well as put their rights in grave danger.[98] One clear area is the uncertainty of working conditions, which puts great stress on the worker.[99] Benedict reaffirms his predecessor's conviction that "poverty results from a violation of the dignity of human work";[100] this is due in part to limited work opportunities, either through unemployment or underemployment or by not paying a fair wage or not providing social security.

Development has become a multilayered and complex reality.[101] Integral development includes material as well as spiritual growth.[102] As a vocation, "integral human development presupposes the responsible freedom of the individual and of peoples."[103]

Although the primary concern of *Laudato Si'* (2015) is the environment and the ecological crisis, a reckless economy and a certain idea of development are its preferred targets. "Work is . . . a path to growth, to human development and personal fulfillment."[104] Financial help to the poor must be temporary since the broader aim should be for them to have a dignified life through labor.[105] Pope Francis thinks that technological progress should be a help to human work but not replace it entirely because this is detrimental to humanity.[106] This is the case where massive layoffs occur or when small producers disappear.[107]

Francis mentions the introduction of genetically modified (GM) cereals as a showcase. Not only are small producers put out of business or made dependent on large operations, but also temporary laborers and rural workers have to move up to cities for a life of misery.[108] Francis denounces the savage exploitation of raw material by multinational corporations in the Third World leaves in its wake "great human and environmental liabilities such as unemployment, abandoned towns . . . the impoverishment of agriculture and local stockbreeding, open pits, riven hills, polluted rivers, and a handful of social works which are no longer sustainable."[109]

For Francis, "our human ability to transform reality must proceed in line with God's original gift of all that is."[110] Authentic development assumes respect for the human and nonhuman world.[111] "Social love is the key to authentic development."[112] Contrary to Paul VI and the other popes who preceded him, Francis rejects demographic growth as an obstacle to development.[113]

THE QUESTION OF THE EMPOWERMENT
OF WORKING WOMEN IN OTHER
MAGISTERIAL DOCUMENTS

The previous subsections looked at the question of empowerment of workers in general in CST. I shall now look at some Church official documents or statements addressing the specific situation of working women.

The apostolic exhortation on the family, *Familiaris Consortio* (1981), tackles the issue of women's role in society. John Paul II underlines "the equal dignity and responsibility of women with men"[114] that flows from the divine creation. This ground "fully justifies women's access to public functions."[115] However, this does not mean that women's maternal and family roles should be overlooked. To the contrary, society should recognize them and be "structured in such a way that wives and mothers are not in practice compelled to work outside the home."[116]

John Paul II opposes the objectification of women, which depersonalizes them and treats them as mere objects of sensual gratification or exploits them as mere commodity.[117] This violates their dignity, and results in discrimination against them "in the fields of education, employment, [and] wages."[118]

As such, the apostolic letter *Mulieris Dignitatem* (1988) does not address the situation of working women, but it does affirm some principles, such as the essential equality between men and women, and their difference.[119] While John Paul II rejects discrimination against women, he states that "in the name of liberation from male 'domination,' women must not appropriate to themselves male characteristics contrary to their own feminine 'originality.'"[120]

The *Letter to Women* (1995), written at the time of the Beijing's international conference on women, has many references to working women. It acknowledges that "women's dignity has often been unacknowledged and their prerogatives misrepresented; they have often been relegated to the margins of society and even reduced to servitude."[121] John Paul II regrets the fact that women have contributed a lot in the history of humanity, and yet their achievements have been barely acknowledged in history.[122] He praises working women for their "indispensable contribution"[123] to the growth of humanity, and particularly women involved in various areas of education outside of the home.[124] He also addresses "the obstacles that . . . still keep women from being fully integrated into social, political and economic life."[125]

He urges the necessity achieving "real equality in every area: equal pay for equal work, protection for working mothers, fairness in career advancements."[126] He commends, in a special way, women and institutions who have been fighting to promote women's rights and full dignity.[127] As John Paul II renews his discourse on the essential equality and difference between men and women, he brings some nuance to the difference perspective by claiming that the difference between men and women is not an "irreconcilable inexorably conflictual difference."[128] The *Letter to Women* is the first document from the magisterium where "women's work outside the home is praised as a vital cultural contribution not just tolerated as an unfortunate economic necessity."[129]

The letter on the *Collaboration of Men and Women in the Church and in the World*, issued by the Congregation for the Doctrine of the Faith (CDF) in 2004, is aimed at "certain currents of thought which are often at variance with the authentic advancement of women."[130] The CDF aims at showing that the promotion of women should not lead to confrontation between genders and deny women's ontological difference from men.[131] Hence, the CDF insists on that difference to the point of claiming that "from the first moment of their creation, man and woman are distinct, and will remain so for all eternity."[132]

By virtue of their genius, women's contribution is within both the family and the society.[133] Although the CDF insists that women's primary duty in reproductive labor, it also states that "women should be present in the world of work and in the organization of society, and that women should have access to positions of responsibility which allow them to inspire the policies of nations and to promote innovative solutions to economic and social problems."[134]

The CDF reemphasizes John Paul II's point that appropriate policies and attitudes for stay-at-home mothers and for working mothers should be adopted. If it reaffirms the necessity to fight all types of discrimination, the CDF contends that "the defence and promotion of equal dignity and common personal values must be harmonized with attentive recognition of the difference and reciprocity between the sexes where this is relevant to the realization of one's humanity, whether male or female."[135]

Pope Francis, in the post-synodal apostolic exhortation *Amoris Laetitia* (2016), rejoices in the growing disappearance of old forms of discrimination and the growing reciprocity within the family as a manifestation of a sense of equal dignity of men and women.[136] Moreover, he sees "in the women's movement the working of the Spirit for a clearer recognition of the dignity and rights of women."[137]

NOTES

1. Paul VI, *On the Development of Peoples, Encyclical* Populorum Progressio (Rome: Libreria Editrice Vaticana, 1967), 9, http://w2.vatican.va/content/paul-vi/en/encyclicals/documents/hf_p-vi_enc_26031967_populorum.html.

2. Allan Figueroa Deck S.J., "Commentary on *Populorum Progressio* (On the Development of Peoples)," in *Modern Catholic Social Teaching: Commentaries & Interpretations*, ed. Kenneth R. Himes O.f.M. et al. (Washington, DC: Georgetown University Press, 2005), 297.

3. Barker and Feiner, *Liberating Economics*, 112.

4. John XXIII, *Mater et Magistra*, 153–63.

5. John XXIII, *On Establishing Universal Peace in Truth, Justice, Charity, and Liberty,* Encyclical Pacem in Terris (Rome: Libreria Editrice Vaticana, 1963), 121–25, http://w2.vatican.va/content/john-xxiii/en/encyclicals/documents/hf_j-xxiii_enc_11041963_pacem.html.

6. Uzochukwu Jude Njoku, *Examining the Foundations of Solidarity in the Social Encyclicals of John Paul II*, European University Studies. Series XXIII, Theology, v. 819 (Frankfurt am Main; New York: Peter Lang, 2006), 167.

7. Paul VI, *Populorum Progressio*, 7.

8. Ibid., 44.

9. Ibid., 13.

10. Ibid., 27.

11. Ibid.

12. Ibid.

13. Ibid., 28.

14. Ibid., 21.

15. Ibid., 14.

16. Ibid., 47.

17. Lamoureux, "Commentary on *Laborem Exercens*," 393.

18. John Paul II, *Laborem Exercens*.

19. Lamoureux, "Commentary on *Laborem Exercens*," 394; John Paul II, *Laborem Exercens*, 25.

20. Ibid., 1.

21. Ibid., 3.

22. Ibid., 8, 27.

23. Ibid., 5–6.

24. Ibid., 6.

25. Ibid., 7, 13.

26. Ibid., 12–13.

27. Ibid., 16.

28. Ibid.

29. Ibid.

30. Ibid., 17.

31. Lamoureux, "Commentary on *Laborem Exercens*," 399.

32. John Paul II, *Laborem Exercens*, 17.

33. Lamoureux, "Commentary on *Laborem Exercens*," 390.

34. John Paul II, *Laborem Exercens*, 20; Lamoureux, "Commentary on *Laborem Exercens*," 390.

35. From here onward see John Paul II, *Laborem Exercens*, 19.

36. Ibid., 7.

37. Ibid.

38. Ibid.

39. Ibid., 21.

40. Ibid.

41. Ibid., 9.

42. Reproductive labor is defined as "the care and maintenance of the household and its members, including bearing and caring for children, food preparation, water and fuel collection, shopping, housekeeping and family care"; see Fondo Sikod, "Gender Division of Labour and Women's Decision-Making Power in Rural Households in Cameroon," *Africa Development* XXXII, no. 3 (2007): 64.

43. John Paul II, *Laborem Exercens*, 19.

44. Christine Firer Hinze, "Women, Families, and the Legacy of *Laborem Exercens*: An Unfinished Agenda," *Journal of Catholic Social Thought* 6, no. 1 (2009): 67.

45. From here onward see John Paul II, *Laborem Exercens*, 19.

46. Hinze, "Women, Families, and the Legacy of Laborem Exercens," 80.

47. Paul VI, *Octogesima Adveniens*, 46.

48. Ibid., 14.

49. Ibid., 18.

50. Ibid., 13, 16.

51. Ibid., 13.

52. Ibid., 14.

53. Ibid., 23; Christine E. Gudorf, "Commentary on *Octogesima Adveniens* (A Call to Action on the Eightieth Anniversary of *Rerum Novarum*)," in *Modern Catholic Social Teaching: Commentaries and Interpretations*, ed. Kenneth R. Himes O.f.M. et al. (Washington, DC: Georgetown University Press, 2005), 323.

54. Paul VI, *Octogesima Adveniens*, 15–16.

55. Gudorf, "Commentary on *Octogesima Adveniens*," 323.

56. Njoku, *Examining the Foundations of Solidarity*, 183.

57. Paul VI, *Octogesima Adveniens*, 22.

58. Synod of Bishops, "Justice in the World" (The Holy See, 1971), 6, http://www.shc.edu/theolibrary/resources/synodjw.htm.

59. Ibid., 34.

60. Ibid., 13, 15.

61. Ibid., 10.

62. Ibid., 9.

63. Ibid., 18.

64. Ibid., 16.

65. Ibid.

66. Ibid., 41.

67. Ibid.
68. Ibid., 42.
69. John Paul II, *Sollicitudo Rei Socialis*, 29–34.
70. Ibid., 29–30.
71. Ibid., 33.
72. Ibid., 34.
73. Ibid., 33.
74. Ibid., 46.
75. Ibid.
76. Ibid., 37.
77. Ibid., 15.
78. Ibid., 18.
79. Ibid., 33.
80. Ibid., 42.
81. Charles E. Curran, Kenneth R. Himes O.f.M., and Thomas A. Shannon, "Commentary on *Sollicitudo Rei Socialis* (On Social Concern)," in *Modern Catholic Social Teaching: Commentaries & Interpretations*, ed. Kenneth R. Himes O.f.M. et al. (Washington, DC: Georgetown University Press, 2005), 420.
82. John Paul II, *Sollicitudo Rei Socialis*, 43.
83. Ibid.
84. Ibid.
85. John Paul II, *Centesimus Annus*, 31.
86. Ibid., 32.
87. Ibid., 33.
88. Ibid., 57.
89. Ibid.
90. Ibid., 15.
91. Ibid., 19.
92. Ibid., 35.
93. Ibid., 29.
94. Benedict XVI, *Caritas in Veritate*, 63.
95. Ibid.
96. Ibid., 64.
97. Ibid., 32.
98. Ibid., 25.
99. Ibid.
100. Ibid., 63.
101. Ibid., 21.
102. Ibid., 76.
103. Ibid., 17.
104. Francis, *Laudato Si*, 128.
105. Ibid.
106. Ibid.
107. Ibid., 134.
108. Ibid.

109. Ibid., 51.

110. Ibid., 5.

111. Ibid.

112. Ibid., 231.

113. Ibid., 50.

114. John Paul II, *On the Role of the Christian Family in the Modern World, Apostolic Exhortation* Familiaris Consortio (Rome: Libreria Editrice Vaticana, 1981), 22, http://www.vatican.va/holy_father/john_paul_ii/apost_exhortations/documents/hf_jp-ii_exh_19811122_familiaris-consortio_en.html.

115. Ibid., 23.

116. Ibid.

117. Ibid., 24.

118. Ibid.

119. John Paul II, *Mulieris Dignitatem*, 6, 10.

120. Ibid., 10.

121. John Paul II, "Letter to Women," 3.

122. Ibid.

123. Ibid., 2.

124. Ibid., 9.

125. Ibid., 4.

126. Ibid.

127. Ibid., 6.

128. Ibid., 8. This looks like an attempt to affirm the unity of man and woman while affirming that this unity does not mean uniformity. The only difficulty is that John Paul II does not fully elaborate on areas of similarity between both genders, and he is only concerned on how practically this unity works.

129. Lisa Sowle Cahill, "Commentary on *Familiaris Consortio* (Apostolic Exhortation on the Family)," in *Modern Catholic Social Teaching, Commentaries & Interpretations*, ed. Kenneth R. Himes O.f.M. et al. (Washington, DC: Georgetown University Press, 2005), 377.

130. Congregation for the Doctrine of the Faith, "Letter to the Bishops of the Catholic Church on the Collaboration of Men and Women in the Church and in the World" (Libreria Editrice Vaticana, May 31, 2004), 1, http://www.vatican.va/roman_curia/congregations/cfaith/documents/rc_con_cfaith_doc_20040731_collaboration_en.html.

131. Ibid., 2.

132. Ibid., 12.

133. Ibid.

134. Ibid., 13.

135. Ibid., 14.

136. Francis, *Amoris Leatitia*, 54.

137. Ibid.

Chapter 3

African Bishops on Workers' Empowerment

In this chapter, I shall focus on the teachings of the African bishops who contextualize the general principles and teachings of magisterial documents. I will proceed here in three stages. The first looks at pastoral letters and statements addressing the workers' condition and women. The second focuses on the propositions from the two African synods of bishops (1994 and 2009). And finally, the third part surveys the Cameroonian bishops' pronouncements on economy and work.

AFRICAN BISHOPS CONFERENCES ON WORK AND WORKERS

I cover the period from 1969 till today. There are numerous references in pastoral letters related to work and/or economy that renders it almost impossible to discuss all of them in detail. Therefore, I will simply show the main characteristics. The emphases of the bishops portray the sociopolitical and economic struggles of Africa as a whole, and individual African countries in particular. My focus in all of these will be specifically on the treatment of labor and working women in episcopal documents.

Labor

Labor is simultaneously a gift from God as well as a command.[1] Labor is a faithful response to God's command to subdue the earth, as a collaboration in God's creative work and as a personal contribution to God's providential design in history.[2] The idea of labor as a divine curse, which past bishops upheld, has been rejected recently by some bishops.[3] Labor is the first task

47

given to Christian.[4] Given this, it comes as no surprise that bishops encourage people to work hard, especially in manual labor.[5] They also scold those—especially state agents—who do not do their job properly either by being sloppy, lacking conscientiousness, or by demanding bribes.[6]

Labor fulfills the person;[7] through manual and intellectual work, human beings humanize the earth, are able to feed themselves, and are useful to society. Labor puts the worker in solidarity with other human beings. Through labor, one improves his or her well-being as well as that of humanity.[8] In fidelity to the work of creation, one's work should make the earth more hospitable to the next generations.

Despite this, African bishops acknowledge that the condition of workers in African nations is far from glamorous. One key question is that of wages. They complain about low wages, back pay, or lack of proper compensation in many sectors of the economy, but in a special way, in the public sector.[9] Along with the issue of wages, there is concern for social security and safety nets for workers, which are nonexistent for the majority.

Concerning the issue of how the Church could help in improving the situation, the Senegalese bishops suggest that the Church should start first by treating its own workers fairly, by giving them decent wages and decent housing and working conditions.[10] Another important issue is that of discrimination, which prevents people from gaining job opportunities.[11] For most bishops, though gender discrimination is very evident, ethnicity and religion tend to be the main factors of discrimination.[12] Bishops replicate the equality-difference discourse present in magisterial teaching.

The other issue is unemployment that affects every social category, especially youth and university graduates in particular.[13] Growing unemployment is a source of tension in social life, where cities become pooling areas for the unemployed.[14] As a result many are underemployed,[15] and in activities that have no formal legal recognition. These factors should encourage governments to reflect and provide conditions for job creation.[16]

Bishops look at some categories of workers. Farmers are mentioned most often and are commended for their hard work to feed entire nations.[17] Farmers are facing difficulties caused by endogenous and exogenous factors. Among endogenous factors are the meager profits, the use of outdated techniques, weather uncertainties, the lack of basic infrastructure, the deregulation bringing cheaper imported goods, and the absence of sustained support from local governments for farmers and rural communities.[18] The exogenous factors are a combination of depreciation of exchange rates, the collapse of cash crop prices, and the liberalization of the local market under the pressure of international financial institutions.[19] The bishops regret the rural exodus that is caused by the lack of appeal of agriculture because farmers cannot sustain

themselves and their families.[20] Moreover, the fact that manual labor is dis-
valued in the popular culture explains why many do not want to practice
farming.[21]

African bishops see a close relationship between work and development.
Work is the first path toward development of self, family, and nation.[22]
Development is simultaneously a conversion of the heart and response to
God's project on everyone.[23] Development involves the liberation and flourishing of the human person as a creature, *imago Dei*, saved in Jesus Christ,
and called to divine life.[24] Development is one of the concrete forms that the
liberation of the human person takes along with decolonization, social justice,
and respect for inalienable human rights.[25] Development presupposes creativity and must correspond to the originality of particular people.[26]

Working Women

Women's work contribution is widely acknowledged and commended.[27]
However, the bishops recognize the imbalances and discriminations against
women.[28] Women are deprived of their due place in the social, economic,
and political realm.[29] Moreover, they are exploited in family life where they
need to carry out reproductive labor along with an outside job, while they
assume the entire burden of the family. Husbands should become aware
of the load of the domestic and agricultural work of their wives and find
suitable technological solutions.[30] Women are encouraged to carry on the
fight for the promotion of their rights and to take their due place in their
families as well as in all levels of social life.[31] Their role as agents of change
remains vital.

The letter of the episcopal conference of Congo-Brazzaville is one of the
rare documents devoted to women's place in society.[32] The economic role of
women has evolved from a central to a marginal one.[33] Women's contribution
is limited by the combination of cultural, juridical, and political hindrances.
They particularly observe that domestic violence hampers the flourishing of
married women by preventing them from studying or having an outside job.
The condition of single women is not better since they are among the poorer
people of society, and the bishops call on the Church and government to
intervene. The Congolese bishops suggest improving women's production,
income, and empowerment of the organization and management of women's
activities. They suggest concrete strategies, such as promoting private initiatives and access to micro-credit finance, supporting women in creating small
businesses, supplying seeds and working tools, facilitating women's access to
equipment and means of production, and women's training in local processing of agricultural products.

THE AFRICAN SYNODS ON WOMEN AND WORK

I shall now discuss the propositions of the African bishops that inspired the content of the apostolic exhortations, *Ecclesia in Africa* and *Africae Munus*.

The 1994 African Synod of Bishops

This synod was centered on evangelization with inculturation as its main articulation and the sixty-four propositions by the bishops reflect this emphasis. Proposition 2, for instance, does not list the economy or labor among the challenges facing Africans.[34] Nevertheless, one finds here and there allusions to work or the economy. Proposition 15 sees idleness among some of the problems the youth encounter and recommends, among others, items, human formation and vocational training.[35]

The role of Catholic cultural centers as spaces of dialogue is critical, and proposition 26 sees labor and the economy as some of the topics where the Church can share her conviction as she dialogues with non-Catholics and Christians. The synod fathers see inculturation as a way toward full evangelization and full reception of Jesus Christ.[36] Inculturation touches people at the personal, cultural, economic, and political levels.[37]It is this holistic approach that should inspire the relationships of African Christians with local political powers and international, political, economic, and cultural institutions to develop a dialogue between rich and poor countries.[38]

Political leaders should insure the liberation and flourishing of their people. Governments are exhorted to adopt sound economic strategies to boost growth, productivity, and job creation.[39] The Church condemns the looting of national resources because it affects the marginalized members of society first.[40] The Synod demands that industrialized countries fix fair and stable prices for Africa's raw materials.[41] The attention of governments is called to focus particularly on rural workers and people who reluctantly have to leave their villages to relocate to the city due to economic hardships.[42] On another matter, the workplace is seen as a space of interreligious dialogue.[43] The synod regrets the damage done to the environment by human activity, noticeably deforestation and industrial pollution.[44]

Although the synod fathers only devote one paragraph (48) to women, they are mentioned in other parts of the document in propositions 2, 16, 26, 40, 53, and 61.[45] Most of these references are either marginal or part of a list, and refer to the subjects of evangelization, religious life, women's sexuality or migration. Only paragraph 48 associates women and labor.[46] Like the episcopal regional bodies, the synod appreciates the vital contribution of women to family, the Church and society. It denounces customs and practices that deprive women of their due rights and respect. It recommends that the

Church should include women at levels of decision-making and that national episcopal conferences should defend women's rights in family-related issues (widowhood, bride price, single mothers, justice within marriage), and a suitable wage for women's work. It suggests that subsequent committees should reflect on women's place in the Church and in the society, and whenever possible, work with governments.

The 2009 African Synod of Bishops

This synod focused on justice, peace, and reconciliation. In contrast to the first synod, work and the economy are mentioned numerous times. Bishops in their propositions refer either to workers in general, categories of workers (businessmen and women, journalists, security agents, migrants), working conditions (methods of farming, environment-friendly behavior, priests working outside their dioceses), the wages issue, sectors of activity (agriculture, trade, business, education, judiciary, mass media), the conception of labor (an expression of grace and solidarity), unemployment, and job creation.[47]

Most of the propositions on labor target governments, national, transnational and international institutions, and corporations, which are the "indirect employer" and hold the primary responsibility in organizing the working environment. For instance, it is the responsibility of the government to improve the overall living conditions of their people or to create the framework to improve working conditions that will encourage professionals and graduates to stay in Africa; otherwise, the brain drain that plagues African nations will continue (16).[48]

However, this does not mean that the Church simply folds her hands and stands on the sidelines. For instance, on the issue of youth unemployment, local churches are asked to raise resources for the training of youth, but also to provide career orientation programs and training skills for entrepreneurship (48).[49] To go back to the environment, the synod displays an acute ecological sensitivity by linking natural resources to labor. Access to land, water, and basic infrastructures are essential goods to the human person (17, 30).[50] This ecological sensitivity is related to the attention due to the most vulnerable of people. Hence, natural resources like water should not be commodified without proper attention to the interests of ordinary people (30).[51] Micro-credit financing and agrarian programs should benefit the poor and marginalized (17).[52] Given that agriculture remains the main activity for Africans, and that the majority of Africans live in rural areas, it comes as no surprise that the bishops make the connection between environment and work.

The Church addresses not only the direct or indirect employer but also workers or potential workers. They are invited to show a spirit of self-sacrifice and service of their own people (17).[53]

However, labor is better understood within the context of the whole economy. The economy is one of the social areas where the laity are called to witness to the gospel (37).[54] The economy should be working for the poor and the synod denounces an economic order that generates poverty (17).[55] African bishops raise the issue of a global economic system that keeps on marginalizing Africa (29).[56] Governments are called to redistribute growth benefits fairly to the most deprived among citizens (15–16).[57] Good governance and protections of rights (equality among human beings) especially social, economic, political, and religious are important for the stability of a country (24–25).[58] The synod regrets the massive violation of human rights that characterize many African countries. It condemns the looting and over-exploitation of African countries as a result. In addition, pandemics, such as HIV/AIDS, constitute a serious threat to the socioeconomic well-being of Africans (51).[59]

Women are mentioned in several propositions either as a side-subject[60] or as a primary subject.[61] The synod mostly refers to women in connection with family life (marriage, domestic life, sexual life, or reproduction). Proposition 47 focuses entirely on women. The first statement merely repeats the previous synod's commendation of women's contribution to family, society, and the Church, and the fact that this contribution is not always valued. The proposition recognizes the gender gap in education despite progress made. Violence against women is condemned: the disinheritance of girls, sexual trafficking, and sexual tourism.

The synod condemns all inhuman actions and injustices against women. The Church recommends the professional, intellectual training of women, a better integration of women in Church's bodies and in decision-making processes, and the creation of diocesan and national commissions on gender to help women to accomplish better their mission in Church and society. Oddly, there is no explicit and direct mention of women and work in the 2009 synod's propositions apart from the "business women" phrase of proposition 22. Propositions 33 and 38 respectively mention the respect of woman as a mother, and the service of Christian wives as a ministry. Both are indirect references to reproductive labor although nothing in the text can confirm that.

This absence of clear association of women with labor is not corrected in the post-synodal apostolic exhortation *Africae Munus*. Benedict XVI asserts that giving women "opportunities to be heard and to express their talents through initiatives that reinforces their worth, their self-esteem, and their uniqueness would enable them to occupy a place in society equal to that of men."[62] The inclusive language in the short section on laypeople leaves no doubt that women are also considered in the economic sphere.[63] However, the connection with labor remains implicit.

CAMEROONIAN BISHOPS ON WORK

Since this book focuses on the reality in Cameroon, it is necessary to also discuss how the country's bishops have faced the issues related to work and working women. Although, there is no specific communication of the Cameroonian episcopal conference devoted to labor, there are two pastoral letters that extensively mention labor within the general context. These are the letters on economic crisis (1990) and corruption (2000).

Outside of these, the bishops also mention the condition of workers in many instances. In their 1975 final statement, they note the wage gap between teachers from private schools and public schools.[64] They revisited that issue in 1993, saying that teachers in Catholic schools work almost without wage, yet they remain committed to their work.[65] The 1978 final statement focuses on youth and denounces the exploitation of young workers in urban and rural settings, who do not get fair wages and work under inhuman working conditions.[66] The following year, the bishops issued a statement that was a follow-up of the previous year. They reiterated the great difficulty experienced by rural youth and young wage workers, and unemployed youth.[67] In 1983, the episcopal conference spoke against the exploitation of farmers by middlemen who do not buy their goods at a fair price.[68] They also added that young people are victims of the world of labor and money.[69] A later statement sees unemployment as one of the many hindrances the youth encounter.[70]

The 1990 pastoral letter on the economic crisis deals with the economic downturn that hit Cameroon at the end of the 1980s.[71] I focus here only on labor-related issues. The effects of these situations are layoffs, high unemployment rate, impoverishment of masses, and back pay for state agents (4).[72] The bishops understand the causes of this downturn related to social sin that dominates today's economy.

At the international level, social sin appears in the form of an economy that focuses solely on profit and on exploiting the weak and the poor, and by imposing on African countries new models of dependency (7).[73] For instance, the decrease of the prices of cash crops, such as cocoa, coffee, cotton, rubber, tobacco, banana, or groundnuts, in the international market, has put millions in difficulty in Cameroon. This reduction of prices is the result of stock market speculation and of large corporations that flood the market with supply higher than the demand (7).[74] The poor, the weak, and the destitute are the most affected by this situation (13).[75]

Although the bishops call for everyone's responsibility in this matter, they seem to adopt a kind of Manichean thinking when they look at the categories of workers. State agents and security forces are scolded for exploiting the vulnerable, for their lack of conscientiousness, corruption, and embezzlement of funds (15–18).[76] Farmers suffer mostly from the low prices of crops; the bishops only mention here cash crops or exportation crops (25).[77] The epis-copal conference suggests that other alternatives may be found such as devel-oping food crops and targeting local and African markets (27).[78] Farmers also need solidarity and homegrown initiatives, such as village cooperatives, credit unions, and saving and credits institutions (28).[79] Overall, the bishops think that people need to master updated working techniques and better suit-able technology (28).[80]

On the other hand, the country's labor market cannot absorb the number of university graduates and senior technicians who choose to leave the country for the industrialized world (26).[81] They also denounce the reality that many workers waste their hard-earned wages in life of dissipation without consid-eration for their own family (19).[82]

The general picture that one gets from the Cameroonian episcopal confer-ence's declaration is the growing precariousness of labor. The bishops do not define labor specifically, but they see some values and rights attached to work, although some remain implicit like fair wage. Caring about the com-mon good, being conscientious, hardworking, and acting in solidarity are some of the qualities that they unmistakably expect of workers.

Yet, they do not look thoroughly at specific sectors. First, they target mainly agriculture and the administration and do not look at industry or trade. Second, they only look at whatever is directly affected by the economic crisis in a particular sector. For instance, in agriculture, they will only target cash crops, but do not pay attention to food crops.

In addition, the primary audience of the conference's declaration is public officials, and then Cameroonians of good will.[83] Thus, it comes as no surprise that most of their words seem directed to civil servants or the government. Even as the conference acknowledges subsidiarity, it recognizes that certain things are beyond the reach of individuals (29).[84] The educative system, labor policies, homeland security, cultural life, building roads and bridges, and regulation of mass media are among the items that fall under the responsibil-ity of the state (29).[85]

The 2000 pastoral letter against corruption mentions labor too.[86] If in the 1990 pastoral letter there were external factors then, this is not the case in the 2000 letter, which sounds more introspective of Cameroonian society. Going back to terminology used in the previous letter, they describe corruption as social sin (8) and something that destroys the national economy (2).[87] Due to corruption, people cheat in trade; others receive unfair wages; public work is not properly done, or common goods are misappropriated (6).[88]

The conference grounds its reflection on biblical sources by quoting the Pentateuch, the Prophets, the Gospels and even the Epistles (11).[89] The warn-ing not to exploit the humble worker and the poor resonates throughout the sacred Scriptures. Even the Symposium of Episcopal Conferences of Africa and Madagascar warned that the disorganization of public administration was primarily affecting the rural and working classes, as well as lower state agents (17).[90] Among those who could help curb the phenomenon, they see journalists as well as artists (39) and educators (42) as useful agents.[91]

The conference singles out categories of workers affected by corruption: civil servants in general, administrators, educators, medical personnel, and the judiciary (25–29).[92]They see the decrease of wages among state agents in general as one of the causes of corruption (22),[93] and they recommend that the state improve the working conditions and wages of its agents (46).[94]

Although the tone of the letter is negative, one can deduce the assumptions about workers that animate the episcopal conference. The worker should labor with consideration for the common good, in a spirit of solidarity and justice, and he or she should receive a fair wage. The consideration for the common good is manifest when the conference laments that the state wastes vast sums of money due to corruption, which could have served to build basic infrastructure, like roads, schools, or health facilities (24).[95] Solidarity appears as a concern when bishops mention the disrespect, victimization, and ill-treatment that the poor endure (27–28, 31), and when the bishops suggested sharing as a way of overcoming selfishness and promoting solidarity between rich and poor (35).[96] Justice is manifest when the bishops support honest and hard work (36).[97]

Probably due to the emphasis on corruption, the bishops focus mostly on the public and formal sector. The informal and primary sectors of the economy are barely mentioned. In both letters, work is never mentioned in relationship to women. One needs to look at other declarations to find such an association.

In their 1974 final statement, the Cameroonian bishops briefly write about the dignity of the woman, who is not to be thought of as bound to her family-in-law as a property.[98] She can freely enjoy the fruit of her labor, open a bank account, and contribute to domestic expenses. The *Directory of Family and Marital Pastoral* (1981) introduces the question of work when it surveys special family cases, among which are single women. They observe the fact that some educated women refuse marriage because of their stable job and advantageous economic position.[99] For other women, the conference states that difficulty in finding a job is a reason why they remain single.[100] In the 1983 final statement, they mention the mother at home or at her work. The post-jubilee pastoral guide "Proclaiming the Word" (2002) briefly mentions women too.[101] Looking at the issue of Church self-reliance, the national episcopal conference of Cameroon states that the development of local dioceses will take place through the organization of the youth and women.[102] It acknowledges that the women hold a large portion of the national economy, in the informal sector in particular. In general, references to working women are quite scant.

NOTES

1. Cheza, Derroitte, and Luneau, *Les évêques d'Afrique parlent, 1969-1991*, 316; Evêques du Rwanda, "Résoudre le problème de l' "ethnisme," Message des évêques du Rwanda pour la fin du grand Jubilé et le centenaire de l'évangélisation du pays," *La Documentation Catholique*, no. 2246 (April 15, 2001): 393; Evêques du Congo, "Eglise-Famille et développement, Message des évêques du Congo aux chrétiens et aux hommes de bonne volonté," *La Documentation Catholique*, no. 2121 (August 6, 1995): 763.

2. Evêques du Zaïre, "Le chrétien et le développement de la nation, exhortation pastorale des évêques du Zaïre," *La Documentation Catholique*, no. 1992 (October 15, 1989): 905.

3. Cheza, Derroitte, and Luneau, *Les évêques d'Afrique parlent, 1969–1991*, 300; Evêques du Congo, "Eglise-famille et développement," 763.

4. Cheza, Derroitte, and Luneau, *Les évêques d'Afrique parlent, 1969–1991*, 300.

5. du Zaïre, "Le chrétien et le développement de la nation," 910; du Congo, "Eglise-famille et développement," 763; Cheza, Derroitte, and Luneau, *Les évêques d'Afrique parlent, 1969–1991*, 1087.

6. Evêques du Sénégal, "Bâtir ensemble un Sénégal de justice et de paix, lettre pastorale," *La Documentation Catholique*, no. 2107 (January 1, 1995): 42; du Congo, "Eglise-famille et développement," 762; CERAO, "Démocratie et promotion humaine, Lettre pastorale de la Conférence épiscopale régionale de l'Afrique de l'Ouest francophone (CERAO)," *La Documentation Catholique*, no. 2128 (December 17, 1995): 1084; Cheza, Derroitte, and Luneau, *Les évêques d'Afrique parlent, 1969–1991*, 315.

7. From here onward see Cheza, Derroitte, and Luneau, *Les évêques d'Afrique parlent, 1969–1991*, 316.

8. From here onward see Evêques du Zaïre, "Le chrétien et le développement de la nation," 902.

9. Ibid., 890–92, 895; Conférence Episcopale du Tchad, "Tout est possible quand le droit remplace la force, message de la conférence épiscopale du Tchad," *La Documentation Catholique*, no. 2087 (February 6, 1994): 134; Evêques de Centrafrique, "Tenir bon face à la crise, Message des évêques de Centrafrique aux fidèles et aux hommes de bonne volonté," *La Documentation Catholique*, no. 2244 (March 18, 2001): 291; Evêques de Centrafrique, "La population centrafricaine paie le prix fort, Message des évêques de Centrafrique," *La Documentation Catholique*, no. 2285 (February 2, 2003): 159; CENCO, "Changeons nos coeurs, Appel à un engagement réel pour la reconstruction, Message des évêques du Congo (RDC)," *La Documentation Catholique*, no. 2399 (April 6, 2008): 343.

10. Cheza, Derroitte, and Luneau, *Les évêques d'Afrique parlent, 1969–1991*, 390.

11. Ibid., 275, 289, 370.

12. Ibid., 289; IMBISA, "Justice et paix en Afrique australe, lettre pastorale," *La Documentation Catholique*, no. 1980 (March 19, 1989): 304.

13. Cheza, Derroitte, and Luneau, *Les évêques d'Afrique parlent, 1969–1991*, 289; du Zaïre, "Le chrétien et le développement de la nation," 895; Conférence

Episcopale du Togo, "Pour un esprit et un comportement nouveaux, lettre pastorale," *La Documentation Catholique*, no. 2117 (June 4, 1995): 558, 561.

14. Conférence Episcopale du Tchad, "L'an 2000, une ère nouvelle pour une vie nouvelle, Message de Noël," *La Documentation Catholique*, no. 2220 (February 20, 2000): 182.

15. Cheza, Derroitte, and Luneau, *Les évêques d'Afrique parlent, 1969–1991*, 290.

16. du Sénégal, "Quel Sénégal pour le troisième millénaire? Lettre pastorale," *La Documentation Catholique*, no. 2247 (May 6, 2001): 434; Cheza, Derroitte, and Luneau, *Les évêques d'Afrique parlent, 1969–1991*, 305–6.

17. CERAO, "Democratie et promotion humaine," 1087.

18. Evêques du Zaïre, "Le chrétien et le développement de la nation," 892, 895–96; CERAO, "Democratie et promotion humaine," 1085; Conférence Episcopale du Congo, "A qui profite la manne du pétrole? Déclaration de la Conférence épiscopale du Congo-Brazzaville," *La Documentation Catholique*, no. 2278 (October 20, 2002): 887; de Centrafrique, "La population centrafricaine paie le prix fort," 159.

19. Cheza, Derroitte, and Luneau, *Les évêques d'Afrique parlent, 1969–1991*, 273.

20. Ibid., 376; du Sénégal, "Quel Sénégal pour le troisième millénaire?," 434.

21. CERAO, "Democratie et promotion humaine," 1087.

22. Cheza, Derroitte, and Luneau, *Les évêques d'Afrique parlent, 1969–1991*, 300.

23. Ibid., 292.

24. Ibid., 299.

25. Ibid., 266.

26. Ibid., 291, 297.

27. Ibid., 393; Conférence Episcopale du Togo, "Pour un esprit et un comportement nouveaux," 561; du Sénégal, "Quel Sénégal pour le troisième millénaire?," 433.

28. du Zaïre, "Le chrétien et le développement de la nation," 899; IMBISA, "Justice et paix en Afrique australe," 304.

29. From here onward see IMBISA, "Justice et paix en Afrique australe," 304.

30. Cheza, Derroitte, and Luneau, *Les évêques d'Afrique parlent, 1969–1991*, 899–900.

31. From here onward see du Sénégal, "Quel Sénégal pour le troisième millénaire?," 438.

32. Conférence Episcopale du Congo, "Le rôle incontournable de la femme dans la société congolaise, Message des évêques du Congo-Brazzaville," *La Documentation Catholique*, no. 2278 (October 20, 2002): 894–96.

33. From here onward see Ibid., 895–96.

34. Maurice Cheza, ed., "Les 64 propositions," in *Le Synode Africain: Histoire et textes* (Paris: Karthala, 1996), 241.

35. Ibid., 247.

36. Proposition 32 in Ibid., 254.

37. Ibid., 254–55.

38. Proposition 43 in Ibid., 260.

39. Proposition 54 in Ibid., 265.

40. Proposition 45 in Ibid., 261.

41. Proposition 54 in Ibid., 266.

42. Proposition 45 in Ibid., 261.

43. Proposition 41 in Ibid., 258–59.

44. Proposition 55 in Ibid., 266.

45. Ibid., 241, 248, 252, 258, 265, 267–68.

46. From here onward Ibid., 262.

47. Propositions 15–17, 22–23, 28, 30, 39, 48, 54, 56 in Synode des évêques pour l'Afrique, "Les 57 propositions pour l'Afrique, document du synode des évêques," *La Documentation Catholique*, no. 2434 (November 15, 2009): 1040–43, 1045–46, 1049, 1052, 1054–55.

48. Ibid., 1040. Propositions' numbers are in brackets.

49. Ibid., 1052.

50. Ibid., 1040, 1046.

51. Ibid., 1046.

52. Ibid., 1040–41.

53. Ibid., 1040.

54. Ibid., 1048.

55. Ibid., 1040.

56. Ibid., 1045.

57. Ibid., 1040.

58. From here onward see Ibid., 1043–44.

59. Ibid., 1053.

60. Propositions 4, 22, 33, 42, 45, and 51 Ibid., 1036, 1042, 1047, 1050–51, 1053.

61. Proposition 20 and 47 in Ibid., 1041–42, 1052.

62. Benedict XVI, *On the Church in Africa in Service to Reconciliation, Justice and Peace, Post-Synodal Apostolic Exhortation* Africae Munus (Ouidah, Benin: Libreria Editrice Vaticana, 2011), 57, http://www.vatican.va/holy_father/benedict_xv i/apost_exhortations/documents/hf_ben-xvi_exh_20111119_africae-munus_en.html.

63. Ibid., 128–31.

64. Conférence Episcopale du Cameroun, *L'enseignement social des évêques du Cameroun 1955–2005*, 314–15.

65. Ibid., 387.

66. Ibid., 331.

67. Ibid., 335.

68. Ibid., 352.

69. Ibid., 355.

70. Ibid., 358.

71. Ibid., 149–69.

72. Ibid., 150–51. Paragraphs are in brackets

73. Ibid., 152.

74. Ibid.

75. Ibid., 156.

76. Ibid., 157–58.

77. Ibid., 162.

78. Ibid., 164.

79. Ibid., 165.

80. Ibid.

81. Ibid., 163.

82. Ibid., 159.

83. Ibid., 149.

84. Ibid., 165–66.

85. Ibid., 166.

86. Conférence Episcopale Nationale du Cameroun, "Lutter contre la corruption au Cameroun: lettre pastorale des évêques du Cameroun," *La Documentation Catholique*, no. 2236 (November 19, 2000): 987–96.

87. Ibid., 987–88. The specific paragraphs are put in brackets.

88. Ibid., 988.

89. Ibid., 989.

90. Ibid., 990.

91. Ibid., 994–95.

92. Ibid., 991–92.

93. Ibid., 992–93.

94. Ibid., 995.

95. Ibid., 991.

96. Ibid., 992–93.

97. Ibid., 993.

98. Conférence Episcopale du Cameroun, *L'enseignement social des éveques du Cameroun 1955–2005*, 309.

99. Ibid., 86.

100. Ibid.

101. Ibid., 213–44.

102. From here onward see, Ibid., 243.

Chapter 4

Evaluation of Catholic Social Teaching on Workers' Empowerment

In this chapter, I intend to look at the strengths and limits of CST from the standpoint of an African theological ethics and from a feminist perspective.

STRENGTHS OF CST

The word "empowerment" is virtually absent from social encyclicals. I argue, however, that empowerment is implied by participation and is necessary to maintain human dignity, basic human equality, and the common good. One needs to look to issues related to justice, human dignity, and development to get a sense of how empowerment is understood by CST. The strengths of CST are its grounding in biblical theology, the emphasis on the dignity of the worker, the recognition of the impact of the indirect employer, the option for the poor, the reality of social sin, participation, and the growing awareness of gender issues. Instead of looking at these as separate elements, they should be viewed as parts of the same structure.

The Holy Scriptures play a critical role in African Christianity. The discourse of CST on human work and workers takes its key principles from Scripture: human dignity rooted in *imago Dei*, labor as God's command, labor as an essential reality for humans, God as the rightful owner of creation, the primacy of human community, the option for the poor and the vulnerable, and so on. These critical insights help articulate an alternative vision of human work rooted in a comprehensive worldview provided by the Holy Scriptures.

Another strong point is the fact that the dignity of the worker as the defining element of any economic system is underscored. Dignity takes precedence over other aspects such as capital, the objective work performed, efficiency, or profit. In virtue of the person as made in God's image and the social nature of human beings, workers should be treated with respect. That humane treatment takes the form of fair wages, just wages, and the right to participate in the decision-making process about his or her work, and allows the worker to thrive individually and socially.[1] The human worker is a person that is a member of a community and through his or her work contributes to the common good. The dignity of the worker goes beyond a simple fair wage, working conditions, and labor union membership. The worker should be treated as a free and responsible subject.

Another strength is to recognize that humans are social beings and that the worker does not work in a vacuum but within a social context. CST understands that the environment or general context plays a critical role in creating conditions for "decent work." A context can be empowering or disempowering. For instance, a sexist society will tend to curtail women's opportunities for jobs. That general context is determined by the "indirect employer," which covers everything at the national level (the government, labor legislations, labor unions, job training) as well as the international one (relations of dependence between states).[2]

"Indirect employer" highlights the interplay between internal/local factors with external/international factors. Moreover, "indirect employer" implies that everyone has some sort of responsibility "for creating a just society and for the laws that govern the workplace."[3] Indeed, "the notion of indirect employer means that employment justice in our world cannot be side stepped."[4] If governments have the primary responsibility of providing a conducive environment for labor, they are not alone.

The option for the poor is also very important in a context where many people are poor, marginalized or oppressed. This principle helps us to see how the most vulnerable are treated, and the workforce and labor policies are working against them. The option for the poor is justified since poverty is the result of the violation of the dignity of human work.[5] In the context of CST, this ideal is connected to the Gospel, and that category is broad enough and not limited to material and economic aspects. The duty of the Church is to stand with the poor and the vulnerable, since this option for the poor is a condition of her credibility.

The next element, social sin, is closely related to the previous ones. This notion reminds us of the mystery but also of the systemic character of the injustice against (female) workers. In addition, sin is not ordinary evil but the result of a human action. Social sin reminds us that in spite of the good ideas laid out earlier, the reality and practice of labor for many is far from being liberating and fulfilling. Indeed, "there are alienating patterns of work and international distribution of labor that threaten human dignity."[6]

Participation is one of the great contributions of CST. The notion of participation gives a concrete substance to human dignity. Participation integrates the individual to the community by contributing to the common good and by sharing in social benefits. Participation demands the inclusion of every member of society and as such it tests the social health of a political community. Labor is inseparable from participation, and the latter, by paying attention to contribution, sharing, and responsibility, probes the way labor enhances, and promotes the flourishing of the individual and community. Participation brings to the forefront the social nature of the individual and the fact that society benefits from individual and group activities.

The last element is the attention to gender shown in post-conciliar magisterial documents with respect to labor. There is a recognition of social imbalances and injustices against women. The popes and bishops condemn all types of discrimination against women and call for more social justice. They state that women should have access to work outside the home and should be promoted to public responsibilities; they also call for equal pay for equal work. They address the tension between employment and reproductive labor.

LIMITS OF CST

Unfortunately, the arguments found in the CST are not trenchant. CST also suffers from an inadequate notion of "development" and has Western and patriarchal views of the role of women in the family.

• Limits in the Form of the Argument

CST's teachings on labor, the interaction between labor and capital, and the use of the Bible need to be improved and nuanced. So, too, does the teaching on gender equality.

The broad definition of work offered especially in *LE*'s introduction, and that remains the prominent one in CST, offers recognition "and appreciation for all types of work,"[7] which is positive. Thus, "work within the home is to be honored as much as work in the marketplace since it is sharing in God's creative activity."[8] It makes sense in this perspective that John Paul II would advocate remuneration for those who care for the family.

However, Patricia Lamoureux points out that this broad definition blurs the reality of work, which makes it difficult to distinguish what counts as work and what does not.[9] Indeed, should actions on behalf of justice or spiritual practices be considered part of human labor? As understandable as this attempt is—to move away from a commodified perception of labor—it still dilutes the meaning of labor. Daniel Finn moves a critical step further in the criticism by stating, "CST, particularly at the level of papal statements, has dealt with issues of employment and labor in largely general terms without much specific analysis of more concrete patterns of development."[10] Accordingly, other areas need better attention, such as "the changing nature of work . . . where fewer and fewer people have lifetime careers."[11]

LE and subsequent documents give prominence to labor over capital, but they are not separate or conflicting realities. Capital is defined by *LE* as "the whole collection of means of production,"[12] and is distinct from labor, which refers to the human beings performing the work.[13] From that standpoint, it seems obvious that the human person is superior to the means of production. However, Daniel Finn contends that John Paul's "analysis eclipses the more common meaning of the conflict between capital and labor, namely the clash between the interests of workers and the interests of owners of the means of production."[14] The argument changes and is no longer about the superiority of persons against things, "since there are persons on both sides of this conflict."[15] Rather, the conflict is one of competing claims between workers and owners or employers.

In that same vein, Lamoureux asserts that the "ethic that gives priority to labor over capital must acknowledge and address the tension that exists between this harmonious ideal and conflicting reality."[16] Divisive issues such as reasonable and legitimate profit, the responsibilities of employers and employees for the common good, or democracy in the workplace, "cannot be resolved simply by stating that the fundamental structure of work is that it first and foremost unites people, or declaring that the priority of labor over capital has always been taught by the Church."[17]

The addition of solidarity to the right to work makes conflict unavoidable. To contextualize Lamoureux's examples for Cameroon, for whom should a job be prioritized when only 10 percent of the active population work in the formal sector? In virtue of solidarity, development aid workers are sent by country donors to help, and sometimes end up with jobs that could be performed by local people; those workers who come to help end up taking precious jobs from those who seriously need them. How can this be avoided? For Uzochukwu Njoku, the ambiguity lies with the way John Paul II articulates solidarity, which does not carry the same meaning throughout his writings.[18] Moreover, Njoku observes a discrepancy in John Paul's approach, which is characterized by a failure to duplicate his methodology to third world countries.[19]

Another critical limit—especially in the case of John Paul II—comes from his personalist approach. He rightfully sees that human beings affect social institutions. However, he fails to acknowledge ways in which social institutions shape individuals in spite of the fact that he uses concepts such as structural sin.[20] In fact, "while John Paul's notion of structural sin stresses how individual acts and omissions culminate into a social system of sin, it does not pay adequate attention on how these social structures could drastically reduce human freedom to the extent that they become uncontrollable forces against human persons."[21] Hence, his approach does not go deep enough "to offer the challenging tools necessary to realize the just world"[22] that he advocates.

The other criticism concerns the way Scripture is used. For Lamoureux, this shows that the "ethic of human labor needs a critical theory of biblical interpretation."[23] Sometimes, "the lack of careful exegesis of a text leads to missing the point of what the text meant in its early form."[24] In addition, the "selective use of the creation story to interpret work's theological significance relies almost exclusively on the Priestly source and neglects the Yahwist tradition."[25] The Priestly source offers a positive view of humanity and its capacity to build bonds of solidarity, while the Yahwist presents a more realistic view, which presents conflicts and flaws in human behavior. "Because achievements of human creativity can lead to rebellion against God and actions that harms persons and communities, the Yahwist account of creation is needed along with the Priestly narrative to formulate a balanced biblical theology of work."[26]

In addition, while it is important to recognize that all types of work involve some sort of toil, its systematic linkage to the suffering on the cross is problematic for three reasons.[27] First, the cross of Christ is "a unique and specific instance of suffering," before being "a symbol of life's difficulties."[28] Second, one should pay attention to the particular causes of toil in specific circumstances to avoid overlooking social injustice.[29] Finally, "John Paul's 'co-redemptive' view of the toil of human labor seems to imply that the more unpleasant work is, the more fully it is a participation in Christ's sufferings, and, paradoxically, the more redemptive it is."[30] In addition, what are the limits of unpleasantness? At what point does the toiling worker break? The human capacity to suffer is not infinite, and there comes a point where toil becomes unbearable. In addition, the cross is the result of human sin. In other words, the crucified exist because of people or institutions that lead them to the cross.[31] Yet, John Paul II's linkage does not distinguish degrees of toil and does not look at situations, which violate the dignity of the worker and thus make the toil inhuman.

Concerning the use of the Bible, the Church is invited to be more critical in its use. Indeed, as Mercy Oduyoye states, "Because of its widespread treatment of the Bible as an infallible oracle, the Church in Africa is slow to change its attitudes, and this is particularly true of its attitudes toward women."[32]

Western and Patriarchal Views of the Role of Women

Recent popes have rejected the inequality defended by Popes Leo XIII and Pius XI and have affirmed equality between men and women, the legitimacy of women's work outside the home, equal pay for equal work, and call for an end to all types of discrimination against women. However, an ambiguity remains, especially pertaining to women's role within the family. That ambiguity is reinforced by the principle of difference that the popes are quick to mention as soon as they affirm the equality of men and women. Christine Gudorf observes, "The dual nod to women's traditional family role under patriarchy and to the application of liberal rights to women served to validate both patriarchal traditionalists and feminist reformers in the Church."[33]

Concerning Paul VI in Octogesima adveniens (*OA*), Gudorf notes that "though he advocated the equality of women 'to participate in cultural, economic and social life,' Paul [VI] never indicated how such participation could and should be integrated with previous papal understandings of women's role as the heart of the home, dedicated to motherhood and domesticity."[34] It appears that Paul VI seemed "oblivious to the need in justice for women's participation in cultural, political, and economic responsibility to be balanced by men's sharing in domestic and childcare responsibility."[35]

John Paul II offers a mixed impression. He proclaims the equal dignity of women and men, asserts their right to work outside of the home, and condemns all forms of discrimination, as shown in the second section of this chapter. At the same time, he claims that their reproductive role is the most valuable[36] and that work at home should be compensated. While he acknowledges reproductive labor as valuable as any other form of employment, there are some reservations with his approach.

Although "difference feminists"[37] basically agree with John Paul, other feminists offer various levels of criticism. First, valuing and insisting on the importance of reproductive labor "can be fused with a feminist affirmation of the rights and dignity of women to produce an adequate valuation of women's traditional contribution without circumscribing opportunities for women in workplace and professions."[38] Second, "[John Paul II] mistakenly attributes domestic activity solely to mothers."[39] It is one thing to recognize the importance of reproductive labor and another to say that this should be left only to women. As Hinze states:

> By too tightly intertwining femininity and family-work, rather than highlighting this work as part of the domestic vocation of every person, the pope's approach to women and labor within the family ultimately contributes to the very problems—the socio-economic disvaluing of women and their contributions, and the socio-economic disvaluing of the work of the home—it seeks to ameliorate.[40]

Indeed, daily experience shows that men can do reproductive labor: cooking, doing the laundry, or being janitors. Third, as a consequence, while it calls for a "social reevaluation" of the mothers' role and the work connected with it, "there is no attempt to redistribute the work of the home between the spouses."[41] There is no corresponding appeal to reevaluate fatherhood.[42]

One would have to wait for Francis to have a pope praising the equal share of domestic chores between husband and wife, as was shown in section 2 of this chapter. Fourth, although the idea about compensating the stay-at-home mother is laudable, "it concedes too much to a market economic model."[43] Unless reproductive labor is valuable in financial terms, it looks as if it has no intrinsic value. Moreover, as Gudorf points out, compensating homemaking mothers is not possible in African nations, given the limited resources and uphill challenges that these young nations face.[44] Moreover, even if one agrees to compensation, there is a more pressing issue, that is, the hardness of working conditions. As I will show in the next chapter, the absence of basic facilities such as running water, electricity, and gas cookers in many households in sub-Saharan Africa adds long hours of hard work to the already existing responsibilities of African women. So the urgent issue is not to compensate them for reproductive labor; rather it is to make their work easier by providing basic facilities. Fifth, this view fails to account for the diversity of household arrangements, and operates within the model of a male breadwinner.[45] Besides, in Africa, the obligation of feeding the family has always been the prime responsibility of women.

On another topic, papal discourse on women's work seems to lack any social analysis. There is a failure to acknowledge

and address the historical realities and effects of systemic, institutionalized devaluation of women, a devaluation grounded in their so-called exceptional or different status and nature from men; and the role of ideology in maintaining this inferiorization of women in homes and in public.[46]

Put more pointedly, there is no recognition of the systemic nature of sexism and unequal wages that exist in the workplace.[47] In addition, women have always worked, and so much so that in Africa they barely have time for themselves.[48] In most African cultures, they played a key economic role through trade and in producing and processing the food. The industrial revolution in the West[49] and the imposition of a colonial economy in Africa have exacerbated the economic marginalization of women. Indeed, the introduction of fiduciary economy, commercial agriculture, Western type of education, modern jobs, and private land ownership has pushed women further to the margins.[50]

This neglect of data is due to the fact that "papal teaching on the nature and role of women still demonstrates a romantic pedestalization of women."[51] This view romanticizes the role of women in society. Even the papal view of the family that consists of a working man and a homemaking wife is a product of the "cult of domesticity" developed in the nineteenth century by bourgeois families to justify the exclusion of upper-class women and children from the industrialized workplace.[52] This cult of domesticity resonates in Africa where women are expected to be mothers, wives, and homemakers.[53]

According to Drucilla Barker and Susan Feiner, "this ideology defined families and households exclusively in terms of nurturing, endearment, and affection."[54] This idealistic picture of the family aimed at concealing the imbalance "of power inequities from a culture increasingly critical of power inequities."[55] One such area has been the division of labor within the household that has always been to the disadvantage of women. This is why "the role of this ideology that perpetuates the idolization of women as mothers should be exposed and exorcised."[56]

Alice Dermience also observes the papal tendency to emphasize difference between genders, without emphasizing what they share in common and what constitutes their equality, which are intelligence and freedom.[57] This tendency to stress difference is pushed to the extreme by the Congregation for the Doctrine of the Faith's 2004 letter. Biological differences between genders are used as an argument to ground the sexual division of labor within society. This predetermines the role of women in society.[58] This physicalist or naturalistic approach has the pernicious consequence to limit women's prospects within the labor market, as I will make clear in the next chapter. Moreover, the letter reproaches feminists to create contestation and competition between genders by overstressing the subordination of women. The letter makes a crucial confusion between legitimate right claims and a quest for power. It seems to adopt a Western and bourgeois perspective[59] that defends at all cost a romanticized vision of women rather than confronting the ugly reality of oppression and domination that the vast majority of women in the world experience.

Most of the reservations formulated above could also apply to African bishops. Indeed, most documents are unoriginal, and simply repeat much that is in papal and Roman curia writings, and mention working women in one paragraph or only in passing. Very few national episcopal conferences have written a pastoral letter on the question of work in general or on gender.

OA indicates that making statements and condemnations is no longer sufficient; concrete actions must follow.[60] Apart from isolated initiatives, gender issues have hardly been touched. For instance, the 1994 Synod enjoined the national episcopal conferences to establish special commissions to deal with gender issues.[61] The 2009 synod repeated the same recommendation, which, to my knowledge, has yet to surface in many dioceses.

In the particular case of Cameroonian bishops, they seem to consider some issues from an androcentric perspective. For instance, when they look at how the economic crisis affects farmers, they name only cash crops, such as cocoa, coffee, and cotton whose prices have dropped.[62] Cash crops are the exclusive domain of men in Cameroon, with women being confined to food crops that are cheaper and meant mostly for sustenance.

Moreover, what the bishops perceive as a crisis for male farmers has been a blessing in disguise for women. Cameroonian social scientists William Tantoh Farnyu and Emmanuel Yenshu Vubo rightly observe that "with the fall in the prices of cash crops in the world market, the value of food crops has risen and with it greater autonomy and economic power for women."[63] When they suggest that the food crop market in Cameroon should be boosted and that the government should technically support it,[64] they fail to notice that women, who are the majority of farmers, tend to be excluded when new techniques are introduced. Moreover, their property rights are limited, but this goes unnoticed by the bishops.

Their 1974 statement where they claim that women can open a bank account and enjoy the fruit of their labor demonstrates how disconnected the bishops are from the reality of the majority of women. They seem unaware of the structural constraints that hamper women from flourishing. One has to agree with Oduyoye that "the experience of women in the church of Africa contradicts the Christian claim to promote the worth (equal value) of every person."[65]

Issues with Human Dignity

The Church's vision of human dignity assumes a lot more than what the reality shows. First of all, where the Church assumes a basic common understanding, human dignity presents itself as a volatile concept in modern public discourse. In theory, it is supposed to be a unifying concept. There is no agreement whether human dignity is a status, value or principle.[66] Is it inherent, a telos, an elevation or something else? Originally, "human dignity represents a claim about human status that is intended to have a unifying effect on our ethical, legal and political practices."[67] However, when one looks at legal practices, the scope of human dignity varies from one place to the other.[68] In some places, human dignity has an absolute role; it is not the case in some other places.[69]

The second issue is the association of *imago Dei* and equal dignity. That link was not obvious in the Church tradition until the 1950s. The Church has long defended a hierarchical vision of society, beginning with the family. Believing in human beings as images of God did not prevent the justification of slavery or the subordination of women in the tradition. Even today, some part of the language remains ambiguous. Cardinal Walter Kasper affirms that thinking of women in terms of roles misses the mark in terms of their dignity.[70] Indeed, the woman cannot be defined by her role as wife nor by her role as mother, friend, partner, colleague, competitor, or even as cheap labor. As an autonomous person a woman is more than all this. She transcends all these roles. Her value does not depend on whether she fits into one or several of these roles and does justice to them.[71]

However, in his further remarks, Kasper limits women to biology. For him, "the sexual is not a specialized zone or sector but a determination of the human being which affects the whole person, all that is human."[72] After saying that women are not determined by their roles, he claims that "responsibility for life and for humane conditions of life" through biological and/ or spiritual motherhood is what should give women "esteem and dignity."[73] John Baker et others reflecting on the dimension of love, care, and solidarity observes that if the gendered division of labor assigns the duty of caring labor to women, carrying this task "does not always give them the love and care they need themselves, and the other conditions of their lives sometimes leave them little space for relationships of love and care."[74] As Pope Benedict XVI observes, "Man cannot live by oblative, descending love alone. He cannot always give, he must also receive."[75] However, not only the destiny and vocation of women is predetermined, but there's never a reflection on how they can benefit from other people's love.

Third, CST incorporates elements of each of the three types of equality that I presented above, although each one of them has its flaws. Basic equality "remains a powerful force for action and for change."[76] However, basic equality is a minimalist idea, which "does not challenge widespread inequalities in people's living conditions or even in their civil rights or educational and economic opportunities."[77] Moreover, "it calls on us to prevent inhumanity, but it does not necessarily couch its message in terms of justice as distinct from charity."[78] This tendency is clearly visible in the work of Benedict XVI who tries to offer a holistic vision of charity that incorporates justice, which may not be always clear to outsiders to whom encyclicals are also destined. CST agrees with liberal equality push for anti-discrimination and affirmative action measures,[79] which promotes equal opportunity. CST would disagree with its individualistic outlook. Liberal equality counts on social institutions to further equal opportunity.[80] CST like liberal equality trusts that governments, global institutions, and people of goodwill help improve the situation, but today one needs to include more actors. At the end, CST lays down principles whose implementation remains problematic because the concerned social institutions do not operate fairly.

CST agrees with equality of condition in giving people the opportunity to exercise real choices among real options. CST is in tune with equality of condition, which calls for a transformation of social institutions, but it differs to the extent it scrutinizes social institutions such as family and religion. Criticism of the family does not challenge its traditional structures that take gender dynamics for granted. CST criticizes practices and attitudes, but it avoids pointing fingers at specific individuals or institutions. CST calls for reform or conversion, but only denounces in general statements a situation of inequality.

The question of equal human dignity is an anthropological one. A discourse on human dignity grounded on an exclusive ontological reading of the *imago Dei* will end up excluding the disabled and all those who cannot use their abilities fully. For instance, the fact that those who do not fully use reason or free will are still images of God shows clearly that the *imago Dei* goes beyond simple functioning. This demonstrates that the emphasis is on God, who creates man and woman in God's own image. Since God is a mystery, what ultimately makes humans in God's image remains a mystery. Moreover, the equal worth of man and woman is not only metaphysical but has to be recognized socially. The extent of the equality of man and woman is not fully articulated in papal and magisterial teaching. What does it look like at these different levels, namely, respect and recognition, resources, love, care and solidarity, power, and working and learning? There seems to be urgency in pointing differences and not pointing the unity celebrated in Gen 2:23: "bone of my bones and flesh of my flesh." Emphasizing women's vocation to life is not bad, but this enshrines inequality in the household in a context where unpaid domestic labor is perceived as women's exclusive prerogative. Encouraging women to service is not per se a problem since it is the vocation of all Christians. However, since women have been subordinated to men throughout history and still remain so in many African societies, such an appeal must be balanced with a similar invitation to men. The denunciation of an undifferentiated equality rather appears as an excuse to apply double standards when it comes to women.

An Inadequate Vision of Development

The criticism I make here is valid for both papal documents and those of the African bishops. The notion of development puts the debate about socioeconomic justice and labor on the global stage. The whole of CST—including African bishops' letters—acknowledge the theological roots of development, which can be found in the individual. An important input of the Church's vision is the holistic view of development that transcends material considerations by being grounded on its anthropological vision of the human person as *imago Dei*. Development is a reminder that human beings are social beings linked through solidarity. This is obviously the case for working women. One must agree with Hinze that "wage-worker justice in one country can no longer be pursued in isolation from the global dimensions of the economy."[81]

Despite these facts, development as a notion remains problematic. One of the aims of *PP* was a criticism of the prevailing notion of development. Nevertheless, "the fact, however, [is] that at the end of the day [PP] accepted the term and did not propose a clear practical alternative leading to the implementation of its exalted vision [which] ironically made it susceptible for falling into a soft kind of developmentalism."[82]

The development model considers the industrialized or modern society as its paradigm.[83] According to this logic, the underdeveloped countries are considered backward and at a lower level when compared to the industrialized ones. For the underdeveloped world to become like the industrialized world, it needs to duplicate the development model. The development approach seems at best reformist, and fails to attack the root causes of the evil,[84] hence, its failure in the vast majority of African nations.

PP hints at "the issue of asymmetrical power relations" in relationship with development, pointing to its political dimension.[85] One cannot ignore that underdevelopment as a social fact is "the historical by-product of the development of other countries."[86] Development is associated with the relationships of dependence, which "presuppose the insertion of specifically unequal structures."[87] Indeed, relationships of dependence and domination among nations in recent decades and centuries originate from the growth of the world market.[88] Striving for development means fighting to maintain this imbalance.

Given this background of the term "development," it is surprising that subsequent documents continue to use the term. Indeed, later popes and African episcopal conferences have embraced it and simply offered an alternative and critical understanding of the notion. One cannot adopt such a problematic term without effect. For instance, Paul VI and John Paul II accepted the demographic negative influence on economic growth.[89] It is only Francis who definitively rejected the linkage.[90] On the other hand, Latin American theologians have replaced development with liberation, which provides the possibility of transformation.

There are other issues with CST's vision of development. CST's vision of the common good is grounded on the sovereign nation-state as I have showed in the first section of this work. Added to that is the firm belief in an emerging system of world government.[91] These assumptions are problematic because we increasingly live in a world where the centers of decision-making are diversifying. In addition, a basic notion in international relations is that of anarchy.[92] Even among the scholars who support the idea of world government, there is a split between those who advocate global governance or a world state.[93] One thing is sure, world government is still in the process, but contrary to Paul VI's vision, "the state is no longer the only source of authority for global governance."[94] The "increased economic globalization and an emerging global civil society"[95] create a situation where centers of decision-making are more scattered. Even the nation-state should not be viewed as a monolithic reality.

Nigerian theologian Agbonkhianmeghe Orobator, SJ, raises other issues with papal treatment of development. In Africa, development as the panacea against poverty is assumed by *CV* for instance. However, the understanding of who the poor are can help nuance this idea.[96] Benedict XVI's presumption about the end of ideological blocs, makes him overlook the fact that external powers still dominate and manipulate Africa to control her mineral resources.[97] Further, John Paul II and Benedict XVI offer solidarity as a solution to corruption in the context of development, assuming a common understanding of solidarity.[98] However, in Africa where practices such as nepotism, favoritism, patronage, and fund embezzlement originate in the emphasis put on community, connections, relations and affectivity, solidarity becomes ambiguous and problematic. In addition, "this vision of solidarity remains very relevant but it does not pay a corresponding attention on how social structures limit human capacities to act."[99]

On another matter, gender is barely mentioned in relationship to development, while all the indicators show how badly women are affected by social and economy hardships and how they are more vulnerable than men in case of a crisis.[100] Such a silence simply reinforces the marginalization and oppression of women in Africa while the vital contribution they make in the economic realm is ignored.[101]

NOTES

1. Lamoureux, "Commentary on *Laborem Exercens*," 398.

2. Ibid., 399.

3. Ibid., 400.

4. Daniel Finn, "Human Work in Catholic Social Thought," *American Journal of Economics and Sociology* 71, no. 4 (December 2012): 883.

5. John Paul II, *Laborem Exercens*, 7; Benedict XVI, *Caritas in Veritate*, 63.

6. Lamoureux, "Commentary on *Laborem Exercens*," 406.

7. Ibid., 407.

8. Ibid.

9. Ibid.

10. Finn, "Human Work in Catholic Social Thought," 884.

11. Ibid.

12. John Paul II, *Laborem Exercens*, 12.

13. Daniel Finn, "John Paul II and the Moral Ecology of Markets," *Theological Studies*, no. 59 (1998): 665.

14. Ibid.

15. Ibid.

16. Lamoureux, "Commentary on *Laborem Exercens*," 407.

17. From here onward see Ibid.

18. Njoku, *Examining the Foundations of Solidarity*, 408. Depending on the writings, solidarity is associated with social justice and has liberative tone, or it is linked to Christian charity, and tends to promote the status quo.

19. Ibid., 335. The bias is visible concerning the situation of Central and Eastern Europe; "[not only] did he fail to make a historical reading of the economic problems of the Third World countries as he did in the case of Central/Eastern Europe, [but also] he merely refers to these problems as if they were secondary to those of eastern/ Central Europe by appealing that the urgent task of rebuilding Eastern Europe should not diminish the readiness to assist the Third World. The task of rebuilding Eastern/ Central Europe is considered a matter of urgent justice while that of the Third World countries becomes a matter of charity, placed on the altar of the willingness of those ready to assist."

20. Ibid., 423.

21. Ibid. In fact, John Paul's approach "does not take sufficient account of the effect of international economics and politics on the ability of the local groups to struggle for social justice."

22. Ibid., 424.

23. Lamoureux, "Commentary on *Laborem Exercens*," 406.

24. Ibid.

25. Ibid.

26. Ibid.

27. John Paul II, *Laborem Exercens*, 9; Lamoureux, "Commentary on *Laborem Exercens*," 406.

28. Lamoureux, "Commentary on *Laborem Exercens*," 406.

29. Ibid.

30. Ibid.

31. For more details on various theologies of the cross, see Andrew Sung Park, *Triune Atonement: Christ's Healing for Sinners, Victims, and the Whole Creation*, 1st ed. (Louisville, KY: Westminster John Knox Press, 2009); for links between cross and social sin see Walter Rauschenbusch, *A Theology for the Social Gospel*, Library of Theological Ethics (Louisville, KY: Westminster John Knox Press, 1997), 240–79; for an African perspective on the cross and its implications for the Church, see Jean-Marc Ela, *Repenser la théologie africaine: Le Dieu qui libère*, Chrétiens en liberté. Questions disputées (Paris: Editions Karthala, 2003).

32. Oduyoye, *Daughters of Anowa*, 190. Although Oduyoye is not a Catholic, her remarks can be applied to the Catholic Church in Africa.

33. Gudorf, "Commentary on *Octogesima Adveniens*," 324–25.

34. Ibid., 328.

35. Ibid.

36. Cahill, "Commentary on *Familiaris Consortio*," 364.

37. Hinze, "Women, Families, and the Legacy of *Laborem Exercens*," 83–84. Difference feminists hold the position that "women are, indeed, specially equipped

for the family and home work" (Ibid.). In addition, they "are convinced that pursuing social recognition for women's special qualities and contributions is the best way to assure that women, and the work of home and family, receive the support and resources they need to play their part in contributing to familial and common ground" (Ibid.).

38. Hinze, "Bridge Discourse on Wage Justice," 525.

39. Ibid.

40. Hinze, "Women, Families, and the Legacy of *Laborem Exercens*," 64.

41. Gudorf, "Encountering the Other," 73.

42. Hinze, "Women, Families, and the Legacy of *Laborem Exercens*," 81.

43. Cahill, "Commentary on *Familiaris Consortio*," 377.

44. Gudorf, "Encountering the Other," 73.

45. In Cameroon today women are heads of one household out of five, see Institut National de Statistique du Cameroun, *Annuaire statistique du Cameroun 2014* (Yaoundé: Institut National de Statistique, 2016), 71, http://www.stat.cm/downloads /2016/annuaire2016/. This does not take into account situations where women assume de facto leadership (husband absent, laid-off, or seriously ill), which means that the obligation of feeding the family falls on them.

46. Hinze, "Women, Families, and the Legacy of *Laborem Exercens*," 81.

47. Lamoureux, "Commentary on *Laborem Exercens*," 401.

48. Catherine Coquery-Vidrovitch, *Les Africaines histoire des femmes d'Afrique subsaharienne du XIXe au XXe siècle* (Paris: la Découverte, 2013), 7.

49. Barker and Feiner, *Liberating Economics*, 23–24.

50. Coquery-Vidrovitch, *Les Africaines*, 103.

51. Gudorf, "Encountering the Other," 70.

52. Barker and Feiner, *Liberating Economics*, 23.

53. Oduyoye, *Daughters of Anowa*, 81.

54. Barker and Feiner, *Liberating Economics*, 24.

55. Gudorf, "Western Religion and the Patriarchal Family," 256.

56. Oduyoye, *Daughters of Anowa*, 73.

57. Alice Dermience, *La "question féminine" et l'Église catholique: approches biblique, historique et théologique*, Dieux, hommes et religions, no 11 (Bruxelles ; Oxford: P. Lang, 2008), 93.

58. From here onward, see Ibid., 96.

59. Ibid., 97.

60. Paul VI, *Octogesima Adveniens*, 48.

61. John Paul II, *On the Church in Africa and Its Evangelizing Mission, Post-Synodal Apostolic Exhortation* Ecclesia in Africa (Yaoundé, Cameroon: Libreria Editrice Vaticana, 1995), 121, http://www.vatican.va/holy_father/john_paul_ii/apo st_exhortations/documents/hf_jp-ii_exh_14091995_ecclesia-in-africa_en.html.

62. Conférence Episcopale du Cameroun, *L'enseignement social des éveques du Cameroun 1955–2005*, 150, 162.

63. William Tantoh Farnyu and Emmanuel Yenshu Vubo, "Gender and Rural Economy in the Wimbum Society, Cameroon: Perceptions, Practices and the Land Question," in *Gender Relations in Cameroon: Multidisciplinary Perspectives*, ed. Emmanuel Yenshu Vubo (Mankon, Bamenda: Langaa Research & Publishing CIG, 2012), 84.

64. Conférence Episcopale du Cameroun, *L'enseignement social des évêques du Cameroun 1955–2005*, 164.

65. Oduyoye, *Daughters of Anowa*, 9.

66. Riley and Bos, "Human Dignity."

67. Ibid.

68. McCrudden, "Human Dignity and Judicial Interpretation of Human Rights."

69. Ibid., 699.

70. Walter Kasper, "The Position of Woman as a Problem of Theological Anthropology," in *The Church and Women: A Compendium*, ed. Helmut Moll (San Francisco: Ignatius Press, 1988), 57. I use this reflection of Kasper, because it provides a good summary of the contemporary position of the official Church on women.

71. Ibid.

72. Ibid., 59.

73. Ibid., 61.

74. Baker et al., *Equality*, 45.

75. Benedict XVI, *On Christian Love, Encyclical Letter* Deus Caritas Est (Rome: Libreria Editrice Vaticana, 2005), 7, http://w2.vatican.va/content/benedict-xvi/en/encyclicals/documents/hf_ben-xvi_enc_20051225_deus-caritas-est.html.

76. Baker et al., *Equality*, 23.

77. Ibid.

78. Ibid.

79. Ibid., 25.

80. Ibid., 31.

81. Hinze, "Bridge Discourse on Wage Justice," 526.

82. Deck, "Commentary on *Populorum Progressio*," 309.

83. Gustavo Gutiérrez, *A Theology of Liberation: History, Politics, and Salvation* (Maryknoll, NY: Orbis Books, 1988), 50.

84. Ibid., 17.

85. Deck, "Commentary on *Populorum Progressio*," 305.

86. Gutiérrez, *A Theology of Liberation*, 17.

87. Ibid., 52.

88. Ibid.

89. Paul VI, *Populorum Progressio*, 37; John Paul II, *Sollicitudo Rei Socialis*, 25.

90. Francis, *Laudato Si*, 50.

91. Lisa Sowle Cahill, "The Common Good and Development" (Revisiting *Populorum Progressio* 40 years after: Rethinking Catholic Development Ethics? KU Leuven, 2007), 5.

92. Anarchy in international relations simply means the absence of supranational government; see James D. Fearon, "Bargaining, Enforcement, and International Cooperation," *International Organization* 52, no. 2 (1998): 269.

93. Those who advocate a global governance want a looser system of governance that relies on existing international institutions and organizations; while those who support a world state want a more formal and full-fledged system of government; For more on this discussion read Campbell Craig, "The Resurgent Idea of World Government," in *The Politics of Global Governance: International Organizations*

in an Interdependent World, ed. Paul F. Diehl and Brian Frederking, fourth ed. (Boulder; London: Lynne Rienner Publishers, 2010), 397–407.

94. Paul F. Diehl and Brian Frederking, "Introduction," in *The Politics of Global Governance: International Organizations in an Interdependent World*, ed. Paul F. Diehl and Brian Frederking, fourth ed. (Boulder; London: Lynne Rienner Publishers, 2010), 5.

95. Ibid.

96. Agbonkhianmeghe E. Orobator, "*Caritas in Veritate* and Africa's Burden of (under)Development," *Theological Studies* 71 (2010): 324.

97. Ibid., 325.

98. Ibid., 327–28.

99. Njoku, *Examining the Foundations of Solidarity*, 428.

100. Orobator, "*Caritas in Veritate* and Africa," 330.

101. Ibid.

Conclusion to Part I

In this part, I tried to present the perspectives of CST on the empowerment of (female) workers and where the strengths and weaknesses of this perspective lie. CST refers to the body of literature produced by the popes, the Roman curia, and bishops that present the Church's perspective on burning social issues or challenges. Rooted in biblical and Church tradition, CST continues to evolve. Among its key themes are human dignity, solidarity, participation, and the common good. The comprehensive well-being of human beings and of human communities is at the heart of CST.

In chapter 2, I took the post-conciliar social encyclicals *Populorum Progressio* (*PP*; 1967) and *Laborem Exercens* (*LE*; 1981) as the starting points for my discussion on the CST arguments for the dignity of workers. *LE* offers an updated vision of human work and what workers' justice can look like, while *PP* offers the general context in which this justice is carried out. Both documents take into account the global context within which labor needs to be considered.

For *PP*, the key argument revolves around authentic development and the necessity to solve the question of social injustice globally. *LE* highlights the essential dimension of work for a person's fulfillment and that the worker should be at the center of economic considerations. Subsequent documents expand the vision laid out in the precedent ones. *OA* recognizes gender as one of the social challenges and introduces the preferential option for the poor in the declarations of the magisterium. *JiM* makes the action in favor of justice a constitutive dimension of the gospel. In addition, it calls the Church to witness to its teaching.

SRS looks at the structures of sin that affect the global society and economy in opposition to solidarity. *SRS* revisits the concept of development by giving it a theological grounding and by linking development and underdevelopment with justice in employment. *CA* notices the technological gap between Northern nations and those from the global South. *CV* sees work as something freely chosen, fulfilling, and that allows a worker to thrive. *LS* calls attention to how a reckless economic system only focused on profit endangers the environment and people's work. In a nutshell, worker's justice is understood in terms of decent work that highlights the individual dimension (fairness in opportunities and working condition, freedom, flourishing) and the context (systemic).

Concerning working women, CST, as well as other documents, affirms the right of women to work outside the home; they condemn discriminations against women; they advocate for compensation for homemaking mothers and insist that women keep their originality.

In chapter 3, I have shown that African bishops use a theology of human work grounded in biblical texts to assert the positive value of work. In most cases, they speak of the great difficulties found in Sub-Saharan Africa. They look, in a special way, at the working conditions, the precarious economic environment, and unemployment. They equally condemn the exploitation and discrimination against women, and commend the latter for their great economic contribution. The 1994 and 2009 African synods do not add much to this topic and virtually make no mention of working women.

The strong grounding of its principles on Scripture, the centrality of the dignity of worker in the evaluation of an economic system, the notion of indirect employer, and the reality of social sin are the positive contributions of the CST from an African perspective. Its limitations concern the broad notion of work, the lack of a more detailed analysis of labor, the lack of nuance in some arguments related to human work, and the problematic use of some scriptural references (little use of the Yahwist story of creation, the cross as a symbolism of human toil). The discourse of women still betrays a patriarchal perspective that tends to associate and limit women to reproductive labor. Moreover, there seems to be a lack of social analysis of women's real working conditions. The image of the working woman is a romanticized one. The application of equal human dignity is not always consistent, especially when it comes to women. In addition, the notion of development while important carries many ambiguities that may not go away simply by qualifying it differently.

Overall, the position of the Church on workers' empowerment offers illuminating principles such as the dignity of the worker. However, in some issues, there are limits, especially in the systematic analysis of human work and on the social analysis of women's work. In the case of Africa, there are generous statements on women's economic contribution and denunciation of discrimination, but the practice of the Church does not offer concrete strategies to curb the latter. This is what I will discuss in the next chapters.

Part II

THE REALITY OF WOMEN'S WORK IN CAMEROON

This part begins to address some of the limits of Catholic Social Teaching on human work and offers a systematic analysis of women's work. My understanding of work, as already indicated, follows that of the International Labor Organization that views work as "all productive activities," even unpaid household services and volunteers as work.[1] Simultaneously, employment is distinguished from unpaid work as "work for pay or profit."[2] This idea of employment allows the inclusion of informal activities, such as rural farming in which people contribute to their own or family farm without getting a remuneration. My focus is mainly on women from working and poor classes, who live in either urban or rural areas.

Part II has three chapters. The first (chapter 5) deals with feminist criticism of neoclassical economics' conception of labor. I focus on neoclassical economics because it is the dominant paradigm. Neoclassical economics proceeds by assuming an abstract or ideal economy, outside of any historical specific content with the exception of wants, land as commodity, labor and capital, the market, and a minimal state or government.[3] Neoclassical economics locates gender discrimination outside the economic sphere and in the sociocultural realm.[4] Thus, neoclassical economics is gender-biased.[5] Feminist economists not only reject the universality of rational economic agents, but they "extend the economic horizon to analyze the economic activities that take place in households and families without assuming that these activities parallel behaviors found in markets."[6]

Chapter 6 presents the general characteristics of women's work. When one takes gender into account, the emerging picture shows how the experience of working women is far from empowering.[7] If women work as much as, if not more than men they often occupy jobs that are less desirable or less well paid (horizontal segregation); they are at the bottom of the structures (vertical segregation); they do not receive equal pay for equal work (wage gaps). They spend a disproportionate amount of time on domestic labor, and they have a higher unemployment rate. Women's work seems of lesser value perhaps because most of it falls under the category of unpaid work (reproductive labor, rural farming, and the like). I also look at the limitations of the usual solutions such as education, access to paid work, and better legislation. They are important but not enough in themselves to effect structural change.

The last chapter of this part (chapter 7) presents the reality of women's work in Cameroon by building on the previous section and by adding data specific to Cameroon. Instead of using the traditional division of labor as primary (agriculture), secondary (industrial), and tertiary (services) sectors, which ignores reproductive labor, I look at Cameroonian working women in reproductive labor and the informal sector in agricultural and nonagricultural jobs. The reality reveals that a disproportionate number of Cameroonian women are found in vulnerable work compared to men,[8] and most of the negative trends observed in the second section are confirmed. An ambivalent picture will emerge and will show simultaneously the dynamism of working women and the marginalization and constraints they face. The section ends by looking at the controverted image of the autonomous woman in the African context.

NOTES

1. United Nations, *The World's Women 2015*, 95.
2. Ibid.
3. Guy Mhone, "Gender Bias in Economics and the Search for a Gender-Sensitive Approach," in *Engendering African Social Sciences*, ed. Ayesha Imam, Amina Mama, and Fatou Sow (Dakar, Senegal: Codesria, 1997), 126–27.
4. Ibid., 129.
5. Barker and Feiner, *Liberating Economics*, 5–7; Rebecca Pearse and Raewyn Connell, "Gender Norms and the Economy: Insights from Social Research," *Feminist Economics* 22, no. 1 (January 2, 2016): 30–53, doi:10.1080/13545701.2015.1078485.
6. Barker and Feiner, *Liberating Economics*, 4–5.
7. From here onward see United Nations, *The World's Women 2015*, 87–112.
8. Institut National de Statistique du Cameroun, *Annuaire statistique du Cameroun: recueil de séries d'informations statistiques sur les activités économiques, sociales, politiques et culturelles du pays jusqu'en 2013* (Yaoundé, Cameroon: Institut National de Statistique, 2013), 218, http://www.stat.cm/downloads/annuaire/2013/Annuaire_statistique_2013.pdf.

Chapter 5

Feminist Criticism of Neoclassical Economics

Since labor is primarily addressed within the economy, it is important to look at how economics perceives it. The first section of this chapter tries to argue why the neoclassical economic conception of labor is inadequate and does not properly account for women's work. Neoclassical economics fails to address the reality of women's work for many reasons. The feminist criticism of its approach is located at four levels: fundamental, macroeconomics versus microeconomics, the rational economic "man," and the predominance of money.

ISSUES AT THE FUNDAMENTAL LEVEL

Economics prides itself as the most objective and rigorous among social sciences.[1] This level of criticism addresses "the ontological and epistemological premises of the discipline of economics itself."[2] At a fundamental level, economics is divided into a hard core and a protective belt.[3] The hard core defines what economics is about and what its rules are. The protective belt "complements and extends the 'hard core' with a compendium of subsidiary theories, methodologies and verification agendas, conclusions and outstanding debates in various aspects of the discipline."[4] The ontological premises of economics lie within the hard core, while the epistemological premises are in the protective belt. Most of the criticism against economics refers to the second level.[5] However, as Malawian economist Guy Mhone points out, "gender bias in economics may be located at both the ontological and epistemological levels."[6]

At the heart of economics, there is the question of scarcity of means/goods opposed to the unlimited character of human wants/desires. Economics is concerned with "maximizing ends in the face of scarce resources,"[7] or in other words, "with the efficient allocation of scarce resources . . . for the maximum satisfaction of unlimited human wants which have different priorities."[8] Economics favors a supra-historical approach that takes the distribution of resources, "social, psychological, political, economic, institutional and behavioral relations"[9] as given. It adopts a positivist analysis that considers things as they are in contrast to how they ought to be.

For Guy Mhone, there is a problem here, because economics as a science cannot simply assume the reality of things without asking how they came to be the way they are.[10] Such an approach is unscientific. A scientist does not take things for granted but investigates and questions the reality he or she faces. In economics, this is an "ontological bias [which] extends to the manner in which economists take as given social relations that are inherently constituted to contain relations of domination and subjugation based on class, gender and race."[11] Here, neoclassical economics overlooks the fact that "social facts necessarily embody human values and are not inherently neutral."[12] In fact, "claims about disinterested, and value-free science are as outmoded and inappropriate in economics as they are in all other disciplines."[13]

The fact that gender is treated as a mere case of discrimination is also unsatisfactory. Gender is treated as a side issue, and gender discrimination is seen as an aberration.[14] This point of view underestimates "the pervasiveness of gender discrimination and inequality in society."[15] This pervasive character affects economics at both ontological and epistemological levels. Neoclassical economists try to tackle the issue of discrimination through human capital theories.[16] "Human capital refers to the education, skills, training, and experience necessary for particular occupations."[17] According to these theories, women are less favored than men in the labor market because they have accumulated less human capital than the latter.[18] For the protagonists of human capital theories, "women's investments in human capital are the result of rational, cost-benefit calculations."[19] Women have to juggle between their professional and domestic duties, which is the reason they will "choose occupations that require less investment in training and education and that are compatible with family responsibilities."[20] The human capital argument fails at many levels.[21] First, the differences in human capital may be due to gender discrimination, and may not be the consequence of individual decision. Second, even in occupations "requiring similar levels of training, education, skill, and responsibility,"[22] male-dominated jobs are better paid. Third, by denying the presence of discrimination and flying in the face of the evidence, these theories "serve to perpetuate market inequalities."[23] Last, "the human capital theory . . . is an exercise in circular reasoning."[24] Women are paid less because they invest less human capital, and if they invest less in human capital, it is because they are paid less. It is not surprising that human capital theories fail at explaining why skills acquisition and their returns show a "persistent negative racial and sex bias."[25]

Overall, "the inadequacy of neo-classical theories of discrimination relates particularly to their limited applicability and their inability to address the overall reproduction of gender inequality as embedded in society itself."[26] All these limits explain why neoclassical economics paradigms cannot properly capture the complexity of women's labor.

RATIONAL ECONOMIC MAN OR SUBJECT

The phrase "rational economic man/subject" encapsulates the supra-historical character of economics. Indeed,

> neoclassical economics is defined by its reliance on rational choice theory. By rational choice economists mean that individuals can (and do) arrange their preferences (their likes and dislikes) logically and consistently. Then, given their preferences, and the constraints of time and income, individuals make choices that maximize their self-interest.[27]

The rational economic subject is "referred to as *homo economicus*, or Economic Man,"[28] who is devoid of gender, race, class or any marker of social location.[29] Indeed, "humans are depicted as rational preference-maximizers who compete in markets for scarce resources to fulfill unlimited wants."[30] This reinforces the scientific and universal pretention of economics. This concept also conveys an atomistic conception of individual and economic operations. Neoclassical economists view the market as autonomous and self-regulating with minimal state intervention,[31] and the only regulator is the price of goods and services.[32]

This atomistic trend of economics is what Karl Polanyi called "disembedding," that is, "the separation of economic thought, and practice from older moorings in the thickly relational and normative relationships of households and local communities."[33] "Disembeddedness" is located primarily at the anthropological and economic level.[34] The *homo economicus* is anthropologically disembedded, because he or she is cut from any "social relationships and institutions that embody substantive moral and cultural values, and that enable persons to give and receive recognition and respect."[35] Likewise, at the economic level, economic institutions and activities are separated from "embodied, morally and culturally thick networks of social relations."[36]

Both forms of disembedding are closely intertwined. As Matej Vancura observes, "the individual [is] forced . . . to become an atom in the market mechanism and, as a consequence, he [or she is] forced to become an atom in society as well. Economic disembeddedness [tends] to produce anthropo-logical disembeddedness."[37] It comes as no surprise that the ideal worker is understood "as unconstrained either by dependency or requirements concern-ing job security, schedule, levels of pay, or free time."[38]

Feminist economists contest the concept of *homo economicus* devoid of any context. Since there is no such thing as a universal human subject, the universal rational economic agent does not exist.[39] In fact, "gender, race, ethnicity, and nation are analytical categories, not mere descriptors attached to rational agents who are in all other regards identical."[40] While economics rejects the particularity of context, Odozor reminds that the rational economic subject presupposes a well-developed economy and a literary populace who has "imbibed" every capitalist virtue, which is not the case in Africa.[41] In addition, the neoclassical conception offers a truncated vision of the human subject, far from the holistic one that stems from Church reflections (see, for instance, the idea of integral development from the previous chapter). To the atomistic view of the market and the economic agent, the Church and feminist economists offer a reflection rooted in a political economy that takes into account the full context of the person.[42] Furthermore, for the Church, "economy and state exist for the sake of families and the persons that house-holds comprise."[43]

What has been said above illustrates that neoclassical economics cannot give a fair account and description of working women, since it does not emphasize gender or local contexts. Its ideal worker looks at best like a celi-bate living alone with no dependents or no ties to any community. This will hardly fit most working women worldwide.

MACROECONOMICS VERSUS MICROECONOMICS

Neoclassical economics is divided into macroeconomics and microeconom-ics, which claim to be either gender-neutral or gender-blind.[44] Nonetheless, at both levels, "neo-classical economics is male-biased."[45] Macroeconomics focuses on the bigger picture: "gross national product [GNP], its level and growth; imports, exports and the balance of payments; tradable and non-trad-able; investment, savings, efficiency and productivity."[46] Macroeconomics is male-biased, because "it assumes that the unpaid reproductive labor . . . can be ignored in economic analysis; and it assumes that all other [labor] can be treated as interchangeable and aggregated."[47] In recent years, there have been efforts to integrate unpaid reproductive labor to gross domestic product (GDP) in many countries.[48] However, even such attempts exclude services that the household produces for its own benefit such as cooking, cleaning, care for household members, and volunteer community services.[49] Since unpaid reproductive labor is associated with women, ignoring it "renders much of women's work invisible,"[50] and their valuable contribution to economic growth is not fully appreciated. Moreover, ignoring unpaid labor "also means that the true costs of many macro-economic policies are obscured."[51] Diane Elson provides an example in Zambia in the 1980s where the government cuts on public health expenditures. This meant less hospital staff and more work for women who had to spend more time in hospitals with family members to care for them.[52] Finally, macroeconomics overlooks the sexual division of labor that creates structural constraints. This means that shifting from one occupation to another may not be as smooth as believed, especially for women.

This illustrates that the foregoing assumptions on labor do not allow macroeconomic theory to give an adequate analysis of real economic processes or "to identify some important structural constraints and costs of economic change."[53] Hence, its measurements as technical as they are, fail to capture the complexity of what happens on the ground. Simona Beretta contrasts attributional (which refers to women as individual agents or as a group) to relational (which measures women's roles and positions within networks) data, and notes that the predominance of the former in economic analysis and the virtual nonexistence of the latter.[54] Beretta further observes that while attributional data offers valuable information on women's economic and social condition, one "cannot ignore their structural limitations: they are embedded in a cultural framework dominated by the individualistic paradigm."[55] Attributional data tend to overlook relevant issues to women, such as childbearing and its effects for instance. The question of women and the missing GDP (unpaid labor not counted and the cost of women's discrimination to the economy) highlights the missing contribution of women.[56] However, this does not include childbearing, which "is the single most evident and least considered case of feminine contribution (investment) to society and to the economic system."[57] This single example highlights the inadequacy of indicators such as GDP in accounting for the full contribution of women to economic life. Beretta suggests that the value of care cannot be quantified and that care must be evaluated in terms of results instead of valuing in terms of their market price or opportunity cost.[58]

Microeconomics deals with unpaid labor and the sexual division of labor, but views "gender differentiation patterns as, on the whole, rational, efficient and mutually advantageous."[59] Again, economists emphasize individual choices over a thorough study of social structures that influence the economic agent's decision.

> The sexual division of [labor] between household members is explained in terms
> of the preferences and skills of household members, and the opportunity cost

of their time, as measured by the remuneration they could get from paid work outside the household.[60]

Women's lower economic position and achievements are explained in terms of their lower aspirations.[61] Gender discrimination in the labor market is due to individual irrational decisions (prejudice or lack of information) more than structural factors.[62] On the whole, the focus is directed on women than on their employers, customers, and others, and "on the characteristics of individuals rather than on the structural characteristics of [labor] markets, such as the nature of [labor] contract and [labor] processes."[63]

Again, neoclassical economics cannot give a good account of women's work and analyze the deep reasons that hamper women from achieving their full potential. It overlooks the power dynamics at play that may dictate a person's choice. As Beretta asserts, "Individualistic approaches in monitoring the economic situation of women are not adequate in highlighting the specificity of the "feminine" in economics."[64]

THE PREDOMINANCE OF MONEY

I need to make a qualification before moving forward. I do not advocate a return to barter economy. The issue is the logic of market and profit when overemphasized leads to underestimating economic processes that do not yield immediate financial gains. This overemphasis may also lead to a reversed tendency seen even in some feminists: the need to quantify all economic contributions as if their value depends on the fact of being monetized.

For working women, the emphasis on money works in very pernicious ways. There are three ways in which the logic of the market plays out: the undervaluation of unpaid work, the commodification of labor, and the application of partial solutions.

Concerning the undervaluation of unpaid work, I have already indicated in the previous subsection how women's unpaid reproductive work is left out of macroeconomic indicators of many countries. This lack of consideration for unpaid labor is embedded within a gendered division of labor that removes any economic significance to homemaking activities and simultaneously makes them priceless and worthless.[65] Indeed,

> paid work is absolutised and fixed as the sole form of work to afford people an income, and social security, status and power. Domestic [labor], on the other hand, in spite of its essential significance for the survival of the individual family as well as for that of the human family, is altogether discriminated against.[66]

The commodification of labor is driven by the neoliberal tendencies of recent trade agreements, which have made work flexible and have thrown Third World workers—mostly women—into more precarious conditions. Human labor is now treated as any other commodity in the market,[67] and is exploited by market forces in places where people experience economic hardships. It leads to cheap labor often performed in subhuman conditions.[68] Cheap labor means low wages, job insecurity (absence of health and safety protections, employee benefits, and social insurance), and flexibility (short-term contract, no employment security, requires minimal training).[69] This growing commodification shows more interest in profit than in the human worker as transnational corporations ship more of their production to the global South.

The application of false solutions is visible in the thinking that improving women's economic status means increasing their financial income. These approaches have all failed in bringing substantive changes to women's condition. The Women in Development (WID) approach in the 1970s thought that integrating Third World women into the market economy would change the society and bring an end to women's economic oppression.[70] Unfortunately, WID was unsuccessful because it failed to recognize that in a capitalistic economy, women are still exploited.[71] It is undeniable that women's integration into the paid workforce has its advantages for the individual. However, these individual benefits do not solve the structural problems: quality of the paid work, structure of relationships, supportive environment, status and roles of women, and other cultural constraints women may face.[72] The same can be said of the microcredit[73] solutions. If microcredit has improved the conditions of individual women and their family, "it does nothing to change the structural conditions that drive women into the informal sector in the first place."[74] Moreover, "microcredit fits nicely with the prevailing neoliberal ideology that defines poverty as a problem of individual failing. . . . This rhetoric shifts poverty solutions away from collective, social efforts and onto the backs of the poor women."[75]

NOTES

1. Mhone, "Gender Bias in Economics," 118.
2. Ibid., 119.
3. From here onward see Ibid., 118.
4. Ibid.
5. Ibid., 119.
6. Ibid., 121.
7. Ibid., 122.
8. Ibid., 123.
9. Ibid., 124.

10. Ibid.

11. Ibid., 125.

12. Ibid., 121.

13. Barker and Feiner, *Liberating Economics*, 11.

14. Mhone, "Gender Bias in Economics," 130.

15. Ibid.

16. Ibid., 129.

17. Barker and Feiner, *Liberating Economics*, 67.

18. Ibid.

19. Ibid.

20. Ibid., 68.

21. From here onward see Ibid., 68–69.

22. Ibid., 68.

23. Ibid.

24. Ibid., 68–69.

25. Mhone, "Gender Bias in Economics," 129.

26. Ibid., 131.

27. Barker and Feiner, *Liberating Economics*, 5.

28. Ibid.

29. Ibid.

30. Hinze, *Glass Ceilings and Dirt Floors*, 61.

31. Mhone, "Gender Bias in Economics," 126–27.

32. Hinze, *Glass Ceilings and Dirt Floors*, 65.

33. Ibid., 63.

34. Ibid., 64.

35. Ibid.

36. Ibid.

37. Quoted in Ibid., 65.

38. Ibid., 74.

39. Barker and Feiner, *Liberating Economics*, 5.

40. Ibid.

41. Paulinus I. Odozor C.S.Sp, "Truly Africa, and Wealthy! What Africa Can Learn from Catholic Social Teaching about Sustainable Economic Prosperity," in *The True Wealth of Nations: Catholic Social Thought and Economic Life*, ed. Daniel K. Finn (Oxford ; New York: Oxford University Press, 2010), 279.

42. Hinze, *Glass Ceilings and Dirt Floors*, 53.

43. Ibid., 97.

44. Diane Elson, "Gender Analysis and Economics in the Context of Africa," in *Engendering African Social Sciences*, ed. Ayesha Imam, Amina Mama, and Fatou Sow, Codesria Book Series (Dakar, Senegal: Codesria, 1997), 158.

45. Ibid.

46. Ibid.

47. Ibid.

48. For more on gender-aware macroeconomic models see Nallari and Griffith, *Gender and Macroeconomic Policy*, 35–36.

49. United Nations, *The World's Women 2015*, 90.

50. Elson, "Gender Analysis and Economics in Africa," 158.

51. Ibid., 162.

52. Ibid.

53. Ibid., 158.

54. Simona Beretta, "What Do We Know about the Economic Situation of Women, and What Does It Mean for a Just Economy?," in *The True Wealth of Nations: Catholic Social Thought and Economic Life*, ed. Daniel K. Finn (Oxford: Oxford University Press, 2010), 240.

55. Ibid.

56. Ibid., 246.

57. Ibid.

58. Ibid., 247.

59. Elson, "Gender Analysis and Economics in Africa," 163.

60. Ibid.

61. Ibid., 166.

62. Ibid.

63. Ibid., 167.

64. Beretta, "What Do We Know about the Economic Situation of Women," 239.

65. Hinze, *Glass Ceilings and Dirt Floors*, 66–67.

66. Marita Estor, "Women's Work Is Never at an End: Paid and Unpaid Labour," in *Women, Work and Poverty*, ed. Elisabeth Schüssler Fiorenza and Anne E. Carr, Concilium 194 (Edinburgh: T. & T. Clark, 1987), 5.

67. Hinze, *Glass Ceilings and Dirt Floors*, 87.

68. Barker and Feiner, *Liberating Economics*, 110.

69. Ibid.; Nallari and Griffith, *Gender and Macroeconomic Policy*, 114.

70. Barker and Feiner, *Liberating Economics*, 106.

71. Ibid., 102.

72. Hinze, *Glass Ceilings and Dirt Floors*, 80–82.

73. "Microcredit (sometimes referred to as microfinance) refers to extremely small loans made to poor women to enable them to start small-scale enterprises in the informal sector." Barker and Feiner, *Liberating Economics*, 124.

74. Ibid., 126.

75. Ibid.

Chapter 6

General Characteristics of Women's Work

Having quickly discussed the reasons why the neoclassical economics approach to labor in general, and women's labor in particular is unsatisfactory, I now present the main features of women's work worldwide.

Globally, half of the women participate in the workforce against three-quarters of men.[1] Women work mostly in the service sector (education, health, social work, and in private households). In Sub-Saharan Africa, women find themselves mostly in the informal sector whose main characteristics are precariousness and vulnerability. Women are in charge of unpaid reproductive labor, and when this is combined with employment, women spend more time working than men. Women's wages are lower than men, and they suffer from an unfriendly environment that limits them to some professions and positions (occupational segregation). Societal biases (marriage and land customs) also hinder women from flourishing.

I will now analyze in more detail the issues of reproductive labor, informal economy, occupational segregation, and unfriendly environment.

REPRODUCTIVE LABOR

Reproductive labor refers to household work, and it is called so because it fosters social reproduction.[2] Indeed, it "contributes to human well-being and overall economic development through nurturing people who are fit, productive and capable of learning and creativity."[3] Some refer to it as domestic work; others as care labor. Care labor is defined "as the relationships and activities involved in maintaining people on a daily basis and intergenerationally."[4] Care labor involves three types of activities: (1) direct caring of the person through physical and emotional care and services; (2) upkeep of the immediate physical surroundings; (3) and promoting "people's relationships and social connections."[5]

The United Nations sees two main categories in care and domestic work, namely, production of goods (collecting water or firewood) and services (cleaning, person-to-person care) for self-consumption.[6] While Drucilla Barker and Susan Feiner think that the term "reproductive labor" is more comprehensive than "caring labor,"[7] Christine Hinze argues that both terms are equivalent. I subscribe to the notion that reproductive labor is equivalent to caring labor. In this section, my focus is on unpaid labor.

Barker and Feiner indicate that reproductive labor cannot be overlooked when one considers women's economic roles.[8] Most unpaid reproductive labor falls into the hands of women who spend close to two and half times more than men doing it, with large disparities in cooking, cleaning, and caring for the members of the household.[9] In developing countries, women spend an average of 4 hours 30 minutes per day while men spend only 1 hour 20 minutes per day on unpaid reproductive labor; and cooking alone takes up to 1 hour 40 minutes daily on average for women.[10] In Sub-Saharan Africa, unpaid reproductive labor entails long working days that for most women starts as early as 4.00 a.m. and ends as late as 10:00 p.m. The absence of running water in the majority of households and of electricity especially in rural areas renders their task more difficult.

The importance of reproductive labor for the well-being of society and the economy is progressively acknowledged. However, it continues to be undervalued. Although it is part of Systems of National Accounts since 1993, it is rarely included in macroeconomic indicators.[11] In fact, most of the unpaid reproductive labors are referred to as "self-contained activity with limited repercussion on the rest of the economy."[12] The perception of reproductive labor suffers from the gender division of space and labor for eighteenth- to nineteenth-century Europe and North America, which was duplicated in Sub-Saharan Africa through colonization. The household is associated with the private sphere, where women belong according to this ideology. Moreover, in the modern economy, the household is no longer a unit of production, but rather a sphere of consumption.[13] In addition, the household is contrasted to the public sphere as a space where empathy reigns and where noneconomic and noncompetitive feelings and attitudes are the norm.[14] Women find themselves with the following contradiction: on the one hand, reproductive labor is elevated in moral and altruistic term; on the other hand, it is devalued in terms of having economic or political significance.[15] In fact, "market ideology enlists care's supramonetary value as a way to keep that work cheap and underpaid."[16]

Moreover, the most significant factor that explains the underestimation of reproductive labor is its perception as an exclusive prerogative of women.

Women's work tends to lack acknowledgment and is underappreciated.[17] Women's caring labor is "considered unskilled," because it is perceived "as emanating from natural abilities rather than acquired skills."[18] It then comes as no surprise that remunerated reproductive labor is among the least well-paid jobs and that domestic workers for the most part enjoy little legal recognition. What Mabel Sardón-Filipini says about domestic workers' legal condition in Latin America is also valid for African countries:

> Their wages are very low, and even in countries with laws and unions that theoretically protect their interests, their employers usually find ways round the laws, and they do not dare claim their rights for fear of losing their jobs. So they neither receive the minimum wage . . . nor enjoy social benefits such as bonuses or old age pensions, paid holidays, medical insurance, maternity benefit, etc.[19]

Likewise, other "female" jobs that are closely associated with reproductive labor such as cleaning, housekeeping, food serving and cleanup, early and young child education, and providing hands-on care for the frail, ill, and elderly "command chronically lower wages."[20]

There is a need to recognize the importance of unpaid reproductive labor in the economy. In fact, "whether paid or unpaid, caring labor is absolutely essential to economic well-being."[21] This is why without an overhaul of women's unpaid reproductive labor, there cannot be substantive change in the labor market and economy in general.[22] Hinze maps out, in five points, a clear connection between women's unpaid reproductive labor and paid labor. First, "the time and effort women put into unpaid care dictate and constrain their capacities to direct time, energy, and attention to paid work."[23] Second, since unpaid reproductive labor is not financially remunerated, "it reduces practitioners' exercise of 'voice' over decision-making and harms their ability to accumulate savings and assets."[24] Third, the fact that unpaid reproductive labor is looked upon as women's natural work that is carried out in the so-called private sphere "hides away its economic dimensions and contributions."[25] Fourth, paid labor associated with reproductive labor by the fact that it is undervalued is considered "unskilled with low pay, slender options for promotion, and scant social protection."[26] Finally, unpaid reproductive labor "entails a systemic transfer of hidden subsidies to the rest of the economy that go unrecognized, imposing a systemic time-tax on women throughout their life cycle."[27] According to Campillo Fabiola, unpaid reproductive labor subsidizes the economy in at least two significant ways: (1) it subsidizes the entrepreneurial sector through the unpaid segment of the workforce; (2) "Under conditions of economic crisis, housewives must intensify their domestic labour in order to counteract a loss in the acquisition power of salaries."[28]

OCCUPATIONAL SEGREGATION

Occupational segregation refers to the fact that women are disproportionately found in some jobs or positions compared to men. It highlights "the different patterns in the occupations and sectors between women and men."[29] The trends in occupational segregation affect both the formal and informal sector.[30] Occupational segregation can be horizontal or vertical.[31] "Horizontal segregation refers to the over-representation of women in a particular occupation."[32] In other words, women are likely to be found more in certain types of work than others. In that respect, women are generally employed in services, housework, and agricultural occupations.[33] Even in agricultural and fisheries, they are underrepresented in skilled work (37 percent worldwide).[34] Men are present in large number in crafts and trade, and as plant and machine operators, while women are in elementary occupations, clerical, and support jobs.[35]

"Vertical segregation . . . occurs when men and women work in the same occupation, but men more often do work that comes with more responsibilities, better pay and higher status, due to reasons not attributable to their skills or experience."[36] In that respect, men tend to be in managerial and legislative positions, and in skilled jobs, while women's occupations are in the majority concentrated in mid-skill or low-skill positions.[37] Looking at the evolution in the first decade of the millennium (2000–2010), women have increased their representation as managers, professionals, and technicians (between 2 percent and 3.6 percent), while their percentages have declined in male-dominated jobs such as skilled agriculture, plan operators, and crafts and trade.[38]

Occupational segregation is a pervasive and persistent phenomenon "resistant to change even as countries develop economically."[39] Whether vertical or horizontal, occupational segregation follows the same pattern. Jobs or positions that are female dominated tend to be less prestigious, less remunerated and with little prospect of promotion. Among the negative impacts of pervasive occupational perversion are the quality of work available to women, the valuation of their skills and gender pay gaps.[40]

The following case will illustrate this. A textile factory located in Ondo, Nigeria, shows how occupational segregation works.[41] Male and female factory workers both had an acceptable level of education. However, female and male workers were treated differently. This generated different work attitudes in the factory. Due to the fact that there were no prospects of promotion (wage increase, access to top positions) and the low quality of their tasks (too simple and repetitive), women view their work as temporary and merely as an opportunity to gathering sufficient funds to move to the informal sector. In other words, it was a dead-end job. Men, on the contrary, had ambitions to become independent craftsmen, which depended upon promotion within the factory.

Among the causes for occupational segregation are the gender disparities in education and in training, experience, as well as gender discrimination, gender stereotypes and biases, and the unequal distribution of unpaid reproductive labor.[42] The issues of education, training, and experience are clumsily addressed by human capital theories, as shown earlier in this work.

I shall address the issue of education and skills acquisition at the end of this section since it is pervasive in all other sections. What I can say for now is that the data show a mixed trend on education, and taken in isolation education is not a decisive factor in curbing occupational segregation.[43] Concerning gender biases, "deeply ingrained stereotypes about gender roles and differences in aptitudes, and the stigmatization of certain occupations, play an important part in shaping preferences and maintaining occupational segregation."[44] For instance, women are overrepresented in jobs associated with reproductive labor, which is perceived in a patriarchal culture as women's proper work, and less in jobs associated with decision-making or physical strength.[45] This is also perceptible in the phenomenon of globalization. The phenomenon of globalization has not improved the situation since women tend to be stuck in low paid jobs, with difficult working conditions and in vulnerable jobs. Indeed, "women's attractiveness to transnational capital stems from their subordinate gender status."[46] Transnational corporations view women of the developing world as "docile, passive, and highly union resistant and hence easily subject to the discipline required by factory work."[47]

The unequal distribution of unpaid reproductive labor takes its toll on women, for they have to juggle between their employment and their household duties. And already mentioned, the amount of type and energy they devote for unpaid reproductive labor determine what kind of job they may take. "The lack of childcare support in developing countries and the fact that women have to combine childcare with income earning . . . contribute to their segregation in informal self-employment such as home-based work."[48] For those who can access formal employment will choose jobs whose schedules are more flexible or more in tune with their domestic duties, or they will enlist the help of another woman to carry out caring labor in their household.[49] Such a situation just perpetuates the negative pattern, and does nothing to change the unequal distribution of unpaid labor.

WOMEN IN THE INFORMAL SECTOR

My choice of the informal sector is because it is the main source of employment in developing countries—in rural as well as in urban settings. In Sub-Saharan Africa in particular, women and men in formal employment represent, respectively, only 11 percent and 17 percent of the labor force.[50]

According to the 1993 international conference of labor statisticians (ICLS) definition, the informal sector is "employment and production that takes place in small or unregistered enterprises."[51] This notion has been enriched and includes "self-employment in informal enterprises (small and unregistered enterprises) and wage employment in informal jobs (unregulated and unprotected jobs) for informal enterprises, formal enterprises, households, and no fixed employer."[52] In addition,

> The term "informal" denotes jobs that are not covered in law or practice by [labor] laws or social security. Informal employment generally includes lack of protection in the event of nonpayment of wages, compulsory overtime or extra shifts, lay-offs without notice or compensation, unsafe working conditions and the absence of social benefits such as pensions, pay for sick leave and health insurance.[53]

Informal workers comprise the self-employed (street vendors, petty traders in goods or services), subsistence farmers, wage workers in domestic or seasonal agricultural work, and subcontracted industrial outworkers.[54] Wage workers are distinguished from self-employed workers within informal employment.[55]

"Self-employment includes employers, own-account workers and contributing family workers."[56] The term "own-account workers" is used to refer to "self-employed women without employees."[57] Some describe this type of work as women's micro or small-scale enterprises.[58] It involves "food processing and trading, sewing, and domestic and personal services."[59] Roughly 80 percent of working women are self-employed in Sub-Saharan Africa with 57 percent in agricultural self-employment and 23 percent in nonagricultural self-employment.[60] Contributing family work refers to "unpaid work in a family business involving the production of goods and services for sale on the market for no direct pay."[61] A good example of contributing family work is the job women do in small-scale family farms in the rural settings in Africa. This work is meant for the sustenance of the family, with the surplus being sold in local markets. Up to 34 percent and 31 percent of working women in, respectively, Sub-Saharan Africa and South East Asia are contributing family workers compared to respectively less than 20 percent and 10 percent of men in the same regions.[62] Women represent more than 63 percent of contributing family workers.[63] Agriculture is the main source of employment in South East Asia and in Sub-Saharan Africa for men as well as for women, and it is almost always informal.[64]

Informal employment is characterized by low pay, poor working conditions, and lack of social protection and job security.[65] This means that informal employment is more a survival strategy, and people resort to it because they have no other means of livelihood.[66] Informal employees end up in a precarious state than their counterparts of the formal sector.

In addition, the same gender trends observed in other sections of the labor market are visible in informal employment. Women find themselves in the most vulnerable forms of informal employment, namely, contributing family workers and own account workers.[67] Vulnerable employment is characterized by the lack of formal work arrangements and adequate social protection.[68] The lack of pay for women who are contributing family workers, "limits their autonomy and decision-making role within the household, as well as their empowerment more broadly."[69] Own-account workers fall victim to the lack of legal recognition and cannot rely on banks to get credit.[70] They are generally not represented by trade unions and do not benefit from the collective bargaining power that trade unions offer.[71] "Policy frameworks either overlook [them] or in some cases make it harder for them to make a decent living."[72] In fact, "constraints on the productivity of informal self-employed are rarely visible to urban planners and policy makers."[73] Instead, they experience—in the case of street vendors in Sub-Saharan Africa—consistent harassment from revenue services and local city councils only interested in collecting money from them.

The other characteristics of occupational segregation are also present in informal employment. Men tend to be the majority in the more protected and well-paid jobs, while women are for the most part in the least secure and lowest paying jobs such as domestic workers, piece-rate home-based workers, and contributing family workers.[74] Even if the proportion of non-agricultural informal employment is higher for women (23 percent) than men (17 percent) in Sub-Saharan Africa, this does not necessarily mean that women's condition is better since women tend to land in the least favored positions. A good example of this is domestic work, an important source of wage employment for women.[75] Most of the domestic work is informal with poor working conditions. It is estimated that "about 30 per cent of domestic workers are currently excluded from national [labor] legislation, 43 per cent are not covered by minimum wage legislation and 36 per cent are not entitled to maternity protection."[76]

Occupational segregation is also present within the same activity. For instance, in agriculture, "men are most likely to be employed as skilled agriculture and fishery workers, while women mostly work in "elementary" occupations, such as unskilled [laborers] in agriculture, fisheries or mining or in refuse collection, cleaning or food preparation industries."[77]

At the end, one must agree that

the informal sector is unlikely to solve the problems of global poverty, women's subordination, and economic insecurity. To the contrary, the growth of the informal sector actually exacerbates the feminization of poverty in part because it weakens the power of nation-states to enforce labor standards that ensure decent conditions of work.[78]

The growing tendency from the public and formal private sectors in industrialized as well as in developing countries to outsource and subcontract work means that informal and vulnerable employment will not disappear soon.[79]

WORK IN AN UNFRIENDLY
ENVIRONMENT: CUSTOMARY LAW

I review here legal and other practices that hinder working women. In Sub-Saharan Africa, women are hampered by their limited education and by customary laws that exclude them from full property rights. When one thinks about an unfriendly environment, there is the issue of violence in the workplace, which can be verbal, physical, or psychological. There is the legal framework that limits the autonomy of married women and their ability to accumulate personal assets.[80] However, for the sake of concise argument, I shall limit my development to the issue of customary law.

Customary law can be defined as "the indigenous customs of traditional communities."[81] It is essentially oral and is discerned through practices. Customary law regulates issues around family, marriage, and property.[82] Customary courts adjudicate claims pertaining to customary law, and they are in full force in rural areas where modern courts and tribunals are not always available. Their scope of sanctions and penalties is limited to fines, compensation, and other light punishment. There are two types of property rights: control (ownership) and access (user) rights.[83] Traditional customary law only grants women the latter, meaning that it limits their autonomy and decision-making power, and they have no security over the land, which is under the care of a male relative, generally a father, brother, or husband.[84] There are four ways by which women can acquire land in Cameroon: registration, purchase, donation, and inheritance.[85] The first and second possibilities are out of the reach of rural women because they demand money and time that these women lack. Donation happens generally between men, and when rural women are beneficiaries, the donation is conditional.[86] The only way through which rural women can get land is inheritance. However, traditionally, women do not inherit land either from their father or their husband. By and large, in Cameroon between the years 2005 and 2013, 92,245 land titles have been issued among which 72,594 were for men and 17,205 for women.[87]

The fact that most women do not own land precludes them from financial loans, since they can offer no collateral. One needs to remember that most women in Sub-Saharan Africa operate in the informal sector and that they need money to launch their business and keep it alive.

The other area where discrimination in customary land tenure manifests itself is on the kind of crops cultivated. Not only do the kind of crops cultivated by women carry less prestige than those by men but also men cultivate the crops that are more valuable financially and socially.[88] Generally speaking, men grow cash crops (cotton, cocoa, coffee, etc.) while women grow food crops destined for subsistence.[89] In addition, women will work in the land plot of the family to help their husbands or male relatives grow the cash crops, while they will enlist little help from the males for the food crops. In addition, the women will be shut out from the financial profits coming from cash crops. Since food crops are meant mainly for sustenance, it is only the surplus that is sold in local markets.

These kinds of practices limit rural women in their capacity and their productivity. In recent years, the question of land has become more acute in many Sub-Saharan countries due to the tendency of government to dispossess rural communities of large pieces of land to give them to multinational corporations.[90] This increases the vulnerability of entire communities and in particular that of women. In addition to the question of land, women carry their work in an environment where basic infrastructures such as water, tarred roads, electricity, or sanitation are sometimes lacking. I shall explore this point in the section on Cameroon.

LIMITS OF THE USUAL SOLUTIONS

Before turning to the specific situation of women's work in Cameroon, a few points need to be highlighted. These points make explicit what was implicit in what I said previously. First, access to a paid job is important but insufficient and not synonymous with flourishing. Second, access to education is good but insufficient to end gender disparities in the labor market. Third, it is crucial to pay attention to unpaid reproductive labor. Fourth, reforming legislation is insufficient to bring change. Since I have already demonstrated the problems with unpaid reproductive labor, it would not be necessary to return to it here.

Access to Paid Work as Insufficient

Paid labor has positive impacts on gender power dynamics even when it is carried on within a domestic setting.[91] It improves women's self-esteem, gives them their own power and improves their role in a household's decision-making. In addition, positive changes are more evident when waged work occurs in nonagricultural sectors.[92] One of the reasons is that "such employment is generally associated with migration by women out of rural areas and away from patriarchal controls of kinship and community."[93]

However, access to paid work is not a solution in itself unless other imbalances are addressed and working women flourish through it.[94] Indeed, "In almost every region in the world women's work has increased, but the conditions of their insertion into the labour market are becoming less and less favourable."[95] Hence, while access to paid labor is important, availability of quality work is too.[96] Occupational segregation needs to be addressed. As long as women remain stuck in less valued and less paid jobs and positions, their situation cannot improve.[97] In addition, since many women in developing countries labor as informal workers, there is need to give them some minimum legal recognition. I have pointed out that unpaid reproductive labor can put constraints on women's choices. Most women have to reconcile paid work with housework. One of the most acute questions is that of childcare.[98] In addition, it is important to identify the power dynamics at play in the household where the woman lives. Is she in control of her earnings or not? Does she have the freedom to decide how her money will be spent? Moreover, the motivation driving the woman in the labor market is important. For example, in Sub-Saharan Africa, involvement in income-generating activity is a necessity rather than an option for the vast majority of women.[99]

There is also the burning issue of a gender pay/wage gap. This "refers to the differences in pay between women and men."[100] The gender wage gap can be explained by levels and differences in education, occupational segregation, the nature of the job (formal or informal), location (urban or rural), the time spent in paid and unpaid work, the undervaluation of women's work, the underrepresentation of women in trade unions, and the perception of women as economic dependents.[101] However, despite these factors, "a sizeable portion of the gender wage gap remains unexplained."[102]

The unexplained factor which is direct or pure discrimination concerns "unobservable or non-measurable characteristics," such as "risk-taking, flexibility over work commitment, working unusual hours, higher mobility, competition, work effort, and difference in responsibility."[103] It is more subjective and refers mainly to individuals' attitudes; for instance, the tendency of employers to hire and pay women less due to personal prejudices, or the tendency of working women to go for less rewarding jobs. However, pure discrimination cannot be understood outside of the factors enumerated above, which create the context for such behaviors to occur.

An interesting "unexplained" factor is the discrepancy between the financial effects of motherhood and fatherhood. Overall, "parenthood and marriage . . . impose a pay penalty on women while they award a bonus to men."[104] This is observable in industrialized countries as well as in the developing world. In Sub-Saharan Africa for instance, having children in the household produces a gender pay gap of 31 percent, while the latter is only 4 percent in households without children.[105] Another often unexplained fact is that even when women and men have the same level of education, studied the same field of education, and have the same number years of work experience, there is still a gender wage gap.[106]

Problems with Education

Education has been generally perceived as a positive tool for curbing gender inequalities in the labor market and for assessing quality labor. Indeed, many women who are stuck in low-paying jobs and in informal employment lack basic education and training skills.[107] Women account for more than two-thirds of 781 million illiterate adults, who are basically found in developing regions.[108]

If education expands the options of individual women, it does not appear to alter the gender gaps of the labor market.[109] This is due to many reasons. For one, "the changes associated with education are likely to be conditioned by the context in which it is provided and the social relationships it embodies and promotes."[110] In the particular case of Sub-Saharan Africa, the present school system is "a creation connected to colonialism."[111] Indeed, "the philosophical and ideological postulates of the educational systems devised by the Europeans in the 19th and early 20th centuries have not yet been significantly transformed."[112] Girls in the colonial educational system were expected to become good mothers and housewives. Although in postcolonial Africa female students are no longer confined to a "domestic" curriculum, they are not encouraged (especially the poor ones) to remain in school and study hard because reproductive labor is perceived as their primary duties by teachers and classmates.[113] And when they want to pursue a professional career, they are advised to take jobs that reflect their caring and nurturing "nature." In addition, "social inequalities are often reproduced through the interaction within the school system."[114] Status and gender play an important role. In a country like Cameroon, students from the upper class will attend better schools than those from the low-income class. In addition, within a school, teachers tend to pay more attention to students with wealthy parents who can easily pay for extra-lessons. Moreover, the curriculum content tends to enshrine certain inequalities. For instance, there is the denigration of manual and domestic labor and gender stereotyping.[115]

It is instructive to observe that "advances in gender parity in education have not helped reduced sectoral and occupational segregation."[116] On the one hand, higher levels of education certainly give women a better opportunity at a quality job; the higher-level group overall records better participation rates in the labor force.[117] On the other hand, women tend to be over-represented in humanities (social sciences, law, etc.) and business and underrepresented in sciences where they study mainly sciences of life.[118] This segregation in fields of study remains strong worldwide and influences occupational segregation.[119] As I have pointed out, even when women share the same level of education in the same field as men, they still experience gender pay gap.

Even in technical and vocational studies, women's options tend to be limited. In countries such as Cameroon and Côte d'Ivoire, I have observed that girls tend to be clustered into accounting and management, hairdressing, and tailoring, while boys can study electricity, mechanics, electronics, carpentry or get training to become welders, iron crafts workers, bricklayers, or tile workers.[120]

Obviously, women with no or little education are worse off in the labor market than those who have a university degree. Women with low secondary education and primary education record lower rates of participation in the labor force than women with no education.[121] Many women with little and no education come from poor background, forcing them to work as early as possible.

Two things seem clear at this point. The rising rates of women's rate in education have not been the miracle solution that would end the gender disparities in the labor market.[122] Then, "gains in women's education have not had the expected positive impact on gender pay gaps."[123] Education gives mixed results. On the one hand, it is important, because it provides women with multiple and better options in the labor market. On the other hand, it is inefficient in redressing imbalances. Hence, it needs to be associated with other practices and strategies.

Legislation Is Insufficient to Produce Change

Bringing into effect new laws appears a viable solution. However, the ratification and enactment of new legislation does not automatically solve the problem of gender disparities in the workplace. Let us take for instance the Convention for the Elimination of all forms of Discrimination Against Women (CEDAW) that the United Nations adopted in 1979 and that has been ratified by 187 countries.[124] Paragraph one of article 11 of that convention asserts "the right to the same employment opportunities," "to free choice of profession and employment," "to promotion, job security and all benefits and conditions of service," "to equal remuneration," "to social security," and "the right to protection of health and to safety in working conditions."[125]

Paragraph two of the same article targets in a special way married women and mothers and encourages the enactment of provisions to protect this category and to fulfill their family obligations. The ILO Maternity Protection Convention answers the need formulated in that paragraph. It asserts that mothers, either in the formal or in the informal sector, are entitled to fourteen weeks of leave that should be paid collectively and at least at two-thirds of the previous rate.[126] If virtually every nation has adopted some kind of maternity protection legislation in response to CEDAW, only sixty-three countries meet ILO minimum requirements.[127] "Even when laws are in place, practical obstacles prevent women from claiming their rights: it is estimated that only 28 percent of employed women worldwide enjoy any paid maternity leave in practice."[128]

The gender disparities that I have highlighted earlier are still pervasive even after the ratification of CEDAW and other treaties and conventions that combat discrimination. On some levels (closing the wage gap, women's rate in the labor force), there has been some improvement, but overall problems remain. This tells us that enacting legislation is not enough and that there is a need for comprehensive action. Indeed, passing legislative reforms needs to be accompanied by additional supportive measures. For instance, granting the same employment opportunities cannot be achieved if there are still gender gaps in education at the expense of women or if there are not mechanisms to encourage or discourage corporations that would discriminate on a gender basis.

NOTES

1. From here onward see United Nations, *The World's Women 2015*, 87.
2. Note 5 in Hinze, *Glass Ceilings and Dirt Floors*, 123.
3. United Nations, ed., *Transforming Economies, Realizing Rights*, Progress of the World's Women 2015–2016 (New York: UN Women, 2015), 83.
4. Evelyn Nakano Glenn quoted in Hinze, *Glass Ceilings and Dirt Floors*, 9.
5. Ibid., 9–10.
6. United Nations, *Transforming Economies, Realizing Rights*, 83.
7. Barker and Feiner, *Liberating Economics*, 103.
8. Ibid.
9. United Nations, *Transforming Economies, Realizing Rights*, 84.
10. United Nations, *The World's Women 2015*, 111.
11. United Nations, *Transforming Economies, Realizing Rights*, 83.
12. Ibid.
13. Hinze, *Glass Ceilings and Dirt Floors*, 65–66; Barker and Feiner, *Liberating Economics*, 103.
14. Hinze, *Glass Ceilings and Dirt Floors*, 66–67.
15. Ibid., 68.
16. Ibid., 85.
17. Estor, "Women's Work Is Never at an End," 4.
18. Barker and Feiner, *Liberating Economics*, 69.

19. Mabel Sardón-Filipini, "Domestic Service in Latin America," in *Women, Work and Poverty*, ed. Elisabeth Schüssler Fiorenza and Anne E. Carr, Concilium 194 (Edinburgh: T. & T. Clark, 1987), 53.

20. Hinze, *Glass Ceilings and Dirt Floors*, 90.

21. Barker and Feiner, *Liberating Economics*, 41.

22. United Nations, *Transforming Economies, Realizing Rights*, 86.

23. Hinze, *Glass Ceilings and Dirt Floors*, 88.

24. Rania Antonopoulos quoted in Ibid., 89.

25. Ibid.

26. Rania Antonopoulos quoted in Ibid., 90.

27. Ibid., 90–91.

28. Fabiola Campillo, "Unpaid Household Labor: A Conceptual Approach," in *Macro-Economics: Making Gender Matter; Concepts, Policies and Institutional Change in Developing Countries*, ed. Martha Gutiérrez (London; New York: Zed Books, 2003), 107.

29. International Labor Office, ed., *Global Employment Trends for Women: [2012]* (Geneva: ILO, 2012), 5.

30. United Nations, *Transforming Economies, Realizing Rights*, 90.

31. International Labor Office, *Global Employment Trends for Women*, 25; Barker and Feiner, *Liberating Economics*, 65.

32. International Labor Office, *Global Employment Trends for Women*, 25.

33. Ibid.

34. Ibid., 26; United Nations, *Transforming Economies, Realizing Rights*, 90.

35. Ibid., 90.

36. International Labor Office, *Global Employment Trends for Women*, 25.

37. Ibid., 26.

38. United Nations, *Transforming Economies, Realizing Rights*, 91.

39. Ibid., 89.

40. Ibid., 89–90.

41. I take this case from Coquery-Vidrovitch, *Les Africaines*, 216–17. The study carried out in 1970s–1980s remains relevant in today's context.

42. United Nations, *Transforming Economies, Realizing Rights*, 90; International Labor Office, *Global Employment Trends for Women*, 26.

43. United Nations, *Transforming Economies, Realizing Rights*, 92.

44. Ibid.

45. International Labor Office, *Global Employment Trends for Women*, 27.

46. Barker and Feiner, *Liberating Economics*, 111.

47. Ibid.

48. United Nations, *Transforming Economies, Realizing Rights*, 92.

49. Ibid., 92–93.

50. Ibid., 103.

51. Nallari and Griffith, *Gender and Macroeconomic Policy*, 27.

52. Ibid.

53. Note 186 in United Nations, *Transforming Economies, Realizing Rights*, 309.

54. Ibid., 102.

55. Note 186 in Ibid., 309.

56. International Labour Office, *Women at Work: Trends 2016* (Geneva: ILO, 2016), 10.

57. Shawn Meghan Burn, *Women across Cultures: A Global Perspective*, 3rd ed. (New York: McGraw-Hill, 2011), 116.

58. Ibid.

59. Ibid., 115.

60. United Nations, *Transforming Economies, Realizing Rights*, 103.

61. Ibid., 83.

62. International Labour Office, *Women at Work*, 10.

63. United Nations, *Transforming Economies, Realizing Rights*, 102.

64. Ibid.

65. Barker and Feiner, *Liberating Economics*, 118; United Nations, *The World's Women 2015*, 104; International Labour Office, *Women at Work*, 11; United Nations, *Transforming Economies, Realizing Rights*, 102.

66. International Labour Office, *Women at Work*, 11; United Nations, *The World's Women 2015*, 103.

67. United Nations, *Transforming Economies, Realizing Rights*, 102; International Labor Office, *Global Employment Trends for Women*, 22.

68. International Labor Office, *Global Employment Trends for Women*, 22.

69. United Nations, *Transforming Economies, Realizing Rights*, 102.

70. Burn, *Women across Cultures*, 116.

71. Ibid.

72. United Nations, *Transforming Economies, Realizing Rights*, 107.

73. Ibid.

74. Ibid., 102; United Nations, *The World's Women 2015*, 103.

75. United Nations, *Transforming Economies, Realizing Rights*, 106.

76. Ibid.

77. United Nations, *The World's Women 2015*, 99.

78. Barker and Feiner, *Liberating Economics*, 127.

79. United Nations, *Transforming Economies, Realizing Rights*, 115.

80. Ibid., 111.

81. Vera N. Ngassa, "Exploring Women's Rights within the Cameroonian Legal System: Where Do Customary Practices of Bride-Price Fit In?" in *Issues in Women's Land Rights in Cameroon*, ed. Lotsmart N. Fonjong (Bamenda: Langaa Research & Publishing CIG, 2012), 70.

82. R. Gordon Woodman, "A Survey of Customary Laws in Africa in Search of Lessons for the Future," in *The Future of African Customary Law*, ed. Jeanmarie Fenrich, Paolo Galizzi, and Tracy E. Higgins (Cambridge; New York; Cape Town; Madrid; Melbourne: Cambridge University Press, 2011), 26.

83. Susana Lastarria-Cornhiel, "Impact of Privatization on Gender and Property Rights in Africa," *World Development* 25, no. 8 (April 1997): 1318.

84. Lotsmart N. Fonjong, "Equal Rights but Unequal Power over Land: Rethinking the Process of Engendering Land Ownership and Management in Cameroon," in *Issues in Women's Land Rights in Cameroon*, ed. Lotsmart N.

Fonjong (Bamenda: Langaa Research & Publishing CIG, 2012), 20, 24–28; Lastarria-Cornhiel, "Impact of Privatization," 1326.

85. Harmony Bobga, "Discrimination in Women's Property and Inheritance Rights in Cameroon: The Role of Human Rights NGOs in Promoting Gender Sensitive Land Reforms," in *Issues in Women's Land Rights in Cameroon*, ed. Lotsmart N. Fonjong (Bamenda: Langaa Research & Publishing CIG, 2012), 142–47.

86. Patrice Bigombe Logo and Elise-Henriette Bikie, "Women and Land in Cameroon: Questioning Women's Land Status and Claims for Change," in *Women and Land in Africa: Culture, Religion and Realizing Women's Rights*, ed. L. Muthoni Wanyeki (London; New York; Cape Town: Zed Books Lt-David Philip Publishers, 2003), 55; Vera N. Ngassa, "Women's Inheritance Rights in the North West and South West Regions of Cameroon," in *Issues in Women's Land Rights in Cameroon*, ed. Lotsmart N. Fonjong (Bamenda: Langaa Research & Publishing CIG, 2012), 50.

87. Institut National de Statistiques du Cameroun, *Annuaire statistique du Cameroun 2014*, 72.

88. In the Mkako of the Eastern region of Cameroon, corn, which belongs to men is more important than cassava, which is cultivated by women, see Elisabeth Copet-Rougier, "Contrôle masculin, exclusivité féminine dans une société patrilinéaire," in *Femmes du Cameroun: Mères pacifiques, femmes rebelles*, ed. Jean-Claude Barbier (Bondy [France] : Paris: Orstom ; Karthala, 1985), 156.

89. Tantoh Farnyu and Yenshu Vubo, "Gender and Rural Economy in the Wimbum Society," 85.

90. United Nations, *Transforming Economies, Realizing Rights*, 109.

91. Naila Kabeer, "Gender Equality and Women's Empowerment: A Critical Analysis of the Third Millenium Development Goal," *Gender and Development*, Millenium Development Goals, 13, no. 1 (March 2005): 18.

92. Ibid., 19.

93. Ibid.

94. United Nations, *Transforming Economies, Realizing Rights*, 120.

95. Campillo, "Unpaid House Labor," 117; For instance, "Export-oriented manufacturing is associated with extremely long hours of work during busy seasons, often combined with lay-offs during the slack season, and poor conditions," see Kabeer, "Gender Equality and Women's Empowerment," 20.

96. International Labour Office, *Women at Work*, 39.

97. As Naila Kabeer rightfully observes, "it is difficult to see how earnings generated by sex work, domestic service, and daily labour on construction sites—which is where the poor women are likely to be found—will do much to improve women's subordinate status at home or at work," see Kabeer, "Gender Equality and Women's Empowerment," 20.

98. For more, see how working mothers try to cope in a context of inadequate childcare support see Gaia Pianigiani, "Italy's 'fertility Day' Call to Make Babies Arouses Anger, Not Ardor," *The New York Times*, September 13, 2016, online edition, sec. top stories.

99. International Labor Office, *Global Employment Trends for Women*, 21.

100. International Labour Office, *Women at Work*, 48.

101. Ibid.

102. Ibid.

103. Ibid., 57.

104. United Nations, *Transforming Economies, Realizing Rights*, 98.

105. Ibid.

106. United Nations, *The World's Women 2015*, 110.

107. United Nations, *Transforming Economies, Realizing Rights*, 93.

108. United Nations, *The World's Women 2015*, 79.

109. United Nations, *Transforming Economies, Realizing Rights*, 80.

110. Kabeer, "Gender Equality and Women's Empowerment," 17.

111. N'Dri Thérèse Assie-Lumumba, "Educating Africa's Girls and Women: A Conceptual and Historical Analysis of Gender and Inequality," in *Engendering African Social Sciences*, ed. Ayesha Imam, Amina Mama, and Fatou Sow, Codesria Book Series (Dakar, Senegal: Codesria, 1997), 299.

112. Ibid., 301.

113. Ibid., 308; Kabeer, "Gender Equality and Women's Empowerment," 17; Hélène-Laure Menthong, "Les cadres masculins de l'expérience féminine: les représentations collectives des garçons sur les filles et leurs trajectoires scolaires," in *La biographie sociale du sexe: Genre, société et politique au Cameroun*, ed. Luc Sindjoun, La bibliothèque du Codesria (Paris; Dakar: Karthala ; CODESRIA, 2000), 79–153.

114. Kabeer, "Gender Equality and Women's Empowerment," 17.

115. Ibid.

116. International Labour Office, *Women at Work*, 42.

117. United Nations, *Transforming Economies, Realizing Rights*, 80.

118. International Labour Office, *Women at Work*, 42.

119. United Nations, *Transforming Economies, Realizing Rights*, 92.

120. See table 15 in Ministère de la Promotion de la Femme et de la Famille, "Femmes et Hommes au Cameroun en 2012: une analyse situationelle de progrès en matière de genre" (Yaoundé, Cameroon, March 2012), 14, http://www.statistics-cameroon.org/downloads/JIF/MINPROFF_Femmes_Hommes_Cameroun_28_02_2012.pdf.

121. United Nations, *Transforming Economies, Realizing Rights*, 80.

122. Ibid., 80–81.

123. Ibid., 81.

124. Philip Alston and Ryan Goodman, *International Human Rights: Text and Materials* (Oxford, United Kingdom: Oxford University Press, 2013), 179.

125. United Nations, "Convention on the Eliminations of All Forms of Discrimination against Women" (1979), sec. 11, http://www.un.org/womenwatch/daw/cedaw/text/econvention.htm.

126. United Nations, *Transforming Economies, Realizing Rights*, 87.

127. Ibid.

128. Ibid.

Chapter 7

The Reality of Women's
Work in Cameroon

In this chapter, I would like to build on the characteristics highlighted in the previous section. I will offer a general overview of the points highlighted, and will present some specific cases to illustrate the reality better. Before doing that, I will describe the reality of work in Cameroon and discuss related issues to give a better picture of the general situation.

GENERALITIES ON GENDER AND WORK

Precariousness characterizes employment in Cameroon. Opportunities for decent and salaried work are limited. Most workers are in the informal sector and are underemployed.[1] Up to 72 percent of Cameroonians were in the labor force in 2014.[2] According to the International Labor Organization (ILO) standards, in 2010, up to 69 percent of Cameroonians were employed with 74 percent of men and 64 percent of women.[3] Overall, women make only 47 percent of the workforce.[4] When one takes into account unpaid reproductive labor, the participation rate to the labor force climbs to 94 percent with 98 percent of women and 87 percent of men. This is not necessarily a positive feature because most women are in vulnerable and unprotected employment and are stuck with low or nonpaying jobs.

Less than 8 percent of the Cameroonian employed work in the formal sector, either public or private; even there, women are disadvantaged.[5] Close to 12 percent of employed men are in the formal sector against 4 percent of employed women.[6] The number of the formally employed is close to 980,000 workers with more than 329,000 employed in the public sector.[7] These figures are rather anemic, considering that the number of Cameroonians able to join the workforce (15–64 years) is 11,252,165 million, which is more than half of the population of the country.[8] Women represent only 31 percent of workers in the public sector and are only the majority among contractual workers and others who do not have permanent employment.[9] In the formal private sector, less than 25 percent of the employed are women.[10]

The informal sector absorbs the vast majority of Cameroonians employed, as I already pointed out. More than 63 percent of employed Cameroonians are in informal agriculture with, respectively, 68 percent and 59 percent of men and women.[11] Up to 28 percent are in nonagricultural informal employment with close percentages between men (29 percent) and women (27 percent).[12] A closer look shows that women are falling into the most vulnerable categories. Half of the women employed are own-account workers, and close to two out of five are family-contributing workers.[13] This makes almost nine out of ten women in vulnerable employment. Agriculture is women's main activity (69 percent), and they are also involved in trade (10 percent), services (12 percent), and industry (8 percent).[14]

More than 8.1 million Cameroonians live below the poverty line, and they represent 37.5 percent of the population.[15] In addition, more than 90 percent of these poor live in rural areas, and it is estimated that close to 57 percent of rural dwellers are poor in Cameroon.[16] Hence, it comes as no surprise that more than six out of ten involved in informal agriculture are poor, and these make two-thirds of the poor in Cameroon.[17] Most of the people working in agriculture are family-contributing workers like women. I should add that most workers in rural areas are not paid. In fact, less than 9 percent possess a pay-slip, and less than 10 percent have any sort of contract.

The next vulnerable group is made of those who are employed in nonagricultural informal sector, with 20 percent, respectively, being poor and of the total of the poor in Cameroon.[18] Even in this group, men are more likely to be paid compared to women. Waged male workers in informal employment represent close to 20 percent of all male workers, while their female counterparts only represent 12 percent of all female workers.[19] Overall, only 11 percent of informal employees in the nonagricultural sector receive a pay-slip and as few as 14 percent have a sort of contract.[20]

In addition, half of the households headed by own-account workers—who represent more than 80 percent of the poor—are poor.[21] All these figures clearly confirm the feminization of poverty in Cameroon, given that employed women are in the informal sector. Hence, they are working in sectors that are mostly disadvantaged.

Many factors explain why women are clustered into vulnerable and low-paying employment, but there is a critical factor of this phenomenon: the lack of education. Most authors I surveyed pointed to the lack of formal education as one factor explaining that women are disadvantaged in the labor market compared to men.[22] Only 66 percent of girls are able to complete their primary education.[23] Not only is their access to a decent job limited as a result, but also the opportunity to expand their activity since they lack basic skills. In addition, social practices that favor boys' education over girls' are responsible for this situation. A national survey shows that households whose head is illiterate or with only primary education make more than 80 percent of the total poor.[24] Moreover, only 3 percent of employed women occupy managerial or executive positions, and 5.8 percent are classified as skilled workers in contrast to, respectively, 6 percent and 14.6 percent for men.[25] However, as I pointed out earlier, education needs to be associated with other elements to effectively improve women's condition.

The other salient factor is colonization.[26] The colonizers introduced monetary economy and private ownership of land, which had devastating effects on women. Women were prevented from participating in the cash economy, and were only involved in cash crop business as unpaid laborers. Then, their central role as food providers through subsistence agriculture was undermined. New agricultural techniques were introduced mostly to men. In addition, land registration could only occur through the heads of households who were invariably male, resulting in the undermining of women's land rights. There were other policies such as the educational policy that reflected the colonizers' gender bias. Indeed, "the school curricular for girls was centred on basic literacy, religious instruction and domestic science. The general intent of female education was to produce Black Victorian wives and mothers."[27] If this is no longer the case, one enduring legacy is that many still consider formal education a luxury for girls, especially in rural areas. In Cameroon, furthermore, the colonial legacy endures in matters of marriage laws, occupational segregation, as well as educational segregation.

The list of factors that make women vulnerable is far from being exhaustive. I would like to look deeper into three areas of women's work in Cameroon: unpaid reproductive labor, the informal sector, and the formal sector.

UNPAID REPRODUCTIVE LABOR

Most of what has been said in section two about unpaid reproductive labor apply to the situation of women in Cameroon. My interest here is on the specifics of the situation of Cameroon.

Let me first present a case that will provide a window into how unpaid reproductive labor structures the day of an urban woman in Cameroon.[28] I will do this by using a real-life woman story. I will refer to her according to the initials of her name R.N.

R.N. lives in the city of Douala, in a working-class neighborhood with her two little children. Her husband is most of the time away from home because of his job. R.N.'s day begins at 5.00 a.m. with a short prayer, then she heats water and prepares breakfast for her children. Around 6.00 a.m., she wakes up her children, bathes them, feeds them, and dresses them. At 7.00 a.m., she accompanies the oldest child to the bus station, where a school bus comes to pick him. After that she comes back home to clean the house, wash the dishes, and do the laundry. Then, she put clothes in right order and irons them. These chores take between two and three hours to get done. She then goes out at 10.30 a.m. to take care of her own affairs. However, before leaving, she makes sure that lunch is ready. In case there are leftovers from the previous day, she warms them. If there are not, she has to cook and has to wait until 2.30 p.m. to go out. In case she went out earlier, she comes back at 3.30 p.m. to start cooking diner. It takes between thirty minutes and two hours. At 6:00 p.m. she bathes her children, and helps the older with her homework. At 8.00 p.m., she serves dinner, and her day ends at 10:00 p.m. As one can see, caring labor takes R.N.'s whole day, and she is even privileged to have running water in her home and a gas stove. If not, she would spend more time as the following table will show. As the case of R.N. reveals, reproductive labor is intensive and time-consuming.[29].

Interesting features emerge from the above table. It confirms the imbalances on time spent at the expense of women. This betrays the fact that Cameroonian society clearly views unpaid reproductive labor as the primary duty of women. On average, employed women spend three times more than employed men on unpaid caring labor. For the unemployed category, women spend twice as much time as men.[30] The location is an important variable in the workload and time-use. People in rural areas spend more time on reproductive labor than those of the city, and even in this case, urban women's time by far twice that of rural men in any matchup. In addition, matching up the data presented in the table with the experience of R.N., which is typical of many women, shows that the numbers here offer a glimpse of reality. The reality might be uglier for millions of women in Cameroon.

Table 7.1.   Weekly Hours Spent on Unpaid Reproductive Labor in Cameroon

Location	Men Employed	Men Unemployed	Women Employed	Women Unemployed
Urban	6.9	9.0	23.0	19.6
Rural	9.2	10.4	26.4	20.4
Cameroon	8.4	9.7	25.5	19.6

Source: Institut National de Statistique 2012.
Institut National de Statistique du Cameroun, *Annuaire statistique du Cameroun, recueil des séries d'informations statistiques sur les activités économiques, sociales, politiques et culturelles du pays jusqu'en 2010* (Cameroon: Institut National de Statistique, 2012), 136, http://www.stat.cm/downloads/annuaire/2012/Annuaire-2012-complet.pdf.

Employed women tend to have longer hours of reproductive labor compared to "unemployed" women. This contrasts with men who show the reverse tendency. Employed men work less at home than unemployed men. The fact that employed women work even more confirms the notion of "second shift" outlined by feminists: that women, after completing their (in)formal employment, begin another one in their own home. We should bear in mind that most women work in the informal sector, which means that they do not have the means to enlist any help. However, this does not explain why they have to work longer. It is probably true that it is because of motherhood and marriage, which entail more responsibility. Since the statistics takes in even children as young as five, I suspect that motherhood and childcare force the mother to look for an income-generating activity. The literature admits that women who work in the informal sector do it out of necessity and for their family.[31] Moreover, Sub-Saharan Africa has the highest rate of men and women aged sixty-five years old and over—the normal ages of retirement—are still in the workforce due to high poverty rates and low retirement benefits coverage.[32] The fact that women go to work for their children and family is confirmed by a survey carried out in villages of the North-West region of Cameroon.[33] The results showed that women use their cash revenue mostly to pay for their children's education (32 percent) and family health care (31.3 percent). The farm products are mainly served for family consumption (48 percent).

When one looks at specific household tasks such as cooking, childcare, house cleaning, fetching water, collecting firewood, or household shopping, these tasks fall disproportionately into the hands of women.[34] Cooking is performed by almost all women; 50 percent of women fetch water; more than 65 percent collect firewood; 70 percent are involved in childcare; more than 50 percent and 90 percent are, respectively, performing house cleaning and household shopping. Apart from firewood collection where the number of men involved reaches 30 percent, most of the other tasks see less than 10 percent of involvement with cooking and fetching water being the least of chores done by men. What makes the work of women more difficult is the fact that some facilities are not available to the majority of Cameroonian households, as the following table will show.

This table shows that most Cameroonian households lack basic commodities, and even when they are present such as running water, water shortages are likely to throw people on the streets in search of water. The absence of basic commodities increases the time women have to spend on unpaid labor. Cooking, for instance, takes a lot of time because of the amount of time needed for collecting firewood in rural areas or buying and warming charcoal in cities. This is a consequence of the absence of gas cookers or gas stoves in the vast majority of households. They have to carry heavy loads of firewood or water on their head, and many times over long distances in rural areas with little help from the men. And one adds farming in the case of rural women, this takes a heavy toll on women's bodies and health.

As we can see the uneven distribution of caring labor and the conditions in which it is performed, constrains women and limit their options. For a starter, the notion of rest and leisure is a luxury for women and girls in rural areas.[35] In addition, in poor families caring labor, in particular "fetching water and fuel wood, is one of the factors limiting girls' access to schooling and consequently, the woman's inability to participate in certain economic activities."[36] I recall the case of a girl in a primary school who was so tired in the morning that she always slept in school. When asked the reason for her fatigue, she said that she had to wake up as early as 2:00 a.m. to go look for water. Daughters are enlisted to relieve the mothers of their workload like taking care of their younger siblings, cooking and cleaning the house. This is very common in poor and working families both in towns and in rural areas. This does not solve the problem but deflects it and perpetuates the cycle of oppression.

To make things worse, this part of reproductive labor so vital for the economy is not taken into account by the System of National Accounts. This confirms the gender bias against reproductive labor, which strips this type of labor of its economic value as I discussed earlier in this chapter.

One other clear feature from the various data presented above is the blatant discrepancy between urban and rural settings. Workers in rural settings are generally worse off than those in the city. This is due to precarious living conditions where basic facilities are not always available (see table 7.2). It is also caused by the limited opportunities for a decent job. The main activity is farming, which is mostly done as household contributing workers. Those who are paid barely receive the minimum wage.

One fact to take into account is that the economic crisis of the late 1980s and early 1990s has had mixed effects on women in Cameroon. A survey carried out in four Cameroonian cities in 2011 has revealed the changing patterns of childcare in all social backgrounds.[37] The observation showed more fathers involved in childcare: feeding, bathing, taking to school or the

Table 7.2. Percentage of Households with Access to Basic Commodities in Cameroon

	Urban (%)	Rural (%)	Nationwide (%)
Access to running water	75	27	45
Electricity	90	23	48
Sanitation	66	14	33
Gas cooker			10
Gas stove			23

Source: Institut National de Statistique 2016

hospital, and the like. This change is due to, at least, three factors. First, the fact that fewer men have stable jobs and that women are employed and too busy to do childcare alone.[38] Second, the economic downturn has made it expensive to keep a large family in town, so it is difficult to enlist the help of a relative who will take care of the children.[39] Third, well-off fathers, in addition to the material and financial resóurces, do not hesitate to give their own time, because the times are changing. If, in terms of childcare, there is a positive change, it does not mean more free time for women. On the contrary, it allows them an opportunity to be involved in income-generating activities to which I shall return in the next subsections.

INFORMAL EMPLOYMENT: AGRICULTURE

I have already explored the generalities of informal employment. I will, therefore, not return to them. I will now specifically look at the case of farming and nonagricultural informal employment.

Female Gardeners in Buea[40]

Women farmers face a great number of challenges. I take the case of women gardeners in the town of Buea, in the South West region of Cameroon, to illustrate the condition of women farmers.[41] This case is instructive because it illustrates gender dynamics in farming. Moreover, both male and female farmers rent the land which they cultivate. Although the case is located in an urban setting, many features are similar to rural settings. The study shows that married female gardeners are likely to come from a household where at least one member of the family works in the public sector, while it is barely the case for unmarried female gardeners. In fact, only one female head of household is a civil servant, while for the majority of the other unmarried female gardeners, gardening is their principal activity. Even in this case where the policy is supposedly gender-blind, male gardeners tend to have larger plots than female gardeners. The vast majority of women rent plots less than 300 square meter while the majority of men rent plots with a size between 300 and 799 square meter. Married women tend to have smaller plots than unmarried ones. It makes sense because for the latter this is their principal means of survival. The vast majority of women farm to supplement household food supply. However, the unmarried group overwhelmingly is also interested in generating additional income, which is less the case of married women. It is noteworthy that, while a minority of men takes on gardening as a hobby, it is not the case with the women interviewed.

There are other disparities noted in the survey. The first one is in the choice of crops. Men tend to cultivate high-value crops (tomatoes, cabbages, etc.) more than women; those demand high investment and generate high returns. By contrast, most of the unmarried females grow basic food crops such as maize, beans, potatoes, and okra. They do not have enough capital and time to grow high-value crops due to their precarious economic status.

Contrary to social expectations, female gardeners are involved in land preparation (which is usually a man's task), weeding, sowing, watering, and harvesting. While male gardeners enlist the help of female relatives to help them with their work, female gardeners have to do everything by themselves. Married female gardeners receive some masculine help in land preparation, watering, applying chemicals, and harvesting. Most of the work is done during the daytime. However, women and female children prior to gardening have to get up early to carry out caring labor. A good number of men only work in the garden in the evening due to their limited involvement in reproductive labor.

Among the difficulties, women complain almost universally about the high prices of agricultural chemicals, which prevent them from cultivating high-value crops. They also noted their lack of education and training as a crucial limitation. They also reveal that when training was offered, women were not invited, rather the men as heads of household (even though they were not farming). Men complain mostly about the lack of farm equipment and the theft of their produce.

Issues with Female Farmers

Means used for farming is an issue for female farmers. But, the main problem is the insecurity of land tenure, which, in turn, limits the control over the land by female farmers.

Farming is the economic activity that illustrates the bias against women. Indeed, women not only constitute the vast majority of farmers but also they do most of the work:

> Women perform about 90 per cent of the work of processing food crops and providing water and fuel wood, 80 percent of the work of food storage and transport from farm to the village, 90 per cent of the work from hoeing and weeding, and 60 per cent of the work of harvesting and marketing.[42]

In spite of this reality, women tend to be left out when new farming techniques are introduced.[43] This is an unfortunate legacy of colonialism. This is part of the "socio-domestic ideology"[44] prevalent in Cameroon that perceives women mostly "as wives rather than partners with men in development."[45]

And even, when female farmers are targeted, some initiatives fail because, among others factors, women are not participants in designing the project or in decision-making process.[46]

Women are subsistence farmers and men farm cash crops.[47] This means that women work mostly not for personal profit but to feed their family since it is their responsibility. Women have to work in their husband's land to help produce the cash crops, although they are eventually excluded from the profits. Most female farmers work as contributing family workers and as own-account workers, which are the most vulnerable positions in informal employment.[48]

The fact that women do not have secured property rights has many unfortunate consequences. First, their power of decision as to what to grow and how to manage the land is curtailed. For instance, in the Fali community of northern Cameroon, the man decides what types of crops are to be grown. In most communities, such as the Wimbun of the North West Region,[49] the Fali, the Mafa and Mounyang of the Far North region,[50] women have access to land through male relatives. In rural North Cameroon, women are in charge of breeding poultry and livestock. However, pig, goat, and cattle belong to men.[51]

A second consequence of not owning the land is that the plots given to women are smaller and of poorer quality.[52] This means that the level of productivity is very low, and the quantities produced are not enough to be sold in local markets. A third consequence is the distinction between "planters" and "cultivators." A planter is someone who grows cash crops and makes money out of farming, while a cultivator grows food crops, and does not make as much money as the latter. In the popular mindset, being designated as planter is more prestigious than being designated as cultivator. To my knowledge, I do not know a single woman who is referred to as planter. This distinction entails that men are more involved than women in commercial agriculture.[53]

The second challenge that female farmers face is that of means. First of all, they used outdated and rudimentary techniques (use a hoe or/and machete, unimproved seeds, etc.) for their work,[54] which are time-consuming and result in low productivity. Second, they lack financial means to buy pesticides or improve their activity. Third, the absence or little formal education that characterizes the majority of female farmers hinders their activity. Fourth, a critical issue is the question of transport.[55] Transport in rural areas is mainly with donkeys, bicycles, motorbikes and by foot. It is very rare to see a rural woman who owns either of the first three. Even carts and rickshaws belong to men. So women have to carry the products of the farm and firewood on their head. It is a common sight to meet women heavily burdened with children on their back while men carry at best their tools or the load on bicycle, donkeys, or cart.[56] All this takes a heavy toll on women's health.

The economic crisis of the 1980s–1990s was characterized by the drop in cash crop prices in the international market. As a result, food crops have gained more prominence. An unintended consequence is the fact that rural women have gained more financial power and supposedly more autonomy.[57] However, some scholars have reservations about the extent of this change. For them, the situation has brought extra pressure for women to fill in the gap.[58] Others argue that even if women make extra cash the power dynamics at play prevent them from enjoying full control of that money.[59] One thing is sure; women increasingly include a "market-oriented dimension to their farming activities."[60]

Women develop strategies faced with this adversity. The first is to gather in farmers' associations.[61] This is not new and existed prior to colonization. The association's main goal is to improve the living condition of its members.[62] They use these associations to purchase land by pooling their resources.[63]

Another strategy is to help women farmers generate more income to fight poverty.[64] However, this strategy falls short for a series of reasons. They lack financial resources, suffer from the lack or low level of education of their members, and their dependence on external partners.[65] They face other constraints. The associations hardly get permanent holding on the land; hence, they focus their activities on food crops, which do not necessitate heavy investment.[66] In addition, the quality of the land is mediocre, and its surface is limited.[67] "They are less likely to carry out long-term investments, such as constructing a women's cooperative building or the cultivation of economic crops like oil palm, coffee or cocoa."[68] In addition, the work for the association exacerbates the workload of women, which is already taken by family-contributing work and reproductive labor.[69] Moreover, the associations have not changed men's perception of women as inferior beings who cannot manage their own resources.[70]

The second strategy is to get loans from donors through women's associations. These allow them to purchase machines and devices that help them process food faster and efficiently.[71] Not only these loans have improved women's economic status in the various regions but also the machines have helped reduce their workload.[72] However, if the situation of individual women is resolved, the structural issues of the imbalance in the gender-based division of labor or the exclusion of women from public policies of development remain.

INFORMAL EMPLOYMENT: NONAGRICULTURAL JOBS

Many women work in informal employment as domestic help, petty traders, seamstresses, hairdressers, sex workers, or in services. Many women are engaged in this type of activity to support their family.

Because I have already spoken of domestic labor extensively, I shall not dwell on the topic here. I will just add that women make up the majority of paid domestic labor. For the most part, they are informal workers poorly paid (sometimes as low as $ 30/month) with long days of work (they work on average 50 hours a week from what I have observed). They have no social protection or benefits. The same is true of hairdressers and waitresses in restaurants and pubs. The latter work for long hours and are paid sometimes as low as $40/month. I recall the case of a lady who worked for seventeen hours in a restaurant and was paid $2 per day. Starvation wages do not help one to sustain her family or pay the bills. To make things worse, waitresses are frequently sexually harassed by male clients. To make ends meet some waitresses choose to have sexual intercourse with their clients. If something is lost or broken in the shop or business, it is deducted from their already meager salary.

Petty Traders

The female petty traders in Cameroon are called *buyam-sellam* a term from Pidgin English, which literally means buying and selling. Buyam-sellam designates women who are resellers and who mostly supply food in Cameroon's major urban centers.[73] They basically buy food from small farmers, transport them and sell them in urban markets.[74] I shall focus, in a special way, on the case of the buyam-sellam of the Fako division[75] in Cameroon.[76]

An earlier survey revealed that of buyam-sellam in their vast majority are not married.[77] This finding is confirmed by the Fonjong's survey I am using here.[78] Since they are the heads of their households this gives them more freedom of movement: they can travel very far and stay away from their home as long as it is necessary, given that a successful trip takes up to two days. The buyam-sellam from the Fako division go as far as Douala (fifty miles away) to supply food. They get up very early and go to the rural markets to buy food from the markets. After that, they travel to Douala where they spend the whole night selling their goods in the open air before coming back the following day. Some of them rather sell the food in the very region where they live.

These female traders face a number of challenges among which limited access to credit, land and transportation, insecurity, and storage difficulties.[79] Having dealt with the land question extensively, I shall not come back to it. However, the issue of land and credit are intertwined, for land serves as collateral in case one wants to get a bank loan. Very few financial institutions are ready to lend money to women who operate in trading with limited resources. This fact "affects the quantity of production and the amount of labour these women can buy or hire respectively at any given time."[80]

Concerning the issue of transport, the poor state of rural roads complicates the transportation of the harvest from the farms to the nearest urban center. "They transport the crops on their head, backs, hand trucks, which saps a lot of their energy and time."[81] This material difficulty explains why a good portion of the harvest never makes it to the market, for it rots in the farm itself. In addition, women get discriminated in public transportation during the rainy season, because of their alleged physical weakness.[82] The poor state of rural roads coupled with the poor condition of the vehicles leads transporters to limit the numbers of women during that period. A transporter who is covering the route from N'zerekore in Guinea-Conakry to Abidjan in Ivory Coast told a friend that he limits the number of women to less than 40 percent of available seats because they will be of no use in case the car breaks down or needs to be pushed if it falls into a pothole. This anecdote is confirmed by Njoh Ambe's study of Cameroon.[83]

Related to the issue of transport, the absence of storage facilities does not allow these women to stock their product.[84] Whether in the farms or the markets, their products are in open air. In case of overproduction, the products can be lost. To make things worse, security is an issue. The lack of storage facility leads to theft. The women themselves can be robbed or even worse raped as has been reported at least in one site.[85]

Buyam-sellam also deals with constant harassment from city councils who demand daily taxes and security forces on the roads who extort money.[86] Added to the high cost of transport, their margin of profit is very thin.[87]

Buyam-sellam as the female farmers gather in associations called ROSCA[88] also known in Cameroon as njangi.[89] Of the three main categories of njangi (labor, goods and money njangi), they use the money type. It works according to the system of pooled resources that are distributed according to an agreed order. It allows one to accumulate quickly an amount that would have taken more time, if one had to do it on one's own. Given the complexity of contemporary life, the money jangi has developed within its structure many other options. Many money jangi have in addition to the rotating savings, a "trouble bank" where anyone can borrow without interest or at a small interest rate.[90] The njangi money has itself many subcategories, and buyam-sellam use two: the rotating and the fixed period njangi.[91] The rotating njangi follows a cycle, while in the accumulated njangi, savings are accumulated and equally shared among members at the end of a fixed period—generally one year. According to my observations, both can coexist within a ROSCA. The njangi allow women to generate some capital and start their business or expand it. Nonetheless, one needs to consider that given the small amount of the savings in the njangi, these women find it difficult to achieve their project as planned and must settle for something modest.[92]

Another strategy is to enlist the help of relatives, especially children to perform certain tasks.[93] It is not uncommon in Cameroon to find pre-pubescent children selling in shops and markets in place of their parents. This has its limits too. It is temporary and very unreliable. Hired labor is generally used for harvesting. However, it is essentially "unreliable and expensive" outside of the peak period of harvesting.[94]

WORKING IN AN UNFRIENDLY ENVIRONMENT: THE ISSUE OF THE AUTONOMOUS WOMAN

One issue that is implicitly mentioned in the literature is the question of the autonomous woman in the African environment. This critically affects women and enters into their working opportunities. As Oduyoye contends, "in Africa, the very idea of a free woman conjures up negative images."[95] A clear objection to that would be that standing alone is not expected of anybody, so this needs qualification. African societies are communitarian for the most part, and connectedness is important for life in those societies. This connectedness is not limited to human beings but extends to the nonhuman world and to the spiritual realm.[96] The individual as such is just a dead branch detached from the living trunk of the community.[97] Togetherness defines the individual to quote the famous words of John Mbiti, "I am because we are; and since we are, therefore I am."[98] Sharing and harmony are key values.[99]

It becomes understandable that in such a context autonomy is viewed with suspicion. For this reason, Mveng prefers complementarity to equality between sexes, since he thinks that the latter makes men and women independent from one another and strangers to one another.[100] To cut oneself from this being-together is to disrupt the harmony within the community and to endanger it. However, this communitarian orientation does not mean that the individual loses his/her proper identity. Indeed, "individual achievement is encouraged and appreciated as long as it benefits the whole community."[101]

For any observers of contemporary African nations, one wonders how far this idea of community goes. Accusations of ethnocentrism, nepotism, and favoritism are current. People tend to favor their close relatives and associates. In addition, certain groups such as women do not enjoy full membership when it comes to benefits and particular rights, as I demonstrated earlier concerning the land issue. The concept of connectedness and community is very restricted when one looks at concrete practices.

If African communities expect no one to be autonomous, the condition of women is different from that of men. As Oduyoye points out, "A woman's life is defined as male-centered and community-oriented; she achieves nothing if she fails in this respect."[102] If no one is expected to be really autonomous, "society ensures that women feel particularly dependent."[103] It comes as no surprise that there is a certain social aversion to successful and/or independent women.[104] Where marriage confers full responsibility and relative autonomy to men, women remain subjects.[105] This can be illustrated by the following examples taken respectfully from traditional and contemporary Africa. Traditionally, widows were to be remarried to one of their husband's relatives. Although this practice stems from a desire to take care of the needs of the widow, "the woman is imaged as a minor who must be protected and provided for by males."[106] In contemporary Cameroonian family code, where unmarried women can move around without hindrances, married women need their husband's signed authorization to travel.

Attitudes toward women's work vary from place to place. In central and eastern Africa attitudes toward urban women tend to be negative, while in West Africa women have been involved in trade before colonial times.[107] In the rural Far North of Cameroon, Muslim Fulani women are traditionally confined to their homes—although this situation has gradually evolved in the past decades—and do not farm. However, the main activity of the other groups in the same area is farming.[108]

Independent women get labeled either as prostitutes or witches because they fail to conform to the expectation of patriarchal society.[109] This is more so in the labor market. In some areas, the colonizers amalgamated independent to "free" women, that is, sex workers.[110] The category of working women who come under heavy suspicion are factory workers.[111] Most of these women are single and household heads.[112] Their financial autonomy is not accepted by men, and a certain opinion thinks that women working in a factory do that to enjoy sexual liberty.[113] Hence, there is a strong suspicion of promiscuity around them.

Market women have been scapegoated in various countries and blamed for high prices and supply difficulties.[114] Associations of successful women traders like the Nupe women of Nigeria and the Nana Benz of Togo are constantly suspected of witchcraft.[115] Female domination of the marketplace symbolizes a male exclusion from power.[116] Indeed, "when women gain authority in male-dominated societies, male suspicion and resentment is often focused on the concept of witchcraft."[117] A witch is a woman who works against the harmony within the community and, as such, does not promote the good of others or care for others.[118]

Cameroonian sociologist Cécile Abega presents the particular cases of women accused of witchcraft in the rural areas of the Far North region of Cameroon.[119] The economic crisis of the 1980s weakened men's perception as breadwinner and empowered women in that particular region. The fact that women earn more money generates tensions in couples, and one of the most recurrent is the accusation of women witches.[120] Those witches are seen as emasculating and soul eaters.[121] The accusation of witchcraft puts at a symbolic level the social conflict and adjustments that different characters experience. It illustrates the case that "successful, independent women may be just as unusual and suspicious."[122] That accusation coupled with that of sexual impropriety indicates also a social struggle toward the redefinition of gender roles. This context belies the idea of a submissive and docile African woman.

In an environment dominated by a strong socio-domestic gendered ideology, it comes as no surprise that women who do not scrupulously follow the script of the patriarchal society are demonized. Jean-Marc Ela observes that women's employment can create two problems.[123] It gives them access to new networks of relationships, which are difficult for a male partner to monitor. Second, employed women can become financially independent, which generates tensions not only with the male partner/husband but also with his family. These hindrances led Ela to question the type of development projects aimed at women that tend to emphasize their role in social reproduction at the expense of their productive roles.[124] A true empowering project must break away from maintaining the structural constraints that hinder women in Africa.[125]

NOTES

1. "Time-related underemployment concerns employees who work less than a specified number of hours and who are willing and available to work more hours." International Labor Office, *Global Employment Trends for Women*, 11. Underemployment is also used as a synonym to informal work.

2. Institut National de Statistique du Cameroun, *Annuaire statistique du Cameroun 2014*, 141.

3. Ibid., 145.

4. Ibid., 151.

5. Ibid., 149.

6. Ibid.

7. Ibid., 144.

8. Ibid., 63.

9. Ministère de la Promotion de la Femme et de la Famille, "Femmes et Hommes au Cameroun en 2012," 22.

10. Ibid., 21.

11. Institut National de Statistique du Cameroun, *Annuaire statistique du Cameroun 2014*, 149.

12. Ibid.

13. Ibid.

14. Ibid., 148.

15. Institut National de Statistique du Cameroun, *Quatrième enquête camerounaise auprès des ménages (ECAM 4): Tendances, profil et déterminants de la pauvreté au Cameroun entre 2001–2014* (Yaoundé: Institut National de Statistique, 2015), 38, http://www.stat.cm/downloads/2016/Rapport_tendances_profil_determiants_pauvrete_2001_2014.pdf.

16. Ibid., 16.

17. Ibid., 41.

18. Ibid. For a list of their activity see page 25 of the present book.

19. Institut National de Statistique du Cameroun, *Annuaire statistique du Cameroun 2014*, 149.

20. Ibid., 150.

21. Institut National de Statistique du Cameroun, *Quatrième enquête camerounaise auprès des ménages*, 41.

22. Fonjong, "Challenges and Coping Strategies of Women," 5–7; Ngome and Foeken, "'My Garden Is a Great Help,'" 114; Sikod, "Gender Division of Labor," 69; Nana-Fabu, "An Analysis of the Economic Status of Women in Cameroon," 158, 161.

23. Ministère de la Promotion de la Femme et de la Famille, "Femmes et Hommes au Cameroun en 2012," 32.

24. Institut National de Statistique du Cameroun, *Quatrième enquête camerounaise auprès des ménages*, 40.

25. Institut National de Statistique du Cameroun, *Annuaire statistique du Cameroun 2014*, 149.

26. Fonjong, "Challenges and Coping Strategies of Women," 5; Fonjong, Fombe, and Sama-Lang, "The Paradox of Gender Discrimination," 576; Nana-Fabu, "An Analysis of the Economic Status of Women in Cameroon," 148–49, 151–58.

27. Nana-Fabu, "An Analysis of the Economic Status of Women in Cameroon," 153.

28. I directly got this from a friend and from my own observation.

29. Sikod, "Gender Division of Labor," 64.

30. The term "unemployed" has to be used with caution here. This report was published one year before the ILO changed its understanding of employment, which now includes contributing family workers, who are for the most part unpaid family members.

31. International Labour Office, *Women at Work*, 11.

32. United Nations, *Transforming Economies, Realizing Rights*, 77.

33. Fonjong, Fombe, and Sama-Lang, "The Paradox of Gender Discrimination," 585.

34. Sikod, "Gender Division of Labor," 62.

35. Jean-Marc Ela, *Afrique, l'irruption des pauvres: société contre ingérence, pouvoir et argent* (Paris: L'Harmattan, 1994), 77; Abéga, *Les violences sexuelles et l'État au Cameroun*, 210.

36. Sikod, "Gender Division of Labor," 63.

37. For more details on this see Kah, "Changing Social Roles in Child Care."

38. Ibid., 112.

39. Ibid., 113.

40. The town of Buea is located 50 miles away from Douala, the commercial capital of Cameroon, with a population of around 466,000 when its agglomeration is taken into consideration. It is the regional capital of the South West Region.

41. I borrow this case from Ngome and Foeken, "'My Garden Is a Great Help.'"

42. Sikod, "Gender Division of Labor," 63.

43. Nana-Fabu, "An Analysis of the Economic Status of Women in Cameroon," 157.

44. Luc Sindjoun and Mathias Eric Owona Nguini, "Egalité oblige! Sens et puissance dans les politiques de la femme et les régimes de genre," in *La biographie sociale du sexe: genre, société et politique au Cameroun*, ed. Luc Sindjoun, La bibliothèque du Codesria (Paris : Dakar: Codesria; Karthala, 2000), 22.

45. Fonjong, "Equal Rights but Unequal Power over Land," 24.

46. Z. Agheneza, "Why Development Projects Fail in Cameroon: Evidence from Ngie in the NW Province of Cameroon," *International Journal of Rural Management* 5, no. 1 (April 1, 2009): 87, doi:10.1177/097300520900500104.

47. Fonjong, "Challenges and Coping Strategies of Women," 3; Fonjong, Fombe, and Sama-Lang, "The Paradox of Gender Discrimination," 585.

48. Institut National de Statistique du Cameroun, *Annuaire statistique du Cameroun 2014*, 149.

49. Tantoh Farnyu and Yenshu Vubo, "Gender and Rural Economy in the Wimbum Society," 85.

50. Abéga, *Les violences sexuelles et l'État au Cameroun*, 215.

51. Ibid.

52. Fonjong, "Equal Rights but Unequal Power over Land," 27.

53. Nana-Fabu, "An Analysis of the Economic Status of Women in Cameroon," 154.

54. Ibid., 155.

55. Abéga, *Les violences sexuelles et l'État au Cameroun*, 232; Ambe J. Njoh, "Gender-Biased Transportation Planning in Sub-Saharan Africa with Special Reference to Cameroon," *Journal of Asian and African Studies* 34, no. 2 (May 1999): 216.

56. Abéga, *Les violences sexuelles et l'État au Cameroun*, 232.

57. Tantoh Farnyu and Yenshu Vubo, "Gender and Rural Economy in the Wimbum Society," 84.

58. Nana-Fabu, "An Analysis of the Economic Status of Women in Cameroon," 155; Sikod, "Gender Division of Labor," 61; Jean-Paul Komon, "La civilisation matérielle des relations sociales: Genre, organisations paysannes et sociétés rurales," in *La biographie sociale du sexe: Genre, société et politique au Cameroun*, ed. Luc Sindjoun, La bibliothèque du Codesria (Dakar; Paris: Codesria; Karthala, 2000), 223.

59. Tantoh Farnyu and Yenshu Vubo, "Gender and Rural Economy in the Wimbum Society," 82.

60. Sikod, "Gender Division of Labor," 61.

61. It was estimated in the year 2000 that there were more than 13,000 farmers associations among which 200 with exclusive female membership; most associations

admit members from both sexes; see Komon, "La civilisation matérielle des relations sociales," 205.

62. Ibid.

63. Fonjong, Fombe, and Sama-Lang, "The Paradox of Gender Discrimination," 585.

64. Abéga, *Les violences sexuelles et l'État au Cameroun*, 232.

65. Komon, "La civilisation matérielle des relations sociales," 206.

66. Fonjong, Fombe, and Sama-Lang, "The Paradox of Gender Discrimination," 585; Komon, "La civilisation matérielle des relations sociales," 215.

67. Komon, "La civilisation matérielle des relations sociales," 215.

68. Fonjong, Fombe, and Sama-Lang, "The Paradox of Gender Discrimination," 585.

69. Komon, "La civilisation matérielle des relations sociales," 215.

70. Ibid., 216.

71. Nana-Fabu, "An Analysis of the Economic Status of Women in Cameroon," 156.

72. Ibid.

73. Arouna N'sangou, "La contribution des buy'em sell'em au développement," in *Femmes du Cameroun: Mères pacifiques, femmes rebelles*, ed. Jean-Claude Barbier (Bondy [France]: Paris: Orstom ; Karthala, 1985), 385.

74. Fonjong, "Challenges and Coping Strategies of Women," 5.

75. The Fako division, whose main urban center is Buea, is a district located within the South West region of Cameroon.

76. I borrow the case from Fonjong, "Challenges and Coping Strategies of Women."

77. N'sangou, "Les 'buy'em sell'em,'" 386.

78. Fonjong, "Challenges and Coping Strategies of Women," 7.

79. Ibid., 9.

80. Ibid., 10.

81. Ibid.

82. Njoh, "Gender-Biased Transportation."

83. Ibid.

84. Fonjong, "Challenges and Coping Strategies of Women," 11.

85. Ibid.

86. Ibid., 12.

87. N'sangou, "Les 'buy'em sell'em,'" 389.

88. ROSCA is the acronym for Rotating Savings and Credits Association. Shirley Ardener define ROSCA as "an association formed upon a core of participants who agree to make regular contributions to a fund which is given, in whole or in part, to each contributor in rotation." Shirley Ardener, "The Comparative Study of Rotating Credit Associations," *The Journal of the Royal Anthropological Institute of Great Britain and Ireland* 94, no. 2 (December 1964): 201.

89. Fonjong, "Challenges and Coping Strategies of Women," 13.

90. Rogier van den Brink and Jean-Paul Chavas, "The Microeconomics of an Indigenous African Institution: The Rotating Savings and Credit Association," *Economic Development and Cultural Change* 45, no. 4 (July 1997): 751.

91. Fonjong, "Challenges and Coping Strategies of Women," 13.

92. Ibid.

93. Ibid.

94. Ibid.

95. Oduyoye, *Daughters of Anowa*, 4.

96. Laurenti Magesa, *African Religion: The Moral Traditions of Abundant Life* (Maryknoll, NY: Orbis Books, 1997), 64.

97. Engelbert Mveng, *L'Afrique dans l'Eglise: paroles d'un croyant* (Paris: L'Harmattan, 1985), 13.

98. Quoted in Magesa, *African Religion*, 65.

99. Ibid., 65, 74.

100. Mveng, *L'Afrique dans l'Eglise*, 16.

101. Oduyoye, *Daughters of Anowa*, 56.

102. Ibid., 53.

103. Ibid., 136.

104. Ibid., 122.

105. Ibid., 135.

106. Ibid., 137.

107. Coquery-Vidrovitch, *Les Africaines*, 152, 155.

108. Abéga, *Les violences sexuelles et l'État au Cameroun*, 213–15.

109. Oduyoye, *Daughters of Anowa*, 121; December Green, *Gender Violence in Africa: African Women's Responses*, 1st ed (New York: St. Martin's Press, 1999), 76, 80.

110. Coquery-Vidrovitch, *Les Africaines*, 152.

111. Ibid., 208, 215.

112. Ibid., 214.

113. Ibid., 208.

114. Green, *Gender Violence in Africa*, 76.

115. Ibid., 81.

116. Ibid.

117. Ibid. The Far North region was until recently the most populous of Cameroon and remains the poorest.

118. Oduyoye, *Daughters of Anowa*, 121.

119. Abéga, *Les violences sexuelles et l'État au Cameroun*, 201–38.

120. Ibid., 216. Women witches in that area are said to have genitals full of birds.

121. Ibid., 236.

122. Green, *Gender Violence in Africa*, 81.

123. Ela, *Afrique, l'irruption des pauvres*, 82–83.

124. Ibid., 97–99.

125. Ibid., 98–99.

Conclusion to Part II

The goal of this section was to present and analyze the condition of women workers in Cameroon. I first showed, in chapter 5, that neoclassical economics—the dominant paradigm—is inadequate to describe all the complexities of female work. At a theoretical level, economics is limited because it takes social institutions as a given without questioning them. Gender discrimination is, at best, treated as a case of aberration. Its concept *homo economicus*, the rational economic subject, offers an atomistic view of the human person and fails to take into account any local context or gender. Macroeconomics partly ignores reproductive labor while microeconomics looks at women as individuals making their own private decision. The predominance of money leads to an underestimation of any economic process that does not produce immediate financial gains. It can lead to the false solutions that increasing women's access to money will solve the majority of their problems.

With this in mind, chapter 6 offered a description of the general characteristics of women's work. First, I started with reproductive labor or caring labor, which overwhelmingly falls into the hands of women. If reproductive labor is important for the economy at large, it remains undervalued. In addition, it clearly influences women's ability to work outside of the household. Second, I looked at occupational segregation whereby women are clustered into low-paying jobs and lower positions. The same trend is valid in the informal sector. In addition, informal employment is marked by vulnerability and cheap labor. Informal employment is a survival strategy and cannot be presented as a sustainable solution. Then, I showed how women worked in an unfriendly environment. I looked at the case of customary law, which discriminates against women in family, marriage, and property. Women do not inherit land in rural areas; they are not allowed to cultivate cash crops. I drew some provisional conclusions from what preceded: (1) access to a paid job is insufficient to solve the gender imbalance in employment; (2) education is not a panacea and does not automatically alter gender gaps in labor; (3) legislation in itself is insufficient to bring change in the labor market.

Chapter 7 focused on the situation of women workers in Cameroon. The generalities on gender and work showed that the vast majority of female workers are absorbed in informal employment, and especially in the primary sector. This says that most women are in precarious employment in Cameroon. Looking at the situation of unpaid reproductive labor as expected, women spend more time performing it. Marriage and motherhood increase the domestic workload of women. Not only do women work longer, but they also work in conditions where the basic facilities like running water, electricity, sanitation, or gas stove/cooker are still a luxury for the vast majority of households. This makes their work more difficult. Looking at informal employment, I depended upon a survey on women gardeners in a Cameroonian town to describe the concrete challenges faced by women. Access to land, credit, transport, and training appeared as the main challenges. The lack of money in a special way curtailed their possibility. Nonagricultural informal jobs bear some resemblances with agriculture. The question of means such as money, transport, storage facilities, and hired labor is critical for buyam-sellam. Domestic workers, waitresses, and hairdressers have to deal with an environment that does not grant them any legal or physical protection.

Women develop strategies to cope in the face of adversity by creating associations to acquire land, generate income, or accumulate savings to help address some of the structural problems they face. However, as I have shown, as laudable as these attempts are, they simply fall short of the mark and fail to transform the general environment. Even at the individual level, they are at best painkillers.

Finally, I also argued that some of the difficulties attached to employment come from the negative perception of autonomous women. Although this varies from place to place, women who try to break away from the patriarchal script are perceived either as prostitutes or as witches.

This section showed that a discourse on women's work must go beyond the limits set by economics and include other noneconomic dimensions. It must proceed from a broad perspective on labor. In addition, it must maintain a collective outlook to balance the individualistic tendencies of mainstream economics. There is a need for a multifaceted reading of the situation that will offer an alternative vision and better solutions. It is clear that one-sided solutions have shown their limits and have failed to radically change the gender-biased dynamics. The next part will construct an alternative framework.

Part III

ELEMENTS OF A GENDERED AFRICAN SOCIAL ETHICS ON LABOR

This section offers an alternative discourse that attempts to correct some of the limits perceived both in CST and in some secular approaches to women's labor, and it offers a better account of the empowerment of women workers in Africa. This part has two main chapters. Chapter 8 presents African liberation theology as the general orientation of the ethical framework I propose. I dialogue with the ideas of Engelbert Mveng, Jean-Marc Ela, and Mercy Amba Oduyoye. These theologians offer a fair picture of the general condition of Africans that mandates the need for liberation. African theology has had two basic orientations in the past century: liberation and inculturation. Although these two are not to be neatly separated, I make the argument that liberation theology must take precedence over inculturation theology in the case of working women. The postcolonial reality of Africa provides the background and the foundation within which these theologians think. The key elements to their reflection are the Bible, the idea of a liberating God, and Jesus Christ. Each of these perspectives is discussed, and appropriate insights are drawn.

Chapter 9 presents my vision of a gendered African social ethics. I suggest three key dimensions: the preferential option for (poor) working women, women's disempowerment as social sin, and a communal approach to empowerment. These elements are neither exhaustive nor exclusive. I look at the biblical foundations of the option for the poor, and how it applies to working women at two levels, namely, option for herself and option for others. The subsection on social sin not only looks at the structural causes of sin but also envisions the conditions and possibility of social conversion. The communal approach uses intersectionality and institutional approach to challenge the status quo. The notion of intersectionality addresses the multifaceted aspect of oppression, while the institutional approach looks at modifying the general environments through social institutions.

Chapter 8

African Liberation Theology and Women's Work

African liberation theology offers various advantages. It helps us locate the difficult condition of working women within the context of Africa. It also offers a theological criticism of social structures that oppress Africans in general and women in particular, as well as actualizes the meaning of salvation. Finally, African liberation theology offers a vision of a redeemed person. The theologians Mveng, Ela, and Oduyoye offer a fair picture of African liberation theology. The first two are viewed as pioneers of contemporary African liberation theology, and the last is also a pioneer in women's theology. One important feature of their approach is that the Church as a social institution does not escape the criticism that they level against other social structures. Each of them offers an important facet of liberation theology. Mveng provides the important concept of anthropological poverty. Ela locates his reflection within the socioeconomic realities of postcolonial Africa that he articulates in relation to the paschal mystery, and Oduyoye brings in a gender perspective.[1]

ENGELBERT MVENG

African theology is essentially liberation theology,[2] which is a contextual theology.[3] In addition to paying attention to context, liberation theology demands the analysis of that context, a liberating reading of Sacred Scripture and a liberating praxis.[4] The African context is marked by oppression, exploitation, and injustice.[5] It offers the reality of "a fragmented and traumatised continent."[6] The continent has suffered in the last centuries from the slave trade, colonization, neocolonialism, as well as from internal and external forces.[7] Imperialistic forces and foreign ideologies threaten it externally and internally divisions weaken it.[8] These worldly forces produce "poverty, destitution, injustice, tears, hard-heartedness, iniquity, discord and war, intolerance, and persecution."[9]

Africa is under the domination of "dark forces" that threaten its very survival.[10] In such a context, the people need liberation. The inclusion of the latter gives credibility to the Church. Indeed, the Church or any other religious institution loses credibility if it is an oppressive force and an instrument of domination.[11] Perhaps the greatest development in twentieth-century Christian theology, especially prominent in liberation theology, is a renewed recognition of the fact that the Bible reveals the true face of God and of Christ who defend the poor, the weak, the oppressed, and who condemn injustice and oppression.[12] In that respect, the Bible is "the message of salvation and freedom" for the most vulnerable.[13] The God who addresses humanity is savior and liberator.[14] The mission of the Church, which continues Christ's mission, is to bring to the poor, the weak, and the oppressed the good news of liberation.[15]

Liberation is a multidimensional and fluid concept.[16] It is a holistic notion that encompasses human experience.[17] Liberation concerns the religious, political, economic, social, and cultural spheres.[18] It is a freedom from hunger, illness, drought, poverty, oppression, tyranny, fear, anxiety, and despair.[19] Among those various areas of human experience, culture is primordial.[20] Culture is understood as a worldview, a conception of the human person and of God particular to a group, from which its people organize their life, their living environment, and system of thought.[21] Liberation for Africans is primarily cultural. Hence, inculturation and liberation are not distinct, but two faces of the same coin. In fact, inculturation is the process through which the gospel becomes a message of salvation and liberation for African people.[22]

At the heart of cultural liberation lies the anthropological issue, which must be addressed to solve the various problems that plague Africa. The enduring legacy of oppression is the de-structuration of the identity and dignity of the African, which creates anthropological poverty. Mveng coined the phrase "anthropological poverty" in 1970s in an attempt to capture the complexity of the terrible condition of Africans. Anthropological poverty points to the fact that poverty is a multilayered reality that cannot be limited to one aspect. Anthropological poverty also indicates that the dehumanization of Africans is a historical process. In that respect, anthropological poverty partly addresses the limitations I pointed out in chapter 2 with neoclassical economics. On another note, anthropological poverty connects with CST's integral human development presented in chapter 1. If anthropological poverty seems like the reverse picture of integral human development, they both share the idea that human well-being is not limited to economics or material things. In addition, the particularity of Mveng's idea is the identification of culture, understood broadly as the primary element in human flourishing.

Anthropological poverty describes a complex reality, which is simultaneously individual and collective. Africa's poverty is political, economic, sociological, cultural, and spiritual.[23] Anthropological poverty is a state of dehumanization and depersonalization.[24] It is also a condition of precariousness, uncertainty, deprivation and destitution that characterizes postcolonial Africa as well as individuals.[25] Anthropological poverty is realized in a situation where people are not in control of their destiny; where they are uprooted; where they live daily in fear and insecurity, and this affects Africans from all social backgrounds.[26]

Historically, anthropological poverty is a by-product of colonization.[27] Missionary/colonial Christianity has played a role in this anthropological crisis. Indeed, not only colonial Christianity was an ally to colonial imperialism but also the Church never took a position against the colonial enterprise while it was in full progress.[28] The missionary church was opposed to local cultures and this exacerbated anthropological poverty in its converts. The process of depersonalization consists of three phases: (1) a moment of break with the historical roots of personality; (2) a moment of isolation; and (3) insecurity and dependency syndrome.[29]

How is all this relevant to gender? African anthropology, according to Mveng, has two dimensions.[30] The first concerns the tension between life and death. In a situation of anthropological poverty, the forces of death seem to prevail over those of life. The second is the dual dimension of humanity, that is, the inseparable man-woman dyad. The woman appears as an irreplaceable dimension, and plays a vital role in humanity.[31] The relationship between man and woman goes beyond the notion of equality and is better captured by complementarity.[32] Complementarity is what makes one free, adult or responsible.[33] The use of complementarity by Mveng is problematic, since he is reluctant to speak of equality under the pretext that it would make men and women independent and stranger from one another.[34] Complementarity is about differentiation, diversity, embodiment and the fact that we interact with our environment as sexual beings.[35] Complementarity is a reminder that as social beings we need others to thrive and fully realize ourselves. The problem with the Church discourse on complementarity is its essentialist nature. The teaching on complementarity presupposes "that traits and roles are essentially sex-based."[36] One may suspect that Mveng behind the complementarity notion defends a preconceived vision of woman, and encourages the status quo at the expense of women empowerment.

On another matter, women have problems at every level of society that need to be addressed.[37] Indeed, "the social, political, economic and cultural struggles of the African woman rest on more radical demands, precisely because of the spiritual depth and density of their stakes."[38] Since man and woman are closely related, the ultimate goal of women's social struggles is not to defeat men, but to save the latter's own masculine nature.[39]

Before moving to Jean-Marc Ela, let me offer an evaluation of Mveng's perspective on liberation theology. The general context of Africa, which is a situation of oppression and exploitation, gives more substance to the difficulties that working women face. The phrase "anthropological poverty" underscores the importance of the sense of self, which translates in self-identity and self-consciousness. The understanding of culture as worldview and conception of human is critical. The worldview guides foundation assumptions and shapes the way people construct reality. We saw in the previous chapter how the perception of labor and gender negatively affect African working women. Indeed, stereotypes and misconceptions are functions of the worldview that is generated by culture and the human community. In addition, Mveng's anthropology acknowledges the social nature of the person and the interconnectedness of human beings. At the same time, the individual is not diluted. One key reservation that one may have is Mveng's romantic view of African culture. It appears that the changes brought from the outside have corrupted an otherwise pristine reality. There is no hint that African cultures in themselves might be problematic.

Kenyan theologian, Musimbi Kanyoro, offers a more nuanced view of culture. She recognizes that "women in Africa are the custodians of the cultural practices."[40] Culture is primordial since "all questions regarding the welfare and status of women in Africa are explained within"[41] its framework. In addition, culture appears to provide some stability and comfort in the face of oppression, injustice, and constant upheavals that people experience in contemporary Africa.[42] In reaction to colonial Christianity's dismissive attitude toward the African ethos, African theologians have developed a theology of inculturation that uplifts and valorizes African cultures in ways that makes them the starting point of liberation theology.[43] Sometimes, however, the reaction has led African theologians to adopt an uncritical stance toward African cultures, as in the case of Mveng.

To the contrary, "African women question the premises, which celebrate all cultural practices regardless of their negative impact on women."[44] In addition, "inculturation is not sufficient unless the cultures we reclaim are analyzed and are deemed worthy in terms of promoting justice and support for life and the dignity of women."[45] Cultural practices detrimental to women are closely related to their physiology. These practices are, among others, dietary restrictions, menstruation taboos, female genital cutting, polygamy, exclusion from inheritance. Kanyoro suggests engendered cultural hermeneutics as a method to scrutinize inculturation from a woman's perspective.[46]

JEAN-MARC ELA

Justification

More than Mveng, the context that forms Ela's idea is postcolonial. This does not mean that he does not pay attention to colonial and precolonial eras. Actually, he identifies shifts between these periods and the present time. The main shift is that culture is no longer the prime element through which reality is analyzed.

Overall, it is the context of oppression that guides Ela's theological reflection. The general context is one of the disillusionment decades after the political independence of 1960s.[47] The dream of a better and just society where everyone could be treated fairly and could enjoy social goods never materialized.[48] In many cases, the situation worsened. This oppression is the fault of local African elites as well as foreign powers. This hard reality is also known as neocolonialism. Indeed, oppression is not only cultural but also economic and political, and people are oppressed by national and multinational/international institutions.[49]

Ela unmasks the evil effects of neoliberalism on Africans and the fact that African economies are mere extensions of this neoliberalism. The Washington Consensus promoted by the World Bank and the International Monetary Fund—the great promoters of this neoliberal policy—encourages government withdrawal from education and healthcare, reduction of taxes for business corporations, and cuts of subsidies to social services.[50] Neoliberal economy is in continuity with the colonial project that consisted in the outward-looking character of African economies at the expense of its own people. That outward-looking is visible through the presence of industries destined to exportation and not oriented toward the needs of local populations.[51] Indeed, Africa is under the domination of heartless and unhindered capitalism.[52] Neoliberalism is the new catechism whose goal is to usher Africans into the promised land of the market.[53] Neoliberalism informs globalization, which carries with it logics of violence, impoverishment, and exclusion.[54] This "barbarous" economy feeds on the elimination of millions of men and women through unemployment and production of poverty.[55] The market values only quantity and immediacy, and reduces to objects people who are crushed by an economic logic that is foreign to them.[56] The supremacy of the market presents itself as a singular challenge to believers.[57] The god-money at the heart of this logic of profit needs to be desecrated and dishonored.[58]

This neoliberal market and logic promote a distorted view of development that benefits the African upper and ruling classes and privileges urban settings over rural ones. Ela emphasizes the damages of neoliberalism and globalization on ordinary Africans, with its privatization, deregulation, liberalization, and casualization of labor, which have increased impoverishment and marginalization.[59]

The market does not affect all Africans to the same extent, and there is a minority that profits from it. Local governments are turned into mere enforcers of agreements made by expansionist multinational corporations.[60] While big corporations reap huge benefits, the masses, particularly the working and poor classes, are getting poorer by the day.[61] Those who suffer the most are rural farmers, the youth, and the masses condemned to informal labor. Farmers appear as the outcast of African independence. For the most part, they are using outdated techniques and technologies, and have to suffer from the humanly made environmental disasters as well as from the negative effects of the single crop policy.[62] In spite of the government officials' lip service, rural areas are the poor parents of development policies and infrastructure projects that are conceived primarily in relationship to the city.[63] For instance, in the Center region of Cameroon, the culture of cocoa has destabilized local agriculture and has created a diet imbalance by the elimination of cattle breeding and reduction of the diversity of food crops.[64] Indeed,

> In many regions, the entire economy is dominated by one single cash crop grown for export, and nutritional concerns have no role in agricultural planning. Agricultural priorities, investments, research, industry, transportation, and the management of peasants are all determined by the wishes and the interests of the large agribusiness.[65]

The lack of social promotion attached to farming has led to massive migration toward the cities, which increases poverty in urban settings.[66] Farmers are the most miserable, exploited, oppressed, and also malnourished.[67] The youth also find themselves unemployed with no real perspective of the future. Urban youth unemployment or underemployment is paradoxical in societies that lack enough trained professional and senior executives[68] and basic infrastructure outside the main cities (roads, schools, hospitals, etc.). Youth underemployment or informal employment instead of lifting them out of poverty increasingly marginalizes them.[69]

The economic marginalization of the masses is exacerbated by their political nonparticipation. Actually, "There is little effective participation of the people in public affairs, and the masses have practically no way of controlling government power, but only of applauding its use."[70] People are not associated with the decision-making process in issues that affect their lives. Indeed,

> the "little ones" are discovering that the era of Africa independence has brought nothing but unemployment, a loss of buying power, insecurity caused by

uncontrolled elements of government, daily difficulties, and a growing gap between their standard of living and that of the governing classes.[71]

Instead of participation, ordinary people experience bullying and intimidation from local government administrations to such an extent that they are afraid to defend their rights, and remain ignorant of their basic rights.[72] More than anything, it is the process of marginalization and exclusion that is worrisome.[73] Ela seems to be worried about three things: people's dignity, people's participation, and the inclusivity of social institutions.

The Appropriate Theology for Such a Context

Ela's theology of liberation is anchored on the Christ event, from the incarnation to the paschal mystery. Theology must be located alongside men and women who risk their lives to defend human rights for the gospel's sake.[74] It is a theology of evangelical dissidence and insubordination.[75] Liberation theology disturbs because it radically questions both the way the other is treated in Africa since the time of the European Renaissance, and why forms of oppression are constantly renewed.[76] The emergence of a prophetic theology that challenges the prince, priest or Levite as in Jesus's parable must be the task of African Christians.[77] It is not merely enough to denounce injustices and human rights violations, those responsible for these situations must be called out too.[78] Liberation theology is the soul of any evangelization that wants to tackle the challenge brought about by structural poverty in Africa.[79] The relevance of the gospel in a context of oppression is critical. Faith is lived in a particular context, and is expressed through praxis, because it must manifest in clear signs Jesus Christ's liberating message.[80]

Contemporary history is the true desert where God puts our faith to the test.[81] In that perspective, happiness, reconciliation and peace, aspirations of just and free societies, cannot be postponed in an afterlife cut from present realities.[82] The stakes in the fight for human liberation are divine, for a concern for human beings is a concern for God.[83] Salvation has concrete implications to be felt here and now. "Salvation, which is life in its fullness, then presupposes that we Africans take responsibility for our present and our future."[84] Salvation is also a liberation from alienating forces.[85] The gospel must be freed from the power of the forces of death to open a way of hope for African men and women.[86] Only God is God, and the idol of the market must be toppled.[87]

The gospel must be the focus of a special attention. "The real world of the gospel is one of hunger, wealth and injustice, sickness, rejection, slavery and death."[88] The God of Jesus Christ must be perceived from our world where the tragedy of the cross is echoed.[89] If the African Church wants to deepen the meaning of the gospel, it needs to come back under the tree of the cross to rediscover God.[90] The crucified Christ calls us to read God's revelation from the perspective of the poor and the oppressed.[91] God must be apprehended from the "have nothing," the people "from below."[92] That perspective from below is also the one of God.[93] The tree of the cross that many experience, becomes in Jesus Christ an opportunity for the cause of those who fight against oppression and resist being crushed to prevail.[94] The cross reveals to us a God who gives God's self in a vulnerable way among the "wretched of the earth."[95] The tree of the cross becomes the tree of life among Christians.[96]

The cross matters as well as the capacity of the Christian faith to contribute to the rebirth of Africa.[97] The resurrection of the human being in Christ probes the meaning of Christian faith.[98] The cross must necessarily lead to the resurrection. Believing in a dead and risen Christ and recreating the world go hand in hand.[99]

In addition, African theologians cannot ignore socioeconomic analysis as well as the social sciences, such as history, sociology, political science, which are valuable tools to read contemporary signs of times.[100] Christ could be seen as the oppressed Africans since he identifies with the poor and exploited.[101] Christ is the other who is poor, marginalized, oppressed, refugee, and undocumented migrant in a context of the violence of money.[102] Christ not only identifies with them, but he also stands for them.[103]

Reading over the Bible means going back to the source of liberation.[104] Biblical monotheism implies the radical challenge of societies and economies whose power lies on the exploitation of human beings and on slave labor.[105] Indeed, "The most basic feature of our biblical heritage, therefore, is attentiveness to those who live in a state of oppression and suffering under unjust social structures."[106] One cannot rediscover Christ in the poor without sharing their struggle for survival and dignity.[107] Ela likes to remind his readers of this passage from Proverbs: "Those who oppress the poor revile their Maker" (14:31).[108] The experience of faith means commitment alongside men and women involved in projects, which aim at restoring the voice and dignity of the poor.[109]

It is noteworthy that there is hope in Ela's liberation theology. This comes from the fact that Jesus's paschal mystery is critical to his approach. Contrary to Mveng's perspective, which is cosmological and incidentally biblical, Ela sees a possibility of redemption based on Christ's resurrection. This is not to say that Mveng does not envision such a possibility, but he never clearly articulates it as well as Ela.

However, a limitation to Ela's liberation theology is the lack of clear articulation of the relationship between liberation and salvation. Ela uses the paschal mystery, the Reign of God, and the notion of salvation as mysteries that are effective here and now.[110] In other words, the value of salvation is in connection to this word, in such a way that possible nuances between liberation and salvation are blurred. However, for Ela, the use of salvation in colonial and neocolonial Africa has been to the effect of preventing the oppressed from fighting for their rights in the present world while waiting for happiness in the next.[111] This is why eschatological hopes are to be fulfilled in this present age.[112] One can understand why Ela emphasizes the present life compared to the next one. Liberation and salvation should rather be viewed in continuity. Historical liberation is a partial and limited "anticipation" of the salvation that will be realized in eternity.[113] Indeed, salvation is "the result of a historical process that begins here and now and culminates in eternity."[114] Salvation "does not spring up full-blown only at the term of history."[115] In that perspective, "Liberation is the act of gradually delivering reality from the various captivities to which it is historically subject and which run counter to God's historical project."[116]

The Church's Mission

Three historic faces of the Church give a hint on what the mission of the Church looks like: the missionary and colonial church, the African-independent churches (AIC), and the inculturated/postcolonial church. This is partly chronological, and partly based on their issues and solutions offered. The practice of liberation theology is inseparable from the type of church in which one finds himself/herself. For liberation theology, the Church is not spared from criticism since it is also a social institution. Gustavo Gutiérrez clearly points out that theological reflection is to be "a criticism of society and the Church insofar as they are called and addressed by the Word of God."[117]

The missionary church denigrated part of the experience of Africans, and colluded with imperial forces against Africans. Indeed, Christianization was in some way the ideological instrument at the service of the expansion of European capitalism.[118] Christianity appeared as the religion of the dominators.[119] This denigration led to the anthropological crisis, particularly for African Christians, highlighted by Mveng, in the previous subsection. Another weakness of this form of Christianity is the tendency to over-spiritualization to such an extent that one can forget that Christianity is primarily a religion of the incarnation.[120]

AIC emerged in reaction to colonial Christianity in the early parts of the twentieth century. These movements, prophetic in nature, reject the alienating message of colonial Christianity by a liberating rereading of the Bible.[121] The Afro-Christian churches do not advocate a return to traditional religious practices; rather, they seek to affirm a God who stands for the emancipation of Africans.[122] The God of AICs is a God for the poor and the oppressed.[123] The AICs teach us to rediscover God from below.[124] They correct the impression of "irrelevance" perceptible in colonial Christianity. This still affects some today who think that Christianity prepares for the afterlife, and is of little use in confronting life's challenges.

For its part, postcolonial Christianity tries to redress some of the grievances against colonial Christianity by giving credence to the local context. The main issue is to give Christianity an African face, which, under the impulse of Vatican II, is translated into liturgy. The dominant trend of theology is inculturation. However, that does not preclude the Church from involving itself in social justice. Ela observes that the work of inculturation has remained superficial, and that the African worldview and historical experience need to be valorized.[125]

Concerning the promotion of African worldview, there is a caveat. Contemporary AICs—mostly Pentecostal and evangelical churches as well as the charismatic renewal in the Catholic Church—promote the African worldview, which blends the invisible and visible worlds. They endorse a worldview where everything is spiritualized and life's unfortunate events (failures, sickness, unemployment, poverty, etc.) tend to be attributed to the nefarious influence of the devil.[126] These religious movements in so doing demobilize men and women in front the challenges they face daily.[127] They also alienate people, since they prevent questioning the failing policies of local government.[128]

The first task of inculturation is liberation.[129] Culture is "a way of living that is continually challenged by the critical events which shape a people's history."[130] In this perspective, culture is a dynamic reality not fixed once and for all. For starters, inculturation is far from being exclusive to African Christianity.[131] Other places experience it in various ways. In addition, inculturation is much more than translating liturgical and theological texts into vernacular languages, adding dances and exotic curiosity to the liturgy, or replacing a clergy of lighter skin with one of darker skin. Inculturation is not limited to retrieving from African traditional customs, myths, and symbols. The danger for the Church is to become superficial and to turn into something of the past that projects an obsolete image of Africa.[132] To avoid this fate, the Church must listen to the aspirations of younger generations[133] who increasingly live in urban settings that shatter traditional social structures.[134] The success of Pentecostal churches in the continent is due to the fact that they offer solutions to people's concrete problems. However, the fact that at the same time they vilify African traditions should alert mainline churches to the limits in their present practice of inculturation. This is a serious issue for the African Church, either by sinking into anachronism by estranging itself from genuine problems or by becoming bold and prophetic.[135] More than the danger of anachronism, there is the danger of using culture as an element of distraction from real-life challenges.[136] Inculturation should not be the only focus of

African theology, and it should retrieve elements of dissidence within African traditions and integrate contemporary socioeconomic concerns.[137] Indeed, "liberation of the oppressed must be the primary condition for any authentic inculturation of the Christian message."[138]

Another feature of the postcolonial church is its relation of financial dependence, which curtails its decision-making power. The postcolonial African church is a dependent institution in the midst of oppressed people.[139] It is difficult to think that such an institution can behave in a mature way and take bold initiatives. Without real autonomy, the African churches will not achieve much.[140] There is no cultural autonomy without economic autonomy.[141] Local churches like their societies must create new strategies for action to avoid economic alienation.[142]

The Church needs to redefine itself to bring hope to a world deprived of meaning.[143] The Church as a social institution needs to undergo a transformation that will regenerate it. The experience of God demands an activism that frees and transforms the oppressed person. To believe in the gospel means resistance to what is intolerable.[144] Only Christians who stand alongside the weak and lowly can retrieve the authentic meaning of the gospel.[145] To be a Church means to live one's "faith in solidarity with the poor and the exploited in our society."[146]

Gender

Ela does not particularly deal with gender-related issues in his theological writings. But matters regarding women are not left out, though it is brief and sparse, and many opportunities for such matters are missed. For instance, when discussing economic imbalances at the expense of farmers, he never points out that women account for the majority of farmers and that the impoverishment affects them in a special way. In the same way, when he deals with the Church, gender issues as such never surface.

A possible element of explanation is the fact that Ela never shows the complex layers of poverty and oppression. He acknowledges the various faces of the poor and oppressed[147]—among which he lists women—but that diversity is never translated in his theological writings. His analysis seems to suffer from a binary approach. For instance, when he deals with the postcolonial times, he points to the corrupt and predatory elites against popular masses or to capitalist imperialism against vulnerable African societies. Each category is treated as a homogenous body without paying attention to the diversity of situations within a particular group. This is especially strange because this comes from a trained sociologist such as Ela. Likewise, it is never clear whether liberation theology is one done by academics reflecting on their people's condition or that it is the popular expression of the people in their own words and own terms. It is noteworthy that whereas Ela frequently mentions experiences of the working and poor classes, he barely gives them a voice in his writings.

However, one does find in his sociological writings something on gender.[148] Ela raises the difficult condition of women in postcolonial Africa who suffer from political and cultural policies inherited from the colonial era as well as from local cultures. He denounces most of what I singled out in chapter 2: discrimination in farming, unequal access to education and remunerated employment, and imbalances in unpaid reproductive labor. Faced with adversity, women develop strategies by investing themselves in informal economy and creating business associations.[149] Any relevant action should reinforce women's position as economic agents. Ela denounces the approach of women training sessions, which predominantly emphasize domestic labor activities.[150] Respected as mothers and nurturers, women are not valued as producers.[151] Any critical reform must target family life by reforming the family code (inheritance rules, status of the spouse) and labor division within the household.

MERCY ODUYOYE

Oduyoye brings to the picture the voices of ordinary people, particularly women, a gender perspective, and a balanced approach to culture.

Liberation

Liberation theology has many layers affected by the African context: the struggle for political independence in the 1960s, the emancipation of oppressed groups within societies, and the "liberation of theology."[152] Oduyoye grounds her liberation theology in the Scriptures and on the experiences of African women.

Creation and redemption are two faces of the same coin. Key to this affirmation is the use of the exodus paradigm.[153] Indeed, "God's power in the exodus was creative: the power to save [and] to create space in which people could grow."[154] The exodus as a paradigm provides powerful insights: people's involvement in their salvation and salvation as the ushering in of a new political and social order.[155] These insights serve to evaluate liberation claims in Africa and ways in which the Bible is interpreted. "It is clear from that political deliverance that the redemption of a community from unjust systems is not outside God's providence."[156] In addition, the exodus paradigm in Africa "poses not only the question of liberation, but one of 'what shall we do to be saved?'[157] The latter is an ethical issue. The exodus paradigm mirrors the situation of colonial and neocolonial Africa.

Linking creation and redemption provides continuity between the liberating activity of God in the Old Testament and the salvation brought by Christ.[158] God's liberation has one purpose: to make us truly human.[159] Moreover, "God, in sending Christ, has demonstrated the limited power of physical discomfort. He asked us not to accept physical pain fatalistically, but with the power given us to put an end to it."[160] Jesus does not invite us to rely on God "to domesticate or soften people for the kill."[161] On the contrary, Jesus refuses to remain quiet while others are being exploited, oppressed, or abandoned to their death.[162]

Oduyoye rejects the debate on whether Jesus's mission was spiritual (sin's forgiveness) or material (healing physical and social problems).[163] This debate creates a separation between the elements of human well-being while "God is concerned for the wholeness of our be-ing and for our relationship to God and to other human beings."[164] In fact, "the human being is still an integrated person in Africa [and] the private and the political cannot be separated."[165] Likewise, redemption is not limited to religion or bad government, but also touches "the perversions of human nature that make it possible for some to prey on others and for individuals to trample upon the humanity of others."[166]

Women and Liberation

The following citation captures well Oduyoye's feeling concerning the experience of working women:

> Traditional sex roles in Africa operate in such a way as to make both women and men economically productive. However, women make pots that are sold cheaply; men make ritual objects and carvings that are highly regarded. Men plant yams, women have to be content with cassava. The technology that modifies men's labor is welcomed; the modernization of women's work is viewed with suspicion—African women still grind and pound the hours away. Women in Africa did not need wars to make them workers—they have always worked. The question is, what kind of work and how has it been valued by society? What initiatives have we women been allowed?[167]

This citation pinpoints important issues I discussed previously: the undervaluation of women's work, their poor working conditions, and the restriction of their possibility or initiatives. In addition, "women's experience of being persons primarily in relation to others—as mother or as wife—predominates in Africa. A woman's social status depends on these relationships and not on any qualities or achievements of her own."[168] To make matters worse, the situation of marginalization experienced by African countries makes it harder to highlight the difficult condition of women. In addition, local cultures put obstacles in the way of women. Oduyoye uses the image of a woman cooking, who has to absorb the smoke coming from the cooking pot and feels the heat of firewood, as an illustration of women's marginalization. "It is the woman who sleeps by the fire of gender discrimination in the modern sectors of our economy."[169] Indeed, "the position of women in the economy has deteriorated; 'modernization' has bypassed the majority of African women who are still in the age of hoes and mortars."[170] The lack of voice and visibility of working women is a serious issue. Rural women are overlooked when public policies are drafted.[171] And when their situation is taken into account, their own perspectives are ignored.[172] The appearance of large corporations has further marginalized the position of women. For instance, large corporations have nearly taken over food processing (oil and flours) and soap-making from women.[173]

Oduyoye more than Ela and Mveng shows how African culture can be oppressive to women. She agrees with Ela on the dynamism of African culture, but she observes that "like most other cultures, [it] has firm foundations in traditions."[174] Moreover, "these traditions continue to shape women's lives, both directly and covertly."[175] So one cannot overlook African cultures. Moreover, there are good as well as bad elements in African cultures. For instance, I pointed out customary laws that prevent daughters and wives from inheriting rural land. Likewise, there are "empowering myths in African tradition."[176] "What women do in Africa is a critique of our own culture so that we may identify and utilize the values and voices that empower us and give us a sense of dignity and worth."[177] African women use cultural paradigms but only those that are liberating.[178] In addition, "women relate more easily to the Christ who knew hunger, thirst, and homelessness, and see Jesus as oppressed by the culture of his own people."[179] Jesus, the liberator, provides a paradigm for cultural criticism. Likewise, women do not use elements from African culture uncritically. In fact, "in African culture, the voice of the ancestors and the voice of elders reflect patriarchal concerns."[180] The fact that African cultures primarily expect mothering and homemaking from women impact their choices even when they are independent.[181]

Jesus frees African women from all kinds of bondage and captivity, especially "cultural, spiritual and socio-economic."[182] Jesus's ultimate mission is to heal, to bring life and dignity to the suffering and to give voice to the voiceless.[183] Christ becomes relevant for African women because He is a concrete and personal figure who inspires hope in them by being on their side so as to give them confidence and courage to persevere and sustain the fight. "The language of struggle and resistance is the only language that penetrates the barricades of the powers of domination."[184]

The Christ of African women does not only operate at an individual level but also heals broken communities while empowering the downtrodden so that they can appreciate their worth and fulfill their destiny.[185] Jesus's power gives them the capacity and authority to act in societies where "women and power are like oil and water."[186]

Church and Gender

Oduyoye is highly critical of the Church's attitude toward women. This presents challenges and opportunities. The introduction of Christianity has not liberated the African woman. On the contrary, Christianity has added its own set of gender biases to the local ones, and has reinforced "the traditional African views of male superiority and male privilege."[187] Indeed,

> the experience of women in the church of Africa contradicts the Christian claim to promote the worth (equal value) of every person. Rather, it shows how Christianity reinforces the cultural conditioning of compliance and submission and leads to the depersonalization of women.[188]

Oduyoye singles out misuse of the Bible in the oppression of women.[189] There is a form of literalist reading of Scripture that distorts it and prejudices women. The Bible is being absolutized throughout Africa, and people are reading into it for ready-made answers.[190] In the case of women, various churches "have developed a theology of folktalk on what God requires of women."[191] It is as if women are to remain stationary.[192] The Hebrew Scriptures and Pauline literature are used to reinforce traditional gender norms instead of uplifting women.[193] "Because of its widespread treatment of the Bible as an infallible oracle, the church in Africa is slow to change its attitudes . . . toward women."[194] This is contrary to biblical ethics that demand that moral agents stand "on the side of the poor, oppressed, and the marginalized."[195]

In addition, issues concerning women need to be taken seriously and mainstreamed. In other words, women's concerns should stop being considered as "special concerns," and be fully integrated into every dimension of societal needs. "The church in Africa has not always accepted that brokenness exists and this has been shown, for example, in its refusal to see the hurt of women."[196] The Church cannot claim to be a body as long as it ignores the hurt of half of its members.[197] Such sexist practices do not enhance the credibility of the Church.[198] "A church that consistently ignores the implications of the gospel for the lives of women—and others of the underclass—cannot continue to be an authentic voice of salvation."[199]

A genuine Christian theology must not only acknowledge "the interdependence of distinctive beings" but must also affirm "the principles of inclusiveness and interdependence."[200] Inclusiveness is hindered as long as women are restricted in "their exercise of initiative and authority."[201]

As with Ela and Mveng, Oduyoye acknowledges the need of the Church to be liberated but differs on two levels. Ela and Mveng look at oppression from the side of outsiders (non-Africans) and the consequences of this oppression (anthropological poverty, dependency, imbalanced relationships between clergy and laity). Oduyoye does not dismiss this approach but shows how Western Christianity colluded with internal forces for the oppression of women. In addition, she sees the inherent oppressive character of African cultures, which is not articulated by the two other theologians.

Before moving to the next chapter, I would like to sum up key insights from African liberation theology. These are self-identity, the redeemed self, attention to the actual context, and the liberation of/in the Church. Self-identity is important at an individual and collective level. Having a healthy appreciation of oneself is important to explore one's creative potential. The oppressed tend to underestimate themselves and lack a proper sense of who they are. Any meaningful type of transformation must start at this level. The notion of the redeemed self anchors one within the mystery of Christ's life and paschal mystery. It gives the goal where one should aim and provides one with hope. The redemption effected by Christ Jesus through His death and resurrection is real and must be experienced already in this world.

In the attention to context, there are three different realities that must be accounted for postcolonial reality, socioeconomic and political structures, and culture. The present context of Africa is a postcolonial one, and fruitful reflections must take that reality into account. This particular context is characterized by unbalanced relationships between the global North and the global South, which are a legacy of the colonial past. It is also characterized by dynamic changes at various levels in African societies. A thorough analysis of socioeconomic and political structures is important to identify clearly the issues, but also the particularities within political communities. Not everyone is affected in the same way by politics and the economy. Finally, culture cannot be overlooked. Attention to the two previous elements will avoid the pitfall of romanticization. The overall context reveals a situation of oppression and injustice that must influence the reading of the Bible. The latter is identified as an important resource in the process of liberation, but it is also ambivalent, for it can be used to justify oppression.

The point of the liberation of the Church highlights the importance for the Church to live by its message. It also hints that the Church as a social institution is in need of conversion. In the case of Africa, it means shaking up structures of neocolonialism, dependence, sexism, and domination. This liberation must happen at the level of its teaching and practices so as to make it relevant to the African context. Reforming practices is important because the Church's credibility is at stake here. It is common knowledge that local churches and church-run institutions do not always treat their lay workers fairly—especially the blue collar and those at lower positions. Many lack a formal contract, and they are paid a starving wage. This behavior is not consistent with the gospel of life and salvation that the Church proclaims.

NOTES

1. The mutual influence that these authors may have had on one another is unclear. Apart from Ela who clearly uses Mveng when he refers to the origin of liberation theology, there is no clear sign of a mutual influence. This may be due to the language barrier given that both Ela and Mveng primarily wrote in French and Oduyoye in English and that neither group exhibited a good grasp of the other language.

2. Engelbert Mveng, "African Liberation Theology," in *Theologies of the Third World: Convergences and Divergences*, ed. Leonardo Boff and Virgil Elizondo, trans. Barrie Mackay, Concilium 199 (Edinburgh: T. & T. Clark, 1988), 18. What follows in the whole section expresses the views of Mveng not of the author.

3. Ibid., 17; Engelbert Mveng and B. L. Lipawing, *Théologie, libération et cultures africaines: dialogue sur l'anthropologie négro-africaine*, Essai (Yaoundé [Cameroun] : Paris: C.L.E. ; Présence africaine, 1996), 29.

4. Mveng and Lipawing, *Théologie, libération et cultures africaines*, 29–30.

5. Ibid., 25.

6. Mveng, "African Liberation Theology," 19.

7. Mveng, *L'Afrique dans l'Eglise*, 87, 162, 167.

8. Ibid., 165.

9. Mveng, "African Liberation Theology," 19.

10. Mveng, *L'Afrique dans l'Eglise*, 165; Mveng and Lipawing, *Théologie, libération et cultures africaines*, 25.

11. Mveng, *L'Afrique dans l'Eglise*, 164.

12. Ibid., 174.

13. Mveng, "African Liberation Theology," 27.

14. Mveng and Lipawing, *Théologie, libération et cultures africaines*, 48.

15. Mveng, *L'Afrique dans l'Eglise*, 200.

16. Mveng and Lipawing, *Théologie, libération et cultures africaines*, 50.

17. Ibid., 49.

18. Ibid., 34.

19. Mveng, *L'Afrique dans l'Eglise*, 164.

20. Mveng and Lipawing, *Théologie, libération et cultures africaines*, 40.

21. Ibid., 58.

22. Ibid., 34.

23. Mveng, *L'Afrique dans l'Eglise*, 211.

24. Ibid., 109.

25. Mveng and Lipawing, *Théologie, libération et cultures africaines*, 32, 40, 65.

26. Mveng, *L'Afrique dans l'Eglise*, 210.

27. Ibid., 207.

28. Ibid., 101, 135, 205.

29. Ibid., 80.

30. From here onward see, Mveng, "African Liberation Theology," 29–30. Mveng understands anthropology as "the conception of humanity" (Ibid., 26).

31. Mveng, *L'Afrique dans l'Eglise*, 16.

32. Ibid.

33. Ibid.

34. Ibid.

35. Kasper, "The Position of Woman," 57–58.

36. Christine E. Gudorf, "Encountering the Other: The Modern Papacy on Women," in *Feminist Ethics and the Catholic Moral Tradition*, ed. Charles E. Curran, Margaret A. Farley, and Richard A. McCormick, Readings in Moral Theology, No. 9 (New York/Mahwah, NJ: Paulist Press, 1996), 75; Oduyoye adds that "In assigning roles based on gender the theory of complementarity plays a negative role for women in domestic organizations and in the church. In practice, complementarity allows the man to choose what he wants to be and to do and then demands that the woman fill in the blanks. It is the woman, invariably, who complements the man," see Oduyoye, *Daughters of Anowa*, 177.

37. Mveng, *L'Afrique dans l'Eglise*, 32.

38. Mveng, "African Liberation Theology," 32.

39. Ibid.

40. R.A. Musimbi Kanyoro, "Engendered Communal Theology: African Women's Contribution to Theology in the 21st Century," in *Talitha Cum! Theologies of African Women*, ed. Nyambura J. Njoroge and Musa W. Dube (Pietermaritzburg: Cluster Publications, 2001), 159.

41. Ibid., 164.

42. Ibid., 166.

43. Ibid., 167.

44. Ibid., 168.

45. Ibid., 167.

46. Ibid., 169.

47. Jean-Marc Ela, *Le cri de l'homme africain: questions aux chrétiens et aux Églises d'Afrique* (Paris: L'Harmattan, 1980), 163.

48. Ibid.

49. Ela, *Repenser la théologie africaine*, 18.

50. Ibid., 98.

51. Ela, *Le cri de l'homme africain*, 81.

52. Ela, *Repenser la théologie africaine*, 103.

53. Ibid., 98. Ela also calls it the new gospel or the unique thought, because it is the only viable economic model presented to poor countries that do have only one option if they do not want to disappear: embrace it.

54. Ibid., 99.

55. Ibid., 105.

56. Ibid., 107.

57. Ibid.

58. Ibid., 105.

59. Ibid., 97–98.

60. Ibid., 113.

61. Ela, *Le cri de l'homme africain*, 81.

62. Ibid., 103.

63. Ibid., 81.

64. Ibid., 104.

65. Jean-Marc Ela, *My Faith as an African*, trans. John Pairman Brown and Susan Perry (Maryknoll, N.Y. : London: Orbis Books ; G. Chapman, 1988), 69.

66. Ela, *Repenser la théologie africaine*, 106.

67. Ibid., 104.

68. Ela, *Le cri de l'homme africain*, 101.

69. Ibid.

70. Ela, *My Faith as an African*, 90.

71. Ibid., 155.

72. Ela, *Le cri de l'homme africain*, 48.

73. Ela, *Repenser la théologie africaine*, 105.

74. Ibid., 87.

75. Ibid.

76. Ibid., 106.

77. Ibid., 112.

78. Ibid., 226.

79. Ibid., 114.

80. Ela, *Le cri de l'homme africain*, 108.

81. Ela, *Repenser la théologie africaine*, 146.

82. Ela, *Le cri de l'homme africain*, 47.

83. Ibid., 121.

84. Ela, *My Faith as an African*, 121.

85. Ela, *Le cri de l'homme africain*, 43.

86. Ela, *Repenser la théologie africaine*, 83.

87. Ibid., 105.

88. Ela, *My Faith as an African*, 105.

89. Ela, *Repenser la théologie africaine*, 48.

90. Ibid., 73.

91. Ibid., 77.

92. Ibid., 75.

93. Ibid., 226.

94. Ibid., 87.

95. Ibid., 144.

96. Ibid.

97. Ibid., 143.

98. Ibid.

99. Ibid., 146.

100. Ibid., 102.

101. Ibid., 73.

102. Ibid., 109.
103. Ibid., 225.
104. Ibid., 224.
105. Ibid., 61.
106. Ela, *My Faith as an African*, 104.
107. Ela, *Repenser la théologie africaine*, 88.
108. Ibid., 105, 225.
109. Ibid., 148.
110. Ibid., 208, 212.
111. Ibid., 81.
112. Ibid.
113. Leonardo Boff and Clodovis Boff, *Salvation and Liberation*, trans. Robert R. Barr (Maryknoll, NY: Orbis Books, 1984), 19.
114. Ibid., 54.
115. Ibid., 56.
116. Ibid., 57.
117. Gutiérrez, *A Theology of Liberation*, 9.
118. Ela, *Le cri de l'homme africain*, 55.
119. Ela, *Repenser la théologie africaine*, 71.
120. Ibid., 79.
121. Ela, *Le cri de l'homme africain*, 63.
122. Ela, *Repenser la théologie africaine*, 63.
123. Ibid., 48.
124. Ibid., 72.
125. Ibid., 147.
126. Ibid., 140–41.
127. Ibid., 138.
128. Ibid., 139.
129. Ela, *My Faith as an African*, xvi.
130. Ibid., xv.
131. Ela, *Repenser la théologie africaine*, 94–95.
132. Ibid., 147.
133. Ibid.
134. Ibid., 268.
135. Ela, *Le cri de l'homme africain*, 159.
136. Ibid., 137, 152, 155. Ela rightfully points that local governments use the slogan of authenticity to quash any opposition, and promote the romanticized idea that precolonial Africa did not know argument or dissidence; in fact, peasants and people from the working classes are well ingrained in African culture and do not need to be schooled in it by deculturated elites.
137. Ela, *My Faith as an African*, xv.
138. Ibid., xvi.
139. Ela, *Le cri de l'homme africain*, 15.
140. Ibid., 160.
141. Ibid., 159.
142. Ibid.

143. Ela, *Repenser la théologie africaine*, 111.

144. Ibid., 148.

145. Ibid., 84.

146. Ela, *My Faith as an African*, 98.

147. Ela, *Repenser la théologie africaine*, 114, 234. He cites among others the youth, women, street children, peasants, victims of structural adjustment, thinkers and creators, artists and writers, and exiled intellectuals. Elsewhere he names those who are deprived of basic rights, the refugees, disable, victims of underemployment, exploitation, and discrimination on the motives of race, language, religion, sex, or opinion.

148. See notably Ela, *Afrique, l'irruption des pauvres*; Jean-Marc Ela, *Fécondité et migrations africaines: les nouveaux enjeux*, Etudes africaines (Paris: L'Harmattan, 2006).

149. Ela, *Fécondité et migrations africaines*, 89–91, 98.

150. Ela, *Afrique, l'irruption des pauvres*, 100.

151. Ela, *Fécondité et migrations africaines*, 102.

152. Mercy Amba Oduyoye, *Hearing and Knowing, Theological Reflections on Christianity in Africa* (Eugene, Oregon: Wipf & Stock Publishers, 2009), 2–3.

153. Mercy Amba Oduyoye, *Beads and Strands: Reflections of an African Woman on Christianity in Africa*, Theology in Africa Series (Maryknoll, New York: Orbis Books, 2004), 3–4.

154. Ibid., 9.

155. Ibid., 3–4.

156. Oduyoye, *Hearing and Knowing*, 103.

157. Oduyoye, *Beads and Strands*, 16.

158. Oduyoye, *Hearing and Knowing*, 102–6.

159. Ibid., 105.

160. Ibid., 106.

161. Ibid.

162. Ibid.

163. Oduyoye, *Beads and Strands*, 21.

164. Oduyoye, *Hearing and Knowing*, 105.

165. Oduyoye, *Beads and Strands*, 21.

166. Oduyoye, *Hearing and Knowing*, 105.

167. Ibid., 123.

168. Ibid., 122.

169. Oduyoye, *Daughters of Anowa*, 73.

170. Ibid., 105.

171. Ibid., 101.

172. Ibid., 105.

173. Ibid., 100.

174. Ibid., 80.

175. Ibid.

176. Mercy Amba Oduyoye, "Spirituality of Resistance and Reconstruction," in *Women Resisting Violence: Spirituality for Life*, ed. Mary John Mananzan et al. (Maryknoll, NY: Orbis Books, 1996), 167.

177. Ibid.

178. Mercy Amba Oduyoye, "Jesus Christ," in *Hope Abundant, Third World and Indigenous Women's Theology*, ed. Kwok Pui-lan (Maryknoll, New York: Orbis Books, 2010), 168.

179. Ibid.

180. Oduyoye, "Transforming Power," 225.

181. Mercy Amba Oduyoye, "Christian Feminism and African Culture: The 'Hearth' of the Matter," in *The Future of Liberation Theology: Essays in Honor of Gustavo Gutiérrez*, ed. Marc H. Ellis and Otto Maduro (Maryknoll, NY: Orbis Books, 1989), 446.

182. Oduyoye, "Jesus Christ," 176.

183. Ibid., 172.

184. Oduyoye, "Spirituality of Resistance and Reconstruction," 170.

185. Mercy Amba Oduyoye, *Introducing African Women's Theology*, Introductions in Feminist Theology 6 (Cleveland, OH: Pilgrim Press, 2001), 61.

186. Oduyoye, "Transforming Power," 225.

187. Oduyoye, *Daughters of Anowa*, 129.

188. Ibid., 9.

189. Ibid., 124–25.

190. Ibid., 174.

191. Ibid.

192. Ibid., 189.

193. Ibid., 174.

194. Ibid., 190.

195. Ibid., 184.

196. Ibid.

197. Ibid., 182.

198. Ibid., 181.

199. Ibid., 182.

200. Ibid., 181.

201. Ibid., 183.

Chapter 9

Key Elements of a Gendered African Social Ethics

The liberationist approach gives the hermeneutic lenses through which the issue of working women must be analyzed. I suggest the following elements as elements of a gendered African social ethics: the preferential option for (poor) working women, women's disempowerment as social sin, and the communal approach to empowerment. These elements helped to flesh out the liberationist framework and substantiate the analysis of women's labor.

THE PREFERENTIAL OPTION FOR POOR (WORKING) WOMEN

On the Option for the Poor

This is the obvious consequence of the liberationist approach, which asserts faith in a biblical God that sides with the poor, the oppressed, and the excluded. As I previously showed, the experience of working women is one of oppression, marginalization and injustice. The fact that God takes up the cause of the poor provides the foundation for the preferential option for the poor and the oppressed.[1] Opting for the working woman is not an exclusivist position that blinds one to the other forms of oppression. The emphasis on working women comes from the fact that not everybody is necessarily included under the term "poor." If the option for the poor includes women by their class, it is not certain that their gender is taken into consideration.[2] This is why other phrases like "option for the oppressed," "option for the excluded or the marginalized," or "option for the poor and the oppressed" have been suggested.[3] I shall not get into the discussion of whether the term "poor" is appropriate or not. I want to simply point out that the term "poor," while useful, can sometimes hide certain particularities—such as that women constitute the majority of the poor and oppressed worldwide.[4] There is also the risk to refer to the poor as an "undifferentiated mass."[5] The reference to women not only substantiates the idea of the poor but is also an indication that poverty is a multifaceted reality that entails more than socioeconomic dimensions.[6]

The revealed God gives us a hint of what the preferential option for the poor entails. God's proximity to the poor can be seen in God's election of the younger child at the expense of the elder (Abel over Cain, Isaac over Ismael, Jacob over Esau, etc.). The expression of the option for the poor is also evident in the Exodus narratives, the Covenant Code, the Holiness Code, prophetic literature, and in Jesus's ministry toward the outcast, the sick, and the vulnerable.[7] In addition, "God's option for the poor includes not only God's solidarity and accompaniment in tribulations and struggles but also God's identification to the degree that the rights of the poor are considered as God's rights."[8] Jesus Christ, the Emmanuel (God-with-us), exemplifies this. During his earthly ministry, he rehabilitates social outcasts through his healings and exorcisms, by forgiving sins, and through table fellowship. His ministry reaches out to sinners, tax collectors, prostitutes, lepers, non-Jews, women, and the "physically impaired."[9] Through his incarnation and by embracing the cross, he identifies with the poor. By his humble birth in a manger and by his death like a slave, he unites his fate to that of the poor. He also identifies with the persecuted, the hungry, the prisoners, and the sick (Mt 25). Moreover, the poor are the primary recipients of the good news (Lk 4).[10] Jesus's praxis provides key insights into what the option for the poor and marginalized consists. It is about welcoming, including restoring, standing with, and identifying with them. Not only does God identify with the poor and oppressed, but also they are "the focus [of] God's concern and the centers of God's redemptive action."[11] The poor enjoy an epistemological privilege to such an extent that one could say, following Shawn Copeland, that "poor is the color of God."[12]

Option for the Working Woman

There is still a need to show the specificity of the option for the working woman. I take into account the insights already developed to which I now add elements from a gendered perspective. The first element is the working woman's option for herself.[13] This comes from the fact that the working women are made to look insignificant and are silenced by the society. Those who are "in-significant," "do not count in society," have no "social or economic weight," are socially looked upon with contempt, and are culturally marginalized.[14] This is the condition of the working woman.

In addition, there is a sort of a culture of silence about the condition of women. The silence is the condition of African women whose voices are barely heard because they are burdened by daily struggles to survive.[15] As I showed in the section on caring labor, African women have long days that start early and end very late. This barely leaves time for one to reflect on one's condition, let alone talk about it. Indeed, "the oppressed rarely have time for such luxuries."[16] Further, Anne Nasimiyu-Wasike concurs that "in most African communities, women . . . have no voice in the social, political, or economic affairs of the community."[17] At this level, silence is imposed on women by the society and "leads to stigmatization and exclusion while allowing ruling authorities to control the lives of others by way of rigid rules and harsh condemnations."[18] Nasimiyu-Wasike speaks of women's "missing voices."[19] This phrase points to the fact that women's contribution to society is unacknowledged because they remain "unnamed and unremembered."[20] This forced anonymity is a general characteristic of the poor[21] and is one of the greatest burdens of African women.[22] Tina Beattie confirms:

> Poor women are particularly vulnerable to this kind of silencing, for they live at the crossroads where the oppressive powers of religious and cultural patriarchy intersect with the no less oppressive powers of the global economic order.[23]

Poor women are ignored and not taken into account as economic agents and in Systems of National Account such as GDP. And they only appear simply as statistics, and never with their own names.[24]

The option of the working woman for herself is important because "the persistent inequality of power . . . leads to internalized oppression, whereby women believe the judgment of their inferiority and behave accordingly."[25] This option is a way of reclaiming herself anew as a woman. It is a rebirth or rediscovery of the self.[26] It is "a deep acceptance of the wonder of the self, body and mind, in its harmony and contradiction."[27] This means that the woman should work on herself, and fight the false, acquired image of herself from within.[28] It is vital to undo "internalized sexism and socialized self-depreciation," and to move toward "transforming their own consciousness in order to deal with the enemy within that is an obstacle to their path to freedom and justice."[29] Far from being an appeal for narcissism or egotism, this call for self-love is located at the heart of Christian revelation. The horizontal dimension of the great commandment states: "love your neighbor *as* yourself" (Mk 12:31). In other words, there cannot be a healthy love of neighbor without the proper love of self. Aquinas in his *ordo caritatis* reminds us that genuine self-love is grounded on the love a person has for God.[30] Stephen Pope, commenting on Aquinas, opines: "Self-love is embedded in human nature by God."[31] That is an important precision that Pope makes: that self-love is a gift from God. As Benedict XVI asserts, "Anyone who wishes to give love must also receive love as a gift."[32] Indeed, a person "cannot live by oblative, descending love alone," for she "cannot

always give," but "must also receive."[33] How could someone who has low
self-esteem properly love others? Love of self and love of neighbor "are two
poles of the same loving movement and one cannot develop fully without
the other."[34] Pope Francis states that appreciation of one's body is necessary
to self-awareness when encountering other people.[35] Proper love of the self
helps to strike a balance and to avoid "becoming alienated"[36] from oneself.
This call for proper self-love is important because, while women are hailed
by the Church and society as caregivers, little attention is paid to their own
personal care.

The second aspect of the option for the working woman is tied to the
first one, and it is the option for others, who suffer as she does.[37] As Yvone
Gebara points out, the option for the self "is a personal act but not a solitary
one. It also means being open and welcoming to others."[38] The person has
to help others to experience this rebirth too if she wants her own rebirth
to become effective.[39] The personal and individual rebirth has to become
a collective one, and working women have "to rediscover themselves as a
human group."[40] They remember their humanity, the dignity it entails, and
the fact that they should not be objectified.[41] Women at this level begin to
break the oppressive silence and raise their issues. Indeed, "growing in love
and trust for self and others, women will share their struggles and common
challenges."[42]

The option for the poor is not a paternalistic project. Rather, it is a way to
help the marginalized and oppressed become subjects of and actors in their
own destiny. Indeed, "the option for the poor is a contribution that empowers
them to take ownership of their own voice by proclaiming the Gospel's challenge to remember their human dignity as daughters and sons of God."[43] The
option for the poor is not limited to working women as individuals or groups
but also concerns social institutions. The latter must not only take them into
account but also learn to partner with the poor. Pope Francis has championed
the notion of a poor Church working for the poor.[44] This primarily means that
the Church allows itself to be taught and to learn from the poor.[45] This act of
listening is important, because it allows the Church to be attentive to the signs
of times. Moreover, "listening is constitutive of a church that is constantly
attuned and open to receiving what the Spirit says to the church."[46] That dis-
cerning activity is primarily the task of the local church.[47] This means that the
community is called "to analyze the local situations," then "draw principles
of judgment, norms of judgment, directives for action from" CST, and finally
"to discern in light of the above the options and commitments to bring about
social, political, and economic change."[48]

Being a Church of the poor also means that the poor are the first recipients
of the Church's mission.[49] This commitment to the poor helps the Church not
to lose focus on her mission[50] and calls for sensitivity to the new forms of

precariousness.[51] It helps to acknowledge ways in which the Church fails to provide adequate pastoral care and support to the poor.[52]

In the precise situation of working women, the lack of specific ministerial outreach is blatant. It is necessary to create safe spaces where they can share their experience and be listened to. Attention to the poor is vital for society at large. Only a durable and viable solution to the condition of the poor can provide a sound answer to the problems of the world.[53] There cannot be peace if poor people are silenced or simply appeased for the benefit of a dominant group.[54] This is why the church must move beyond "episodic tokenism"[55] where women are occasionally allowed to raise their issues. The church should give women "the opportunities to fully express themselves and their desire for fullness of life as God-given gifts."[56] Church-led institutions need to treat their workers more justly and humanly especially those accomplishing humble and vital tasks such as janitors, cooks, and laundresses. The church exploits their work by keeping it informal for the most part with starvation wages, lack of contract, and social security, thus exacerbating their already precarious living conditions. The notion of a Church for the poor acts as revelatory of unjust structures and practices and as a device for self-criticism. Here, one has to pay attention to how gender dynamics prevalent in society are reproduced in the Church: subordination of women (lay and religious) workers to a male hierarchy,[57] occupational segregation (horizontal and vertical),[58] and the wage gap. The option for the (poor) woman worker needs to be acknowledged not only in nice words and statements but also in concrete actions.

SOCIAL SIN

The goal of this section is not to emphasize the evil character of the marginalization of women workers. This has been already illustrated above. The focus of this section is rather to identify key sinful structures that feed and reinforce marginalization and to finally highlight hope through the possibility of social conversion. The notion sin alerts us to the fact that there is harm done to the sinner as well as to the people sinned against. Moreover, "the effort to address any social problem will require understanding its complex historical and structural roots."[59] The notion of social sin gets at the root of social dysfunction.

On Social Sin

I understand sin as anything contrary to God's will and God's salvific project on creation, and in a special way on human beings—either on oneself or on one's neighbor. It is not easy to offer a comprehensive definition of social sin because authors offer various understandings grounded in a certain understanding of sin.[60] One can safely say that social sin refers to "the reality of sin as a social phenomenon."[61] I understand social sin as sin by analogy[62] since "no structure is a conscious agent."[63] Social sin is as old as the Old Testament (OT) that knew the ideas of corporate sin and solidarity in sin. John Paul II's first two meanings of social sin are in tune with the biblical tradition.[64] In the first one, by virtue of human solidarity, every personal sin affects others. The second meaning sees social sin as any direct attack on the neighbor either at the interpersonal level or at the community level. Social sin allows us to locate personal sin within a larger context. Social and personal sin are in a dialectical relation. Social sin can be understood in relationship to individual sin as (1) its social effects, (2) the embodiment of injustice and sin in social structures, (3) co-essential or (4) primary to personal sin.[65] Although I have a broad understanding of social sin, I will favor the third position that puts both social and personal sin in an interdependent relation without neglecting either ones. The parallel with original sin is noteworthy. Original sin provides an explanation for human disposition to sin but does not excuse this disposition or the particular sins. Likewise, social sin does not negate the individual's responsibility or excuse the person's sin. Social sin has a political dimension because sin is embedded in structures of injustice, violence, and domination that deprive men and women of their basic dignity, and enables a state effectively to starve and kill through massive violation of basic human rights.[66]

Another term used is structural sin or structures of sin, which "places great emphasis on the embodiment of sin in structures or systems."[67] Social structures are established and ordered patterns of relationships that become routine.[68] They "involve policies and institutions that make up the patterns of societal organization as well as the worldviews, perspectives, and value systems by which we interpret our experiences so as to bring coherence and meaning into our lives."[69] This means that social structures are both external and internal to the individual.[70] John Paul II points out that structures of sin

are rooted in personal sin, and thus always linked to the concrete acts of individuals who introduce these structures, consolidate them and make them difficult to remove. And thus they grow stronger, spread, and become the sources of other sins, and so influence people's behavior.[71]

Although it is true that "people make social sin" because of their sinful choices/actions and their effects, a sinful society "not only perpetuates injustice" but also conditions individuals "to further personal sin."[72] The analogy of original sin can help to understand how social sin works. Human beings are victims and authors of sin.[73]

Gregory Baum provides a helpful typology of social sin by offering four distinct levels.[74] The first level concerns how social institutions embody injustices and dehumanizing practices. The second level is symbolic and refers to ways in which those unjust practices are legitimized in culture and religion. The third level looks at the twisted effects on individuals' mindset (false consciousness and distorted understanding of the good). The fourth level concerns the collective decisions flowing from the false consciousness that exacerbates the harm done.

The case of the oppression of women workers illustrates how this typology works.[75] First, the various economic institutions pay little attention to women's work, practice occupational segregation, or pay women less. Second, this practice is legitimized through cultural and religious gender stereotypes that construct romanticized female anthropology, which works at the expense of women. Third, the persons within the system do not perceive its injustice and do not think that there is a way out. Generally, it is at this level that conversion must occur. Fourth, different institutions will choose to give girls less education, bar them from certain types of jobs, deny the economic value of reproductive labor, not recognize them as economic agents, or deny them training opportunities.

Kyriarchy and Colonialism as Structures of Sin

In the case of working women, I think that "kyriarchy" rather than "patriarchy" captures better the unjust structures of domination and oppression that they experience. Elisabeth Schüssler Fiorenza, who coined the term "kyriarchy" from the Greek *kurios* (lord) and *arche* (principle, rule), defines it as "the rule of the father/lord/master/husband."[76] It is

a socio-cultural, religious, and political system of elite male power, which does not just perpetrate the dehumanization of sexism, heterosexism, and gender stereotypes but engenders other structures of women's oppression, such as racism, poverty, colonialism, and religious exclusivism.[77]

Kyriarchy seems to describe better the dynamics of power. It can be perceived as a specific form of patriarchy[78] or vice versa. Kyriarchy relates better to other structures of domination, such as racism, sexism, colonialism, and classism. Kyriarchy that pervades social systems is a structural sin[79] and tends to exacerbate gender oppression by the multiplication of oppressive structures.[80] The ideological legitimization of these structures occurs

not simply by androcentrism which privileges the experiences, knowledges, and belief-systems of men, but much more so by kyriocentrism that interprets the world and human life from the perspective and in the interest of kyriarchal domination, exploitation and dehumanization.[81]

What Fiorenza calls the "gendered economic system of kyriarchal capitalism" is maintained through the socialization and education of women that leads them to accept and conform to pre-ordained social roles.[82] The Church participates in this system through its "theology of the woman," which, by overemphasizing women's differences and particularities in opposition to men, leads to differential treatment in the labor market.[83] In many African cultures, a kyriarchal conception of labor is based on seniority (the domination of the younger by the elder), child labor, and overburdening women with extra work.[84] Maria Pilar Aquino notes that the present globalization is a "kyriarchal globalization," which reinforces "kyriarchal relationships of domination" and extends them to the whole world.[85] Under this kyriarchal globalization, "patterns of social disparity and sexual violence against women are bound to be repeated and multiplied again and again."[86] Similarly, because of "its asymmetric and unequal nature,"[87] globalization is in line with a pattern established by colonialism.

Colonialism is a relevant kyriarchal structure to understand working women's condition in Africa. Under this term, I look at the legacy of colonialism, and the reality of neocolonialism. Colonialism established in Africa and in the rest of the world a pattern of relationships, especially relationships with labor and economics that still persists today and negatively affects workers, and, in a special way, women. Colonialism is characterized by top-down planning where decisions concerning economic priorities not only come from the leaders but also are dictated from the outside. The base is never consulted or associated in the decision-making process. In the context of globalization that is in continuity with colonialism, "women and those who depend on them, are excluded from the table that defines social agendas [and] from design of social dynamics."[88]

As a result, economic activities are destined for the satisfaction of the needs of the national elites or the outside actors (transnational corporations, foreign governments, international institutions) and not of ordinary people. One of the main characteristics of a colonial economy is its extraversion where the main impulse and initiative comes from the outside. In fact, under colonialism vital sectors of the local economy are in the hands of non-Africans. To take the case of Cameroon, the ports, the railway company, the electricity company, the textile industry, the main breweries, telephone companies, and the construction of major infrastructures are all in the hands of foreign corporations. In addition, under colonialism, the economy of the colony does not have a value in itself. It is meant to complement the economy of the colonizer.[89] This case illustrates how problematic the notion of complementarity can be, especially in relation to gender.

The second characteristic is the casualization of labor, which entails poor working condition, commodification of labor, and cheap labor. The colonial economy exploits the workforce. Another characteristic is that leadership disposes of unchecked powers that results in a lack of accountability on its part.[90] There are few mechanisms for holding them accountable, since most of the time their power does not emanate from the people. This is not only at the level of political leaders, but employers regularly violate their written or oral agreements with workers. In addition, colonialism does not foster autonomy but produces a situation of constant dependency.[91]

On another matter, there is the denigration of manual labor, which is problematic in countries where (1) the majority of the workforce is made of manual laborers, and where (2) skilled workers are needed for the construction of basic infrastructures. This denigration of manual labor mentally uproots the individual from his/her environment, which is especially true for rural dwellers. Colonialism marginalizes women by excluding them from fiduciary economy through discriminatory policies in land acquisition, access to credit, in educational institutions, and through occupational segregation. Colonialism marginalizes the work of women by making food crops less valuable than cash crops destined for exportation. Moreover, colonialism simply does not view women as economic actors regardless of the reality of the ground.

Colonialism is truly a kyryarchal system where the concept of work and economy is constructed not from the perspective of the practitioners. Colonialism is also a system of domination, which imposes itself through violence. The Church, due to its implication in the colonial system in most African countries, participates in the casualization of labor. As long as work for the Church is not perceived as real work but service, treatments of workers will not improve.[92] It is important to probe the meaning of service to avoid making it a tool for the exploitation of workers.

Social Conversion

Social sin calls for social conversion. Although conversion is primarily a personal experience, salvation is envisioned from a cosmic perspective. If social sins such as kyrarchy and colonialism involve "distorted relationality" and disunity, then social conversion implies building an authentic community of equality and mutuality.[93] This community "involves the overcoming of division and the dispelling of isolation."[94] John Paul II suggests solidarity as a remedy against the structures of sin.[95] Social conversion requires a radical transformation, and a change of paradigms, which in the case of labor will put the (woman) worker and the community at the center.

Having said this, it is important to acknowledge that social conversion does not come about so easily; it takes time. First, social structures, despite their origins in individual actions, get a life independent of the persons' choice.[96] The more they last, the more they come to be viewed as natural and sometimes as the only way to go about things. For instance, the pervasiveness of monarchical leadership makes it difficult for most people to imagine the viability of shared or collegial leadership. This leads to my second point. The structures cannot change without a profound change in individuals who ultimately sustain those structures.[97] Inner perceptions and representations, as well as the behaviors, must be transformed so as to achieve lasting change in people.

Among the strategies for conversion, O'Keefe suggests the option for the poor, conscientization, social analysis, group/community action, and political action, conflict and violence.[98] I have already offered a social analysis in chapter 2 and looked at the option for the poor in the previous section. Chapter 4 will look at possible communal actions. Let me quickly say something about conscientization. Conscientization is "critical awareness" from the oppressed who come to realize "the oppressive consciousness which dwells in them, become aware of their situation, and find their own language."[99] I will add that conscientization affects also the "people of good will" who can be complacent with sinful structures or complicit in sinful structures. Conscientization can help them wake up from the slumber of their resignation ("that is just the way things are") and engage in transformative actions.

In connection with the issue of working women, I would also like to suggest the following areas as ways toward social conversion on women's work: The Kingdom of God, breaking the silence, alternative paradigms of economics and labor, and the integration of caring labor.

The Kingdom/Reign of God

Kyriarchy as a system of relationships is opposed to the Kingdom/Reign of God. The latter provides the eschatological and epistemological horizon against which all realities must be measured. It is important to observe that the distinction made earlier between liberation and salvation applies to the Kingdom/Reign of God and the just society. In fact, "The kingdom, although not of this world in its origin—it comes from God—is nevertheless among us, manifesting itself in processes of liberation."[100] Following the gospels, Fiorenza affirms that the Reign of God, which is God's "intended world, free of oppression and dehumanization, is already incipient historical reality."[101]

John Donahue, S.J., emphasizes this last point: "The reign and power of God is not otherworldly, but embodied in history. Its arrival brings special hope to the poor, the suffering and the marginalized."[102]

Where kyrarchy and colonization emphasize domination, marginalization, and oppression, the Kingdom offers a stark challenge to this picture. The Reign of God demands radical changes of people's concrete living conditions.[103] The Kingdom introduces reversals destined to "challenge deeply held values and [to] invite people to enter imaginatively into a different world."[104] This is notably perceptible in the way Jesus welcomes marginal groups. His table fellowship is inclusive, and constitutes a criticism of social exclusion.[105] By touching the leper—something forbidden by the law—he shows that welcoming the ostracized means putting oneself at the risk of being labeled the same. By taking children as paradigm, Jesus wants his disciples "to renounce dominating power."[106]

Through stories (the rich young man) or parables (the rich man and Lazarus, the rich fool), Jesus shatters the conviction of his audience that those who are preeminent in the eyes of human beings, are not so in the eyes of God. One point also to remember is that the ideal of the Kingdom of God clashes with that of the world. This conflict is apparent in Jesus's ministry: in the exorcisms and the various controversies He faces. This is a reminder to those who try to build alternative visions that they may encounter opposition. This is also a clear indication of the difference between the present age and the Kingdom, and the limited character of human progress and achievements in matter of social justice.[107] However, facing oppositions should not be a source of discouragement for those who choose the way of the Kingdom, but a source of hope in the possibility to transform society.

The paradigm of the Kingdom of God/heaven points to something important. Conversion is not about reforming or amending, but transformation. The Bostwanan biblical scholar Musa W. Dube maintains that transforming is different from reforming, which keeps the basic structure.[108] Rather, "to transform is an attempt to inaugurate metanoia, a complete changing of the current situation." Kyriarchal ways that oppress women workers must be abandoned to give way to visions inspired by the Kingdom of God, which put the dignity of the person and the well-being of the community at the center.

Breaking the Silence

It is generally said that the Church must be the "voice of the voiceless." However, as well intended as this may sound, it could turn into paternalism. In addition, healing cannot begin to occur without some catharsis, which implies voicing one's pain and concerns. Some feminist authors have pointed the necessity for women to break the oppressive silence in which they are kept. Aquino points silence as one of the habits that encourage the violation of human rights and "a sustained repetition of social conflict."[109] Women workers' voices are barely heard in trade unions, or in any relevant matter that concerns them. "In order to be accepted as full equals in Africa, women must raise educated voices against the unjust treatment of women."[110]

By breaking the silence, one brings to the open what has been hidden, and one makes visible the oppression.[111] Silence on the part of the Church is a "sin by omission" that conceals an ugly reality.[112] Breaking the silence means the refusal to remain passive and complicit to social injustice. It is a challenge to the status quo and the unjust order. However, since the hierarchy of the Church may be a participant in women's oppression, breaking the silence befalls the working women who must voice their concerns, and share their joys and pains. In fact, "while those who have been sinned against remember their experiences and honor those who continue to suffer multiple injustices, giving voice to what seems to have slipped into obscurity but continues to harass and shame them is vital."[113] Breaking the silence is not only acknowledging wrongdoing against working women but giving space to their "struggles, hopes, and experience."[114] In addition, by raising their voices, these women begin their healing process and their march toward liberation. Ngozi Frances explores the case of religious women—which could be extended to women workers—and suggests that raising their voices on their suffering is the "first step toward transformative reconciliation."[115] Ultimately, one has to agree that

> every human being must have the right to tell her own story, to explore and discover the meaning of her own life in a mutually transformative dialogue between her personal circumstances and the cultures, traditions, and communities to which she belongs.[116]

Making one's voice heard means participating in the process of reclaiming one's identity, which I underlined above as one of the elements of the option of the working woman for herself. By making their voices heard, women help expose the sinful social structures that oppress them, and challenge the society and the Church to act decisively in their favor.

Alternative Views of the Economy and Labor

Neoliberal economy that accompanies globalization has shown its limits. It centers on making profit and not on the good of the human person. It treats labor as a commodity. It fosters an individualistic and atomistic vision of society, and separates the market from other spheres of society. In Sub-Saharan

Africa, this economy has meant more precarious and more informal jobs for African workers.

Neoclassical economics that feeds neoliberal economy has shown its limits in addressing gender in a relevant way. First, it is due to its lack of critical analysis of the context (history, pervasiveness of gender-based imbalances) in which economic activities are performed. Second, it does not take into account nonmonetary economy such as caring labor. This translates itself in measurements such as the GDP or in public policies that do not take caring labor into account. As a result, many hardworking women's work is unaccounted for. In addition, the unbridled capitalism and industrialization present a threat to the environment and the livelihood of millions of women in Africa.

The official Church through CST has developed a more humane economy that I already presented in chapter 1. Even if CST does not offer a "full-blown alternative socioeconomic system," it contains "very specific convictions about the meaning and purposes of economy for our material, personal, and social lives, and in relation to the mysteries of human-Divine encounter in creation, history and destiny."[117] The primacy of the human person and community, the pursuit of the common good, the promotion of human dignity and equality, and participation are principles that should inform economic activities. "Economy's central aim is to generate material sufficiency for all members, while government is charged with coordinating and overseeing the common good of the whole body."[118] This vision gives a big role to the government, and assumes a context of regulated economy, and a strong and autonomous government. However, globalization is characterized by a deregulated economy. In addition, there are various actors involved in the planning and execution of the economy. In the context of postcolonial Africa, international donors in the form of foreign governments, international institutions (International Monetary Fund (IMF), World Bank), or private individuals may influence government policies.

In the particular issue of development, Ela suggests that local actors such as rural communities, urban neighborhoods, women, and the youth should serve as inspiration when designing development policies.[119] In the specific case of the firm, he suggests the reintroduction of immaterial elements in the process of production.[120] Paulinus Odozor likewise rejects a materialistic vision of human development.[121] Odozor adds that four points should be considered when one speaks about human development: the relationship with God, human flourishing, hope, and solidarity.[122] From these two authors, one understands that a good economy is done from the perspective of the workers and local economies, and that it takes a holistic approach to the person. Moreover, a sound economic system allows for the empowerment of local actors.[123]

Caring Labor

An alternative vision of economy takes caring labor into consideration. Under CST, the family plays a central role in human flourishing, and the "economy and state exist for the sake of families."[124] This in turn produces a threefold moral understanding of labor: (1) "a principal way that people exercise the distinctive human capacity for self-expression and self-realization"; (2) the ordinary way for the fulfillment of human material needs; (3) since it contributes to "the well-being of the larger community," it is not only for oneself.[125] However, these very principles in the abstract do not account for power dynamics and conflicts especially in relation to gender, race/ethnicity, and class. As Christine Hinze contends: "Official Catholic discourse . . . also betrays an insufficiently robust analysis of power, coercion, and social conflict in relation to gender and political economy."[126] For instance, in the African context, the introduction of capitalistic economy was accompanied with violence on the Africans, which sometimes resulted in deaths.[127] In addition, the work in the modern economy is being labeled as the "work of the white man."[128] That work means for workers long working hours under unsafe conditions, with poor remuneration. It also means that those in charge get to sit in an air-conditioned office, do not have to sweat and are well-paid. This second aspect represents the ideal form of work for postcolonial Africans. The "work of the white man" means working out of necessity, being barely rewarded, being exploited, and remaining poor. For executives, it means comfort and good life. As distorted as this notion may sound, it calls for the necessity to locate human labor within the general context of a society.

I pay particular attention to caring/reproductive labor because it was perceived in chapter 2 as a key aspect necessary to change societal gender dynamics in work. Caring labor disproportionately falls on women and affects their possible choices of employment. The fact that caring labor is perceived as feminine and unskilled or requiring less skills creates problematic dynamics. As Fiorenza asserts

> a feminist theological reflection must begin with an analysis of the social structures of domesticity and motherhood that foster wo/men's economic exploitation. It does not suffice to struggle for equal rights in the workplace or advocate salaries for housework as long as only wo/men are believed to be destined by nature and by G*d to do such housework as service.[129]

Caring labor requires a holistic understanding of the economy, which should go back to the root of what economy is according to Pope Francis, that is, "the art of achieving a fitting management of our common home, which is the world as whole."[130] This perception does away with fragmentary ways of looking at the economy. This economy focused on our common home emphasizes the logic of gift alongside the logics of exchange and legal obligation.[131] The essential steps toward developing a culture of care involve: (1) reframing how economy is understood and its assigned purpose, (2) value and adequately provide for care, (3) engender justice in household and waged labor, (4) ensure and embrace "enough" (putting limits to consumption), (5) empower and support dignified wage-force and household participation for all workers, and (6) strengthen the foundations,[132] that is, reinforcing and deepening ethical and spiritual pilings of the society, in view of proper reconsideration of cultural and political-economic priorities.[133] It is about putting relationality, well-being, and human solidarity above the individualist, profit-maximizing, and insatiable economic person.[134] Relationality is not limited to fellow human beings, but concern also nonhuman creation.

These different elements lead to the recognition of the vital place of reproductive labor in people's lives. People who have never experienced and/or given proper care in a healthy domestic environment cannot function properly in a society. Going beyond the simple monetary levels helps to understand the beauty of motherhood/mothering, "which calls for a life of letting go, a readiness to share resources and to receive with appreciation what others offer for the community."[135] This runs contrary to the spirit of grabbing and accumulation of wealth, which is the order of the day in today's economy. Mothering provides us a hint on how caring labor works. Mothering is never the work of one person. It takes a family, neighbors, churches, educational institutions, and the society at large, to provide the proper environment in which a child can grow. Women should not be penalized for becoming mothers in a society that understands the importance of reproduction and caring labor. This calls for mutuality and shared responsibility in providing for care. Indeed, "everyone is vulnerable, needy, and dependent in their bodies, and the work and caring attaching to that fact are the right and responsibility of all."[136]

TOWARD A COMMUNAL APPROACH TO WOMEN'S EMPOWERMENT

I use the word "communal" to avoid using the words "communitarian" and "systemic." Communitarian connotes the idea of the community's primacy over the individual while systemic seems more abstract. The word "communal" puts a face on people, and promotes a dialectical tension between the person and the community/group.

In the previous chapter, it appeared that one of the limits of the different analyses and solutions was their individualistic approach to women's empowerment. The previous section on social sin showed the importance of the context in which one is located, and how influential it is. Social ethical discourse in Africa and elsewhere needs always to locate individuals within the larger picture of the context in which they are historically involved. And unless this general context is affected decisively, there could be pockets of change, which will ultimately not affect the whole picture. The section on social sin revealed how sinful social structures can be. There should be ways to check whether social structures promote the well-being of the community and the individual. In addition, I advocate here a communal approach in strategies and policies. The goal of this section is to make explicit what was implicit in the previous section.

To go back to the larger context concerning the person, that context can be described as the human community or as the individual/groups caught up in the web of relationships. In the life of a person many relationships intersect simultaneously. Thus, the first element that must guide a communal approach must be intersectionality.

Intersectionality

Intersectionality deepens the awareness of structural nature of social sin by looking at how the various levels of social structures crisscross the lives of people and communities to oppress them. Intersectionality is not about diversity, but about the multilayered and complex dimension of marginalization and injustice. Indeed, "intersectionality deliberately seeks to provide a framework for engaging the dynamic complexity of multiple forms of inequality."[137] This assumes that injustice cannot be tackled from a single perspective. Since 1989 when the African American feminist, Kimberlé Crenshaw, coined the term "intersectionality,"[138] the notion has blossomed and expanded in such a way that it is presently difficult to come up with a single definition of the term.[139] Nina Lykke suggests that intersectionality is "a theoretical and methodological tool" that serves

> to analyze how historically specific kinds of power differentials and/or constraining normativities, based on discursively, institutionally and/or structurally constructed socio-cultural categorizations such as gender, ethnicity, race, class, sexuality, age/generation, dis/ability, nationality, mother tongue and so on, interact, and in so doing produce different kinds of societal inequalities and unjust social relations.[140]

Sirma Bilge does not propose a definition as such since intersectionality is a contextual and fluid concept that does not allow for universalization.[141] Instead, she suggests four elements that should characterize any understanding of intersectionality.[142] First, intersectionality is an analysis of power that looks at the imbrication and intertwinement of vectors of power with spheres of power. Second, the vectors of power, that is, identities, social categories or social formations (race, class, gender, imperialism, etc.), obey certain characteristics. None is sufficient to explain injustice and equality. They are not interchangeable and are co-constitutive of one another. The vectors of power have to be analyzed as historical contingencies. The particularity of intersectionality is to pinpoint that "identity is not additive but simultaneous."[143] Third, intersectionality analyzes the various social categories within the framework of spheres of power.[144] Fourth, intersectionality is oriented toward social justice. It is not only an analytical tool but also a critical praxis.

Intersectionality can be understood as a concept, a research paradigm, an ideograph, a theoretical and methodological tool, a broad-based knowledge project, and an analytical sensibility.[145] Leslie McCall suggests three possible approaches to intersectionality: anti-categorical (deconstruction), intra-categorical (analysis of neglected points of intersection), and inter-categorical (analysis of relations of inequality among social groups and changing configurations of inequality).[146]

Furthermore, intersectionality in the context of Africa is very important because it originally arose in the United States as a reaction to what was perceived as hegemonic discourse from middle-class white feminists. That discourse sidelined issues around race. This also was reflected by a certain discourse on Third World women, which inadvertently "reproduced a colonialist tradition of cultural essentialism."[147] Intersectionality as social justice aims at "empowering those who experience multiple dimensions of inequality and of supporting strategic action by coalitions that respect differences while pursuing common goals."[148] Intersectionality as theoretical tool is valuable, because it links the personal and social dimensions.[149] Individuals create and shape unjust social structures and relations. Consequently, the unjust social structures negatively impact the lives of those oppressed by them.

For theologians and CST, intersectionality provides an important tool to analyze power dynamics. In African theology, there is an informal use of intersectionality that is barely mentioned. I will illustrate it through some examples. Oduyoye, in her book, *Daughters of Anowa*, analyses how power differentials in gender, race, ideology, economics, politics, culture, and colonialism negatively affect African women.[150] Jean-Marc Ela acknowledges the importance of race, class, ideology, and location (rural/urban), which he analyzes at the political, economic, and ecclesial level.[151] None of these authors explicitly refer to intersectionality, although they are using an intersectional analysis of some sort. There is a need for a more systematic use of intersectionality that sheds light on the many other areas that can be forgotten. One of these is the failure to analyze social class among many African women theologians—with the notable exception of Musimbi Kanyoro.[152] In most cases, the reader gets the impression that the African women are referred to as a homogenous group.[153] Differences are acknowledged at the ethnic level, but for the most part, the attention to the diversity of situations among women is not always present. Differences in terms of location (rural/ urban), class, instruction, religion, dis/ability, and others are barely mentioned. Intersectionality could prove valuable in probing the claims of communitarianism in Africa by showing who is excluded or who does not fully belong, and how various unjust structures intersect within particular societies to oppress. This is critical because public discourse for the sake of harmony tends to suppress any claim of pluralism and acknowledgment of diversity.[154]

Intersectionality is implicitly present in chapters 6 and 7, where inequalities present on the level of gender, race/ethnicity, location (rural and urban women), education (women with and without instruction), and nation (colonialism) are exacerbated at the ideological (neoclassical economics, neoliberalism, patriarchy), religious, cultural (discriminatory practices such as inheritance), political, and economic (labor market, occupational segregation) levels. Many of the sources I used—especially the reports from international organizations such as the UN and the International Labor Organization (ILO)—acknowledge the various levels of inequalities. What is generally absent is how these various levels work simultaneously. The challenge put forward through intersectionality is not to separate the various levels of oppression and the multiple identities people assume. Feminist scholars acknowledge the limited scopes of the studies on women's labor. Jenny Rodriguez and others observe that "despite the recognition of the workplace as a critical site for the (re)production of intersectional inequalities . . . intersectionality has not been fully utilized to explore structures of discrimination and systems of power and inequality."[155]

Moreover, "intersectionality remains at the margin of dominant work and organization narratives of equality and inclusion."[156] Rodriguez and others suggest two approaches: one focused on individuals and the consequences of intersectionality in their lives; and the second considers the individuals as embedded within larger systems. Since I give priority to a holistic approach, I prefer the second approach, which "relies on systemic analysis of inequality and is characterized by a critical look at how power is exercised simultaneously in all spheres of influence and how these systems of inequality are institutionalized."[157]

As a tool aimed at social justice within the context of labor, intersectionality must not only challenge inequality but also enact change.[158] Rodriguez and others suggest three areas in which intersectional practices can be applied to the workplace: institutional change, organizational change, and in curriculum design and teaching.[159] However, these suggestions only take into account the formal sector of the economy. There must be a more comprehensive approach that can take informal economy into account as well as unpaid reproductive labor. Rodriguez notes the necessity to take into account the changing nature of work, which increasingly becomes "transnational and multidirectional."[160]

As good as it sounds, intersectionality is not, however, immune to abuse. It can "be coopted by neoliberalism mainly because the power of market forces is stronger than the will to promote equality."[161] Bilge observes that over the years intersectionality's anti-establishment character has eroded and that it is not rare to use it for public relations and confuse it with diversity.[162] The co-optation of intersectionality here happens in the academic field where this knowledge is domesticated and turned into a simple object of consumption.[163] This danger looms over most of the revolutionary notions. To avoid falling into this trap, it is important to pair intersectionality with another important approach: the institutional approach.

Institutional Approach

The theory of Christian social ethics must be supplemented by praxis. This subsection's interest is on institutions and levels that can effect positive changes for working women. Taking the specific case of CST, David Kaulemu sees three levels where CST works: (1) dealing with and teaching general values and principles; (2) social policy engagement; and (3) witnessing to Christian values.[164] The first level has been discussed in chapters 1 and 3. The next chapter will address the third level. The institutional approach is located at the second level. The concern is not only to denounce as bad practices "but also to promote best practice, to stimulate creativity in seeking new solutions and to encourage individual or group initiatives."[165]

The institutional approach is taken from development economics. It is born out of an understanding of the importance of institutions in generating economic development.[166] It is primarily an analytical tool that is destined to better understand processes of development,[167] but I primarily use it as a strategic tool not only to identify the social levels, structures, and actors, but also how to act on them, with them, or against them.

"Institutional transformation should focus on generating new forms of correlated behavior aimed at increasing the generalized standard of living of the population of a country."[168] Indeed, "the transformation of human behavior is at the center of the institutional matrix in which humans are both subjects and objects."[169] The institutional approach exploits John Paul II's important idea on indirect employer, which pays attention to actors and critical factors affecting the working environment. Even Pope Francis, in *Laudato Si*, recognizes that there must be an institutional approach and suggested ways that the issues of climate change could be tackled.[170]

Institutions are "durable systems of established and embedded social rules that structure social interaction."[171] Howard Stein identifies five types of institutions, namely, norms, organizations, regulations, capacities, and incentives.[172] "Norms are socially derived behavioral guidelines concerning what is expected, required, or accepted."[173] Organizations "are conceptually (and often legally) recognized entities that combine groups of people with defined common rules and purposes."[174] Regulations are "the legal boundaries that help set the rules of operation in economies."[175] In the context of an organization, "capacities are the abilities of members to operate effectively to achieve the organization's goal and purposes."[176] Incentives are "rewards and penalties that arise from different modes of behavior."[177] Incentives and regulations can change easily. However, their effects may be quite slow.[178] Capacities take time to build up. Organization and norms are difficult to change. These five types of institutions have to be considered together if one wants to bring about an effective change in the situation of women.

Gerry Rodgers and others identify the following as labor institutions: the nature of employment contracts, the mechanisms for controlling and regulating employment contracts, the organization and representation of labor, the organization and representation of employers, the institution of labor market itself, methods by which wage is paid, the process of wage fixing, training and skill institutions, the organization of job within the firm, structure of ownership and control over production, social and state regulation of self-employment, social security and income guarantee systems, conventional standard for life, and the organization of labor supply.[179] Most of these elements work for the formal economy, but not necessarily in the formal economy. In addition, these labor institutions are limited to the national level while there are global elements that may affect the local reality of labor. For instance, the outsourcing of labor in poorer countries by Western corporations creates a situation where local nations deregulate their labor market to attract more investors. This exacerbates the already precarious condition of workers.

The institutional approach is important because factors that influence women's work are manifold: at the theoretical level (neoclassical economics and what count as productive work, financial gain as the primary value), the global context (globalization, economic deregulation), policies (ignoring reproductive labor, trade agreements that weaken social benefits for workers), cultural (undervaluation of women's work), and through practices (occupational segregation). It is clear from what has been said above that economic life is complex and multilayered and it is intertwined with other social spheres. The complexity of these phenomena is the reason why a viable solution cannot be limited at the level of single individuals or to an individual nation. Paul VI acknowledges that "individual initiative alone" is insufficient in solving the issue of development.[180] Communities and nations no longer operate in autarky—if they ever did—and this postcolonial era, international factors affect local and national life, and vice versa.[181] This is why at least three levels—closely intertwined—need to be considered when looking at the type of institutions needed to improve women's conditions. They are international, national, and local.

Moreover, this institutional approach does not mean an impersonal approach. It emphasizes a sense of relatedness, which is present both in CST and in African communitarianism. The institutional approach is enriched by the option for the poor, the awareness of social sin, and intersectionality. In addition, principles of CST such as the common good (at the local and global levels), subsidiarity, participation, and solidarity, operate as guiding principles when thinking on how change must be effected at the institutional level.

Looking at the common good, the dominant understandings of CST are institutional, and relational and solidarity.[182] The institutional approach can be seen in John XXIII's and Jacques Maritain's definitions.[183] This understanding highlights the comprehensive dimension of the common good, which embraces a holistic vision of the person. Life is not limited to the satisfaction of material and physiological needs, and includes relationships and other immaterial goods that are important. The common good is not utilitarian, where it can be achieved at the expense of the few for the good of the many. The promotion of the common good precludes any instrumental use of the person.[184] "The common good of the community and the good of the members are mutually implicating."[185] This is also valid at the global level where common good cannot be achieved at the expense of a nation or local communities.

The institutional understanding of the common good insists on the importance of the social context in providing proper conditions for individuals or communities to flourish. As far as labor is concerned, the notion of "indirect employer" put forward by John Paul II in *LE* seems to fit that context. The "indirect employer" is understood as "all the agents at the national and international level that are responsible for the whole orientation of labour policy."[186] This notion has the advantage of bringing together the individual and the collective, the national and the international, State and non-State entities as well as practices and procedures that affect economic life in general. That will be the key notion with which I want to operate. The notion of "indirect employer" makes it clear that more than simply identifying potential actors and institutions, there are values that must inform interactions at the various levels.

The relational and solidaristic understanding builds on the mutual dependence and the interdependence between people and between States. It fosters the virtues of collaboration and cooperation.[187] In virtue of solidarity, special attention must be paid to the most vulnerable and the marginalized,[188] in this case, women working in the informal sector. The institutional approach is affected by subsidiarity. This means integrating local communities in the decision-making process as well as empowering the local level to act on its own.[189] These have direct impact on working women in the Third World.

At the international level, the indirect employer takes the form of the imbalanced relationships between States, the necessity to reform international institutions (UN, ILO, Food and Agriculture Organization, IMF, World Bank, United Nations Development Program), international legal agreements, and recognize the growing impact of non-States actors (in a special way multinational corporations and transnational NGOs). The involvement of non-State actors results from the awareness of the changing nature of global economics: the diminished power of the State in the financial and business market, as well as the increasing mobility of labor, financial capital, and means of production.[190] In addition, there is a need to address pressing challenges such as the reform of the international trade system, the international division of labor, and the forms of technology and heir transfer.[191] At the local level, one finds the same actors (State, international organizations, corporations, and NGOs), to which one must add the national civil society, intermediary groups, and trade unions.

The diversity of actors and contexts necessitates clarification on "common and differentiated responsibilities."[192] The civil society[193] must act toward other parties as a fulfillment of their obligations and duties. It must not hesitate to put pressure on governments for the latter to play its role.[194] It is the role of the State to create "favourable conditions for the free exercise of economic activity."[195] This means, in the case of agriculture, investing in rural infrastructure, improving farming techniques, and a better organization of local markets.[196] In addition, States should abide by the international legal agreements they commit to. In this particular case, they should enforce the Convention for the Elimination of all forms of Discrimination Against Women and the Protocol to the African Charter of Human and People's Rights also known as the Maputo Protocol.[197]

In general, the Church, at this level, is called to move beyond simple statements and general principles, to work to make its vision for the society a reality. First, it must collaborate through partnership and network with other religious bodies and organizations in civil society. Second, lay people must be at the forefront of this action.[198]

NOTES

1. James B. Nickoloff, ed., *Gustavo Gutierrez: Essential Writings*, The Making of Modern Theology, Nineteenth and Twentieth-Century Texts 8 (Minneapolis, MN: Fortress Press, 1996), 146.

2. Elsa Tamez, "Poverty, the Poor, and the Option for the Poor: A Biblical Perspective," in *The Option for the Poor in Christian Theology*, ed. Daniel G. Groody (Notre Dame, IN: University of Notre Dame Press, 2007), 50.

3. Ibid., 51–52.

4. Maria Pilar Aquino, "The Feminist Option for the Poor and Oppressed in the Context of Globalization," in *The Option for the Poor in Christian Theology*, ed. Daniel G. Groody (Notre Dame, IN: University of Notre Dame Press, 2007), 199.

5. Anne Arabome, "When a Sleeping Woman Wakes ... A Conversation with Pope Francis in *Evangelii Gaudium* about the Feminization of Poverty," in *The Church We Want: African Catholics Look to Vatican III*, ed. Agbonkhianmeghe E. Orobator (Maryknoll, NY: Orbis Books, 2016), 56.

6. Virgilio Elizondo, "Culture, the Option for the Poor, and Liberation," in *The Option for the Poor in Christian Theology*, ed. Daniel G. Groody (Notre Dame, IN: University of Notre Dame Press, 2007), 158–61. Along with socioeconomic poverty, Elizondo lists among others psychological (low self-image, inferiority complex), spiritual (difficulty to find meaning in life), and cultural poverty (internalized prejudices against one's own culture or being, self-depreciation and self-esteem at a collective level). To these dimensions, I would like also to add gender.

7. John R. Donahue, *Seek Justice That You May Live: Reflections and Resources on the Bible and Social Justice* (New York: Paulist Press, 2014), 55–60, 73–86, 205–216; Robert Benne, "The Preferential Option for the Poor and American Public Policy," in *The Preferential Option for the Poor*, ed. Richard John Neuhaus, Encounter Series (Grand Rapids, MI: William B. Eerdmans Publishing Company, 1988), 53; John O'Brien, *Theology and the Option for the Poor*, Theology and Life Series, v. 22 (Collegeville, MN: Liturgical Press, 1992), 79.

8. Tamez, "Poverty, the Poor and the Option for the Poor," 52.

9. M. Shawn Copeland, "Poor Is the Color of God," in *The Option for the Poor in Christian Theology*, ed. Daniel G. Groody (Notre Dame, IN: University of Notre Dame Press, 2007), 220.

10. {Citation}.

11. David N. Field, "On (Re)Centering the Margins: A Euro-African Perspective on the Option for the Poor," in *Opting for the Margins: Postmodernity and Liberation in Christian Theology*, ed. Joerg Rieger, Reflection and Theory in the Study of Religion (Oxford ; New York: Oxford University Press, 2003), 52.

12. Copeland, "Poor Is the Color of God," 217.

13. I freely borrow from Yvone Gebara, "Option for the Poor as an Option for the Poor Woman," in *Women, Work and Poverty*, ed. Elisabeth Schüssler Fiorenza and Anne E. Carr, Concilium 194 (Edinburgh: T & T Clark, 1987), 111.

14. Nickoloff, *Gustavo Gutierrez: Essential Writings*, 144–45.

15. Oduyoye, *Daughters of Anowa*, 82.

16. Ibid.

17. A. Nasimiyu-Wasike, "The Missing Voices of Women," in *Catholic Theological Ethics Past, Present and Future: The Trento Conference*, ed. James F. Keenan (Maryknoll, NY: Orbis Books, 2011), 110.

18. Tina Beattie, "Maternal Well-Being in Sub-Saharan Africa: From Silent Suffering to Human Flourishing," in *The Church We Want: African Catholics Look*

to Vatican III, ed. Agbonkhianmeghe E. Orobator (Maryknoll, NY: Orbis Books, 2016), 178.

19. Nasimiyu-Wasike, "The Missing Voices of Women."

20. Ibid., 107.

21. Nickoloff, *Gustavo Gutierrez: Essential Writings*, 145.

22. Oduyoye, *Daughters of Anowa*, 82.

23. Beattie, "Maternal Well-Being in Sub-Saharan Africa," 179.

24. Nickoloff, *Gustavo Gutierrez: Essential Writings*, 145.

25. Nasimiyu-Wasike, "The Missing Voices of Women," 111.

26. Gebara, "Option for the Poor," 112.

27. Ibid., 111.

28. Ibid.

29. Teresia M. Hinga, "The Dialogical Imperative: Listening to Concerned and Engaged African Women," in *Prophetic Witness: Catholic Women's Strategies for Reform*, ed. Colleen M. Griffith, The Boston College Church in the 21st Century (New York: A Herder & Herder Book, The Crossroad Publishing Company, 2009), 94.

30. St Thomas Aquinas, *Summa Theologiae IIa-IIae*, trans. Fathers of the English Dominican Province, online (Kevin Knight, 2008), q. 26, 4, http://www.newadvent.org/summa/2.htm.

31. Stephen J. Pope, *The Evolution of Altruism and the Ordering of Love*, Moral Traditions & Moral Arguments Series (Washington, DC: Georgetown University Press, 1994), 59.

32. Benedict XVI, *Deus Caritas Est*, 7. However, Benedict XVI does not really dwell on proper self-love.

33. Ibid.

34. Gebara, "Option for the Poor," 112.

35. Francis, *Amoris Laetitia*, 285. However, Francis does not offer a reflection on proper self-love, and only refers to disordered manifestations of self-love.

36. Gebara, "Option for the Poor," 112.

37. Ibid., 113.

38. Ibid.

39. Ibid.

40. Ibid.

41. Gustavo Gutiérrez, "Memory and Prophecy," in *The Option for the Poor in Christian Theology*, ed. Daniel G. Groody (Notre Dame, IN: University of Notre Dame Press, 2007), 31.

42. Anne Arabome, "'Woman, You Are Set Free!' Women and Discipleship in the Church," in *Reconciliation, Justice, and Peace: The Second African Synod*, ed. Agbonkhianmeghe E. Orobator (Maryknoll, NY: Orbis Books, 2011), 123.

43. Gutiérrez, "Memory and Prophecy," 31.

44. Francis, *Evangelii Gaudium*, 198.

45. Ibid.

46. Arabome, "When a Sleeping Woman Wakes," 62.

47. *OA* N. 4 quoted by Mary Elsbernd O.S.F., "What Ever Happened to *Octogesima Adveniens?*," *Theological Studies* 56 (1995): 42.

48. Ibid., 43.

49. Francis, *Evangelii Gaudium*, 48.

50. Ibid., 97.

51. Ibid., 210.

52. Ibid., 70, 200.

53. Ibid., 202.

54. Ibid., 218.

55. Arabome, "When a Sleeping Woman Wakes," 61.

56. Ibid.

57. Ngozi Frances Uti, "Come, Let Us Talk This Over: On the Condition of Women Religious in the Church," in *Reconciliation, Justice, and Peace: The Second African Synod*, ed. Agbonkhianmeghe E. Orobator (Maryknoll, NY: Orbis Books, 2011), 138–41.

58. Ephrem Else Lau, "Women Religious and Lay Women as Workers in the Church," in *Women, Work and Poverty*, ed. Elisabeth Schüssler Fiorenza and Anne Carr, trans. Margaret Kohl, Concilium 194 (Edinburgh: T. & T. Clark, 1987), 79–84; Annekee Schiltuis-Stokvis, "Women as Workers in the Church Seen from the Ecumenical Point of View," in *Women, Work and Poverty*, ed. Elisabeth Schüssler Fiorenza and Anne Carr, trans. David Smith, Concilium 194 (Edinburgh: T. & T. Clark, 1987), 85–90.

59. Mark O'Keefe, *What Are They Saying about Social Sin?* (New York: Paulist Press, 1990), 46.

60. Ibid., 29–32. People such as Peter Henriot define social from the perspective of the objects (evil acts done to others); others like Gregory Baum suggest that social sin should be defined in relation with the subject (individual, communities); some like Thomas Schindler put social sin in relationship with original sin.

61. Ibid., 29.

62. John Paul II, *On Reconciliation and Penance in the Mission of the Church Today, Post-Synodal Apostolic Exhortation* Reconciliatio et Paenitentia (Rome: Libreria Editrice Vaticana, 1984), 16, http://w2.vatican.va/content/john-paul-ii/en/apost_exhortations/documents/hf_jp-ii_exh_02121984_reconciliatio-et-paenitentia.html; O'Keefe, *About Social Sin*, 19.

63. {Citation}.

64. John Paul II, *Reconciliatio et Paenitentia*, 16.

65. O'Keefe, *About Social Sin*, 17.

66. Yao Assogba, *Jean-Marc Ela: le sociologue et théologien africain en boubou: entretiens*, Collection Etudes africaines (Paris: L'Harmattan, 1999), 66.

67. O'Keefe, *About Social Sin*, 34.

68. Ibid., 46.

69. Ibid.

70. Ibid., 35, 46.

71. John Paul II, *Sollicitudo Rei Socialis*, 36.

72. O'Keefe, *About Social Sin*, 62.

73. Ibid., 20.

74. Ibid., 30.

75. I am adapting O'Keefe's example on world hunger to the case of women workers. For more see Ibid., 31.

76. Elisabeth Schüssler Fiorenza, "Introduction: Feminist Liberation Theology as Critical Sophialogy," in *The Power of Naming: A Concilium Reader in Feminist Liberation Theology*, ed. Elisabeth Schüssler Fiorenza, Concilium (Maryknoll, NY: London, England: Orbis Books; SCM Press, 1996), xxi.

77. Ibid.

78. "Patriarchy is a form of social organization in which power is always is the hand of the dominant man or men, with others ranked below in a graded series of subordinations reaching down to the least powerful who form a large base." See Elizabeth A. Johnson, *She Who Is: The Mystery of God in Feminist Theological Discourse*, 10th anniversary ed. (New York: Crossroad, 2002), 23.

79. Schüssler Fiorenza, "Introduction," xxii.

80. Ibid., xxi.

81. Ibid.

82. Ibid., xxiii.

83. Ibid., xxiii, xxv.

84. Jean-Marc Ela, *Travail et entreprise en Afrique: les fondements sociaux de la réussite économique*, Hommes et sociétés (Paris: Karthala, 2006), 240.

85. Aquino, "The Feminist Option for the Poor and Oppressed," 202.

86. Ibid.

87. Ibid., 203.

88. Ibid.

89. Jean-Marc Ela, *La plume et la pioche: réflexion sur l'enseignement et la société dans le développement de l'Afrique noire* (Yaoundé: Éditions Clé, 2011), 67.

90. For more on this aspect of colonial authoritarian leadership and its legacy see Achille Mbembé, *On the Postcolony*, Studies on the History of Society and Culture 41 (Berkeley: University of California Press, 2001).

91. Ela, *La plume et la pioche*, 97.

92. As Fiorenza rightly points out: "as long as wo/men do not understand their ministry in the churches as work but speak of it as service, they cannot see themselves as workers deserving due process and just remuneration," see Schüssler Fiorenza, "Introduction," xxv.

93. O'Keefe, *About Social Sin*, 86–87.

94. Ibid., 86.

95. John Paul II, *Sollicitudo Rei Socialis*, 36.

96. O'Keefe, *About Social Sin*, 92.

97. Ibid., 93.

98. Ibid., 87–90. Concerning the issue of conflict and violence, O'Keefe observes that "political involvement will necessarily involve conflict." He opens the door in case of a repressive and intransigent political regime to violence. Sincerely, I doubt whether violence can be an effective tool of conversion since it inscribes itself in the same coercive logic.

99. Gutiérrez, *A Theology of Liberation*, 57.

100. Boff and Boff, *Salvation and Liberation*, 56–57.

101. Schüssler Fiorenza, "Introduction," xxxiii.

102. Donahue, *Seek Justice That You May Live*, 143.

103. Ela, *Repenser la théologie africaine*, 80.

104. John R. Donahue S.J., "The Bible and Catholic Social Teaching: Will This Engagement Lead to Marriage?" in *Modern Catholic Social Teaching: Commentaries & Interpretations*, ed. Kenneth R. Himes O.f.M. et al. (Washington, DC: Georgetown University Press, 2005), 25.

105. Donahue, *Seek Justice That You May Live*, 148–49.

106. Ibid., 151.

107. Boff and Boff, *Salvation and Liberation*, 61.

108. Musa Wenkosi Dube, "Introduction: 'Little Girl, Get Up!,'" in *Talitha Cumi!: Theologies of African Women*, ed. Nyambura J. Njoroge and Musa W. Dube (Pietermatritzburg: Cluster Publications, 2001), 9.

109. Aquino, "The Feminist Option for the Poor and Oppressed," 196.

110. Arabome, "Women and Discipleship in the Church," 124.

111. Aquino, "The Feminist Option for the Poor and Oppressed," 206.

112. Ibid., 209; O'Keefe, *About Social Sin*, 70.

113. Uti, "Come, Let Us Talk This Over," 140.

114. Mary Catherine Hilkert, "The Poor in the Context of Globalization: A Feminist Vision," in *The Option for the Poor in Christian Theology*, ed. Daniel G. Groody (Notre Dame, IN: University of Notre Dame Press, 2007), 231.

115. Uti, "Come, Let Us Talk This Over," 140.

116. Beattie, "Maternal Well-Being in Sub-Saharan Africa," 180.

117. Hinze, *Glass Ceilings and Dirt Floors*, 95.

118. Ibid., 96.

119. Assogba, *Jean-Marc Ela*, 48.

120. Ibid., 54; Ela, *Travail et entreprise en Afrique*, 208. Ela suggests that unless African cultures and ethos are taken into account in economic planning and activities, strategies of development will continue to fail.

121. Paulinus I. Odozor C.S.Sp, "Theology at the Service of the Church and Human Development," in *Committed in Solidarity: Sist Silver Jubilee Acts*, ed. Gabriel Mendy (Enugu, Nigeria: Kingsley Publishers, 2015), 105–7.

122. Ibid., 105–18.

123. Ela, *Travail et entreprise en Afrique*, 99.

124. Hinze, *Glass Ceilings and Dirt Floors*, 97.

125. Ibid., 92–93.

126. Ibid., 100.

127. Ela, *Travail et entreprise en Afrique*, 268.

128. Ibid., 273.

129. Schüssler Fiorenza, "Introduction," xxiv.

130. Francis quoted in Hinze, *Glass Ceilings and Dirt Floors*, 102.

131. Ibid., 116.

132. Ibid., 105–17.

133. Ibid., 114–16.

134. Ibid., 115.

135. Oduyoye, *Beads and Strands*, 58.

136. Hinze, *Glass Ceilings and Dirt Floors*, 114.

137. Nancy J. Ramsay, "Intersectionality: A Model for Addressing the Complexity of Oppression and Privilege," *Pastoral Psychology* 63, no. 4 (August 2014): 455, doi:10.1007/s11089-013-0570-4.

138. Nina Lykke, *Feminist Studies: A Guide to Intersectional Theory, Methodology and Writing*, Routledge Advances in Feminist Studies and Intersectionality 1 (New York: Routledge, 2010), 50.

139. Sirma Bilge, "Le blanchiment de l'intersectionnalité," *Recherches féministes* 28, no. 2 (2015): 15.

140. Lykke, *Feminist Studies*, 50.

141. Bilge, "Le blanchiment de l'intersectionnalité," 15.

142. From here onward see Ibid., 15–17.

143. Ramsay, "Intersectionality," 457.

144. There is no agreement on what those spheres of power are; Bilge locates them at the structural, hegemonic, disciplinary, interpersonal, and psychic and embodied levels. See Bilge, "Le blanchiment de l'intersectionnalité," 17; Ramsay, "Intersectionality," 455.

145. Jenny K. Rodriguez et al., "The Theory and Praxis of Intersectionality in Work and Organisations: Where Do We Go From Here?," *Gender, Work & Organization* 23, no. 3 (May 2016): 201, doi:10.1111/gwao.12131; Lykke, *Feminist Studies*, 50.

146. Quoted by Lykke, *Feminist Studies*, 70.

147. Ibid., 53.

148. Ramsay, "Intersectionality," 455.

149. Ibid., 458.

150. Oduyoye, *Daughters of Anowa*, 52, 62, 82.

151. For more read Ela, *Le cri de l'homme africain*; Ela, *Repenser la théologie africaine*.

152. Kanyoro distinguishes the categories of rural and illiterate women, and those who are not. See Kanyoro, "Engendered Communal Theology."

153. See, for instance, Hinga, "The Dialogical Imperative"; Nasimiyu-Wasike, "The Missing Voices of Women"; Arabome, "Women and Discipleship in the Church."

154. Aquiline Tarimo, "Ethnic Identities and the Common Good: Considerations on the Social Drama of Africa," *Revista Portuguesa de Filosofia* 65, no. 1/4 (2009): 582.

155. Rodriguez et al., "The Theory and Praxis of Intersectionality in Work and Organisations," 202.

156. Ibid.

157. Ibid., 203.

158. Ibid., 207.

159. Ibid.

160. Ibid., 210.

161. Ibid., 214.

162. Bilge, "Le blanchiment de l'intersectionnalité," 10.

163. Ibid., 19.

164. David Kaulemu, "Catholic Social Teaching at a Crossroad," in *Theological Ethics Past, Present, and Future: The Trento Conference*, ed. James F. Keenan, Catholic Theological Ethics in the World Church Series (Maryknoll, NY: Orbis Books, 2011), 179–80.

165. Francis, *Laudato Si*, 177.

166. Howard Stein, *Beyond the World Bank Agenda: An Institutional Approach to Development* (Chicago; London: The University of Chicago Press, 2008), xvi.

167. Gerry Rodgers, Laurids Lauridsen, and Klárá Fóti, "Introduction," in *The Institutional Approach to Labour and Development*, ed. Gerry Rodgers, Klárá Fóti, and Laurids Lauridsen, EADI Book Series 17 (London; Geneva: Frank Cass in association with the European Association of Development Research and Training Institutes, 1996), 1.

168. Stein, *Beyond the World Bank Agenda*, 112.

169. Stein, 121.

170. Francis, *On Care of Our Common Home, Encyclical Letter* Laudato Si (Rome: Libreria Editrice Vaticana, 2015), paras. 163–201, http://w2.vatican.va/cont ent/francesco/en/encyclicals/documents/papa-francesco_20150524_enciclica-laudato -si.html.

171. Hodgson quoted by Stein, *Beyond the World Bank Agenda*, 123.

172. Ibid., 125.

173. Ibid., 125.

174. Ibid., 128.

175. Ibid., 133.

176. Ibid., 141.

177. Ibid., 139.

178. Ibid., 141.

179. Gerry Rodgers, "Labour Institutions and Economic Development: Issues and Methods," in *The Institutional Approach to Labour and Development*, ed. Gerry Rodgers, Klárá Fóti, and Laurids Lauridsen, EADI Book Series 17 (London; Geneva: Frank Cass in association with the European Association of Development Research and Training Institutes, 1996), 22–23.

180. Paul VI, *Populorum Progressio*, 33.

181. As Hollenbach observes: "The ability of the communities defined by national borders to secure the well-being of their citizens through independently determined policies is declining," see Hollenbach, *The Common Good and Christian Ethics*, 231.

182. David Hollenbach, "The Common Good as Participation in Community: A Theological/Ethical Reflection on Some Empirical Issues" (Empirical Foundations of the Common Good, University of Southern California: Center for Advanced Catholic Studies, 2014), 3–7.

183. Maritain says that the common good "includes the sum or sociological integration of all the civic conscience, political virtues and sense of right and liberty, of all the activity, material prosperity and spiritual riches, of unconsciously operative hereditary wisdom, of moral rectitude, justice, friendship, happiness, virtue and

heroism in the individual lives of its members," see Jacques Maritain, *The Person and the Common Good*, trans. John J. Fitzgerald (New York: Charles Scribner's Sons, 1947), 52; John XXIII defines the common good as "the sum total of those conditions of social living whereby [human beings] are enabled more fully and more readily to achieve their own perfections," see John XXIII, *Mater et Magistra*, 65.

184. Maritain, *The Person and the Common Good*, 67–68.

185. Hollenbach, *The Common Good and Christian Ethics*, 189.

186. John Paul II, *Laborem Exercens*, 18.

187. Paul VI, *Populorum Progressio*, 54; John Paul II, *Sollicitudo Rei Socialis*, 32; Francis, *Laudato Si*, 164.

188. John Paul II, *Centesimus Annus*, 15.

189. Benedict XVI, *Caritas in Veritate*, 47.

190. Ibid., 24; Francis, *Laudato Si*, 196.

191. John Paul II, *Sollicitudo Rei Socialis*, 43.

192. Francis, *Laudato Si*, 170.

193. The civil society here comprises non-state organizations with the exception of business and financial corporations, and is made of religions, intermediary groups and various associations (NGOs notably). It can be local or international.

194. Francis, *Laudato Si*, 179.

195. John Paul II, *Centesimus Annus*, 15.

196. Francis, *Laudato Si*, 180.

197. For instance, the various paragraphs of article 13 of the Maputo Protocol indicate the various areas of economic discriminations and impediments against women to be eliminated, see African Union, "Protocol to the African Charter on Human and People's Rights on the Rights of Women in Africa" (2003), sec. 13, http://www.achpr.org/files/instruments/women-protocol/achpr_instr_proto_women_eng.pdf.

198. This is the point made in Kaulemu, "Catholic Social Teaching at a Crossroad."

Conclusion to Part III

The goal of part iii has been to present elements of gendered social ethics of labor. In chapter 8, I underlined African liberation theologies from Mveng, Ela, and Oduyoye as general orientation of that ethics. Liberation theology emphasizes the importance of theologizing from one's context. The African continent has been oppressed since the past centuries by various forces. Liberation, for Mveng, is a comprehensive concept, and his main concern is anthropological poverty. The latter is a condition of dehumanization and depersonalization that describes groups as well as individuals. It underscores the importance of the sense of self, which translates into self-identity and self-consciousness. For Ela, Postcolonial Africa is oppressed by politico-economic forces from outside and inside the continent. Ela's theology of liberation is grounded in the life of Christ: from the incarnation to the paschal mystery. Both Ela and Mveng suggest a liberating reading of the Bible. Jesus's resurrection provides hope. Oduyoye's Christ stands on the side of women to free them from all sorts of bondage. On the question of the marginalization of women in terms of work, Oduyoye seems to capture the root of the problem better than Ela and Mveng: *undervaluation*. Moreover, these three authors recognize the Church's role in the oppression of the continent and the fact that it needs to make adjustments. The Church is not always exemplary in its labor practices. These theologians ultimately insist on the contextualization of theological discourse.

Chapter 9 looked at the key elements of the gendered social ethics, namely, the preferential option for the poor (working) woman, social sin and a communal approach. The preferential option for the poor is grounded in the Holy Scriptures, which reveal a God who sides with the oppressed and the marginalized. The option for the poor woman has two elements: option for herself and option for others. The option for herself helps the woman to regain a proper sense of who she is. Since this does not isolate her, she turns in solidarity with others who experience the same oppression. The expression "Church of the poor" signals not only a priority for the poor in Church's ministries but also a self-criticism of all Church practices that undermine working women.

Social sin describes the social reality of sin, which is anything contrary to the will of God. Social sin uncovers the structural roots of oppression. It does not wipe away individual responsibility. Social sins, such as kyriarchy and colonialism, plague the lives and relationships of African working women. These social sins are present in economic systems that marginalize working women. The following elements can foster social conversion: the Kingdom of God as the horizon, breaking the silence of women, alternative views of the economy, and caring labor as essential to the economy.

The last element is the communal vision, which assumes that individualistic solutions are very limited in bringing deep social change. This communal vision has two aspects: intersectionality and engaging national and international institutions. Intersectionality shows how multiple power differentials and dimensions of oppression crisscross the lives of individuals. Intersectionality gives a robust analysis of power that can benefit CST. Moreover, it indicates that solutions to labor issues in particular must be comprehensive and not one-sided. For instance, relationships matter in the African context where individuals are defined by being in relation and by belonging. The institutional approach helps identify the levels and structures where change needs to happen. It uses the common good, solidarity, and subsidiarity as its guiding principles. It is grounded on the assumption that working women are affected by factors local as well as international. The institutional approach somehow addresses the necessity for policy engagement to effect concrete change. The next section will deal with some practices that could foster the empowerment of the working woman.

Part IV

EMPOWERING WORKING WOMEN

CONCEPTS AND PRACTICES

This part aims at showing concrete ways in which the Church can participate in the empowerment of working women. The actions of the Church must be grounded on a critical understanding of the notion of empowerment. This, in turn, will lead her to work ad intra and ad extra for the betterment of working women.

This section builds on the previous one, which identified liberation theology as the general orientation of GASE with the preferential option for the poor working woman, social sin, and a communal approach as its key characteristics. While part iii offered theoretical elements of GASE, this current part offers a much practical orientation and demonstrates how concretely GASE works.

This part has two chapters: one on concepts, the other on practices. Chapter 10 centers on clarifying and deepening the notion of empowerment. Part 1 proposed a vision of empowerment according to CST with the various principles (human dignity, participation, subsidiarity, common good, etc.) and key ideas guiding the economic and labor worlds (primacy of labor over capital, integral human development). In chapter 10, I complement this vision from the perspective of social science, philosophy, and biblical theology. The understanding of empowerment is grounded on the analysis of power. In the first section, I use Naila Kabeer's[1] understanding of empowerment and Martha Nussbaum's capabilities approach to draw the basic characteristics of empowerment. Kabeer offers agency, resources, and achievements as indicators to probe the reality of empowerment in a particular context. She also understands the three indicators as capabilities. Nussbaum complements her by offering a deeper analysis of capabilities.

The second section looks at empowerment from a biblical perspective. Given the importance of the Bible within African Christianity, it is important to unearth the gospel's perspective of power to enrich the understanding of empowerment with alternative understandings of power. I approach this from a general perspective, and because the realities of power and empowerment must be understood contextually, the second part of the section explores the reflections on power by African female theologians—especially Mercy Amba Oduyoye and Musa Dube.

Chapter 11 looks at some concrete practices at the Church level that can challenge the *status quo* and improve working women's conditions. My understanding of the Church here is limited to the local level (provincial, diocesan, parish, small Christian communities), and includes individuals and groups, be they lay people or clergy. I see the Church primarily as a humble partner who collaborates with institutions and who strives for the course of women empowerment. My reflection is located within the Roman Catholic Church in Africa.

Building on previous sections of this book, I identify four areas in which the Church *can* and *should* act in a transformative way: socializing the feminine, Church's conversion, biblical storytelling, and partnering with other institutions. Each of these four areas illustrates one of the key elements identified in the previous chapter. The first two, namely socializing the feminine and Church's conversion, address the issue of social conversion identified in the section on social sin as the way forward. Socialization of the feminine, which highlights ways in which attitudes and behaviors are promoted in society, and the way the Church must acknowledge its own role and correct it. Then, the Church's needs of conversion includes acknowledgment of wrongdoing and amending its ways of proceeding. The third practice, biblical storytelling, tackles the question of the preferential option for the poor working woman. The Church must use the Bible to achieve the following empowering goal. It must identify paradigms and practices that will promote a healthy vision of labor and free working women of patriarchy and androcentrism. This is partly addressed by the first concrete practice. The particularity of biblical storytelling as understood by Musa Dube is to shape women's imagination and self-understanding. This is important for women, for the work of reclaiming their own lives. The fourth, partnering with other institution, shows how the Church can carry out the institutional approach. To effect institutional change, the Church needs to partner with women's groups and associations as well as with other institutions. As examples, I shall present the Mbonweh Women's Development Association and the 2000 Jubilee campaign for debt cancellation.

These four areas aim at shaping individuals as well as institutions.

NOTE

1. Naila Kabeer is an Indian-born British social economist who is a professor of gender and development at the London School of Economics and Political Science; she is one of the leading experts on the question of women's empowerment.

Chapter 10

On Empowerment

In chapter 1, equality of condition was mentioned. It is evident that, to secure equality of condition, there must be an open access to real options from which people can make real choices. This cannot be achieved without social transformation. This current chapter, dedicated to empowerment, fleshes out what is meant by the *equality of condition*. This chapter builds on what has been discussed in the previous chapters, namely, the CST's principles (equal dignity, solidarity, common good, and participation), holistic understanding of labor, the shortcomings of the individualistic approach, promoting a liberationist orientation, option of the poor woman for herself, social conversion, intersectionality, and the institutional approach.

Through an understanding of empowerment from the perspective of social sciences (Kabeer) and philosophy (Nussbaum), and public policy, the first section of this chapter complements CST's approach with a notion of empowerment grounded on a critical understanding of power and the way power is distributed in the social sphere. In general, this chapter also argues that empowerment is linked with social change.

NAILA KABEER ON EMPOWERMENT

Defining Empowerment

Naila Kabeer articulates the link between the individual and the social dimensions of empowerment. Her understanding of empowerment is informed by her assessment of power. In relationship to empowerment, power is defined as the ability to make life-strategic choices.[1] The notion of choice makes the difference between empowerment and disempowerment. Indeed, "to be disempowered means to be denied choice, while empowerment refers to the processes by which those who have been denied the ability to make choices acquire such an ability."[2] A choice is genuine if there are alternatives (the ability to choose differently), and if these alternatives are seen to exist.[3] Empowerment is concerned with life-strategic choices, which refer to critical judgments and decisions that people make concerning the type of life they want to live (choice of livelihood, being married or not, whether to have children or not, freedom of movement and association, etc.).[4]

By putting disempowerment in correlation with empowerment, Kabeer makes it clear that empowerment is not an end in itself.[5] Empowerment is a process, and it "entails change":[6] empowerment must be understood "in terms of multidimensional processes of change."[7] The processes touch women at both personal and social level, and concern

> their sense of self-worth and social identity; their willingness and ability to question their subordinate status in society; their capacity to exercise strategic control over their own lives and to negotiate better terms in their relationships with others; and finally, their ability to participate on equal terms with men reshaping society to better accord with their vision of social justice.[8]

Agency, Resources, and Achievements

The ability to make choices is assessed through three closely interrelated notions: agency, resources, and achievements.[9]

Agency is "the ability to define one's goals and to act upon them."[10] It "is about more than observable action. It also encompasses the meaning, motivation, and purpose which individuals bring to their activity, their sense of agency, or 'the power within.'"[11] Agency can have both positive and negative connotations.[12] In a positive sense, it is "power to" and it defines the ability of people to define and pursue their own goals even in the face of adversity. With respect to the negative sense, that is, "power over," it entails the capacity to curtail the agency of others through the use of coercion, violence, and threat. This power over may not necessarily be exerted directly by individuals but can operate through social institutions and various norms and rules that shape people's behaviors. This is close to what we saw with respect to social sin, where a sinful environment can lead people to sinful acts. As far as empowerment is concerned, agency "implies not only actively exercising choice, but also doing it in ways that challenge power relations."[13] Agency is not exercised in a vacuum, but in relation to other agents who willingly or not influence one's choices and actions. Agency can be passive (constrained action) or active (purposeful action).[14] There is also a distinction between a greater effectiveness of agency and a transformative agency concerning women: "The former relates to women's greater efficiency in carrying their given roles and responsibilities, the latter to their ability to act on the restrictive aspects of these roles and responsibilities in order to challenge them."[15]

The term "resources" comprises "not only material resources in the more conventional economic sense but also the various human and social resources which serve to enhance the ability to exercise choice."[16] Resources are "the medium through which agency is exercised."[17] They are accessed and distributed through social institutions and human relationships.[18] The rules and norms that define access to and distribution of resources are important. They indicate "the terms on which resources are made available."[19] Moreover, there is the issue of prioritizing and enforcing claims on resources.

The term "achievements" is Kabeer's appropriation of Amartya Sen's functioning achievements and refers to "the particular ways of being and doing which are realized in different individuals."[20] Simply put, achievements are "the outcomes of people's efforts," and in relation to empowerment, achievements can be considered "both in terms of the agency exercised and of its consequences."[21]

Issues

As a social scientist, Kabeer notes the difficulty to measure and objectively assess agency, resources, and achievements. At the level of agency, scholars tend to focus on decision-making processes. Kabeer warns that "statistical perspectives on decision making" are "simple windows on complex realities."[22] At the level of resources, the notion of "control" is fluid and as "elusive to define and measure as power."[23] On the contrary, achievements as such are not difficult to measure and observe. The issue is whether they indicate a shift in power relations and/or the product of people's greater agency.[24] This points to the necessity to never take agency, resources, and achievements in isolation and always take them in the light of correlation. Agency, resources, and achievements taken as a whole serve to probe various socioeconomic and political indicators (paid labor, educational levels, type of work, access to factors of production, social and political, cultural and legal environment, etc.).

The fact that empowerment is viewed as a process indicates that it is ongoing and as a process of change; it is transformative. Empowerment policies challenge the status quo of individual lives. However, change at the individual level is not enough.[25] In order for empowering policies to have a lasting impact, there must be change at the social level. As Kabeer indicates,

Institutional transformation requires movement along a number of fronts: from individual to collective agency, from private negotiations to public actions, and from the informal sphere to the formal arenas of struggle where power is legitimately exercised.[26]

Indeed, "the project of women's empowerment is dependent on collective solidarity in the public arena as well as individual assertiveness in the private."[27] Concerning the last part of Kabeer's statement, her own studies show how collective solidarity plays even within domestic relationships.[28] Furthermore, agency, resources, and achievement need further probing. In terms of agency, one needs to "know about its consequential significance in terms of women's strategic life choice and the extent to which it had transformatory potential."[29] Likewise, access to a particular resource "tells us about potential rather than actual choice."[30] The value of that resource rests on assumptions about human agency and entitlements embodied in that resource. An empowering achievement needs to be assessed in terms of whose agency is involved and the extent to which it transformed prevailing inequalities and agency.[31]

NUSSBAUM AND CAPABILITIES

For Kabeer, agency and resources are capabilities, and achievements are functioning capabilities.[32] For her, capabilities are people's "potential for living the lives they want."[33] Martha Nussbaum supplements Kabeer's idea and, therefore, offers a more comprehensive guide to understanding capabilities. Drawing from Amartya Sen, Nussbaum defines capabilities as "substantial freedoms," that is, "a set of (usually interrelated) opportunities to choose and to act."[34] Further, "they are not just abilities residing inside a person but also the freedoms or opportunities created by a combination of personal abilities and the political, social, and economic environment." She calls these "combined capabilities."[35] She distinguishes three types of capabilities: basic, internal, and combined.

Basic capabilities are "the innate equipment of individuals that is the necessary basis for developing the more advanced capabilities, and a ground of more concern."[36] Internal capabilities "are trained or developed traits and abilities, in most cases, in interaction with the social, economic, familial, and political environment."[37] Society plays an important role in the development of people's internal capabilities.[38] Combined capabilities are "internal capabilities combined with suitable external conditions for the exercise of the function."[39] I focus here on combined capabilities.

The notion of capabilities asserts clearly the importance of the social context for the sound exercise of one's ability to choose and to act. This is a recognition of the social nature of the human person, although the capabilities approach aims at enhancing the individual's ability. Moreover, the goal of the capabilities approach is to empower people and to make them agents of their own destiny. In addition, capabilities are based on a certain understanding of the human person as "a dignified free being who shapes his or her own life in cooperation and reciprocity with others."[40]

The idea of human dignity is important to the capabilities approach. In Kabeer's version of empowerment, the focus is on social justice and the issue of human dignity never surfaces. As we saw in chapter 1, human dignity touches the core of the person and relates to the inalienable worth of the human person. The capabilities approach points to the fact that the absence of certain elements can lead to an undignified life, or a life that is inhuman or a life that is no longer human.[41]

Nussbaum identifies ten central capabilities as the "bare minimum" that "a life worthy of human dignity" requires:[42] (1) life, (2) bodily health, (3) bodily integrity, (4) senses, imagination, and thought, (5) emotions, (6) practical reason, (7) affiliation, (8) other species, (9) play, and (10) control over one's environment.[43] These central capabilities "have a special importance in making any choice of a way of life possible."[44] Out of these ten basic capabilities, two—affiliation and practical reason—play an "architectonic role" in organizing and pervading the others.[45]

Practical reason refers to the ability "to form a conception of the good and to engage in critical reflection about the planning of one's life."[46] Affiliation comprises two dimensions. The first dimension stipulates that one should be "able to live with and toward others, to recognize and show concern for other human beings in various forms of social interaction; to be able to imagine the situation of another."[47] The second dimension holds that a person should have "the social bases of self-respect and nonhumiliation; being able to be treated as a dignified being whose worth is equal to that of others."[48] Practical reason must inform a person's agency. Affiliation appears critical for the empowerment of women workers especially the achievement of self-respect and nonhumiliation, which precludes all kinds of discrimination. Affiliation relates to bodily health, bodily integrity, and the ability to control one's environment. The latter has two dimensions, namely political and material. The material aspect means, among other things, the possibility to possess property and "having the right to seek employment on a equal basis."[49] When working, this means "being able to work as a human being."[50]

Nussbaum indicates three principles that should inspire public action with regard to gender: importance of options, importance of perceived contribution to the well-being of the household, and importance of a sense of one's own worth.[51] In general, Nussbaum appears in tune with solutions proposed by the main international institutions (access to employment and credit, education, emphasis on human rights and legal reforms).[52] I showed that while these are important, they may not, in themselves, solve the issue of working women's disempowerment (see the last section of chapter 6).

Before discussing theologians, the key insights from Kabeer and Nussbaum need to be highlighted. First, empowerment is inseparable from disempowerment, since it involves moving away from the latter. Second, empowerment is a complex reality that touches on different dimensions of human life. Third, the empowerment of the individual woman is closely tied with collective empowerment and social change. Empowerment is not only about properly equipping the individual but also transforming the general environment. This cannot be done by the individual woman alone. The involvement of intermediary groups and the state are required. Fourth, whether one perceives power as the ability to choose or combined capabilities, the big issue is the person's agency or capacity to make her own choices and set her own goals. Fifth, empowerment is not first about doing or achieving, but the ability to decide and to act. This ability prevents an unhealthy focus on outcomes alone.

The foregoing points are in harmony with the earlier insights on the option for the poor woman, social conversion, intersectionality, and the institutional approach. Moreover, empowerment seems similar to Paul VI's integral human development by its multidimensional aspect and holistic approach. It is important to note before moving forward that the notion of empowerment is not without controversy in public policy discourse among feminists or people fighting for the promotion of women.[53]

THEOLOGIANS AND EMPOWERMENT

This section has two parts. The first looks at how biblical scholars, in particular, articulate the notions of empowerment, especially in relationship to power. I specifically look at the way Jesus's practice subverts and challenges the understanding of power in ways that benefit the marginalized and the oppressed. The second part deals with what female African theologians think about the empowerment of women and how they offer an alternative understanding of power as transformative. The first part offers a general analysis of power in the gospels, while the second one brings in a specific African Christian understanding of power. This section also provides a liberationist view of empowerment, which analyzes power from the perspective of the oppressed. It lays the ground for the reflection on women's empowerment from a theological perspective and for the next section.

Biblical Theology and Empowerment

Theologians' reflections on empowerment are closely associated with that of power. I am not interested here in a general reflection on power, but on how to think critically about empowerment in a way that can inspire action in favor of working women.

Basically, the empowerment trend identifies three forms of power: power over (domination), power to (ability) and power with (relationality).[54] From Kabeer's perspective, as has been shown, empowerment seems to be a move from power-over to power-to and power-with.

In their discussion on empowerment, biblical scholars draw on the earthly activities of Jesus. Their arguments are close to those developed by liberation theologians. Jesus's ministry is primarily directed to the disempowered. The Lucan Jesus appropriates Isaiah's oracle to claim that he is sent "to bring good news to the poor," "to proclaim liberty to captives," "recovery of sight to the blind," and "to let the oppressed go free" (Lk 4:18). Jesus's ultimate mission is to make people live flourishing lives: "I came so that they may have life and have it more abundantly" (Jn 10:10). The ultimate goal of liberation/empowerment is for people to live fruitful lives. Jesus's Kingdom of God captures the key values attached to his liberating project. I discussed this in chapter 9, in the section on social sin. The Kingdom/Reign of God paradigm offers a stark contrast to a kyriarchal society. In the Kingdom that Jesus refers to, contrary to a kyriarchal society, priority is given to the disenfranchised, marginalized, and oppressed. However, this does not come without problems. Jesus is in conflict against forces (demonic powers and religious leaders) that resist his view of the Kingdom.[55] This makes clear that empowerment does not come without resistance from forces that benefit from social imbalances and the status quo.

Jesus's healings and exorcism are understood—at least in Mark's gospel— as *dunameis*, acts of power.[56] "In the healings and exorcisms, Jesus is thus transmitting power to the people of Galilee and beyond that enables them to overcome illnesses and possession by 'unclean spirits.'"[57] The colonial experience of Palestine in Jesus's era and the resulting trauma in people may find echoes among Africans. Richard Horsley sees parallels between the surge of possession by alien spirits in colonized African people to that of the gospels.[58] The specific episode of the Gerasenes demoniac where the demon identifies itself as "Legion" brings this tension to the forefront.[59] Horsley notes:

Like the possessing spirits in Africa whose names were Lord Cromer or the spirits who insisted on their hosts dressing up like the British army, the force that had been driving the possessed man to such violence against himself and his community was that of the conquering Roman army. As in colonial Africa, this symbolic name of the demon means . . . that the Roman army was the cause of the distress among the subjected people, including the possession of this man and his violent destructive behavior. Not only is the demon's name symbolic, but the possessed man is representative of the whole society that had been invaded by the imperial violence destructive of their persons and communities.[60]

The subversion of the colonial domination under demonic possession plays two contrasting roles. First, it is self-protective insofar as it allows "the subject people to avoid direct confrontation with their colonial masters, which would result in their destruction."[61] Second, it is "an effective means of social control in a colonial situation and a mystification" that masks the concrete colonial situation and the powers that create it.[62]

Jesus fights this and defeats demonic forces to restore people's full agency. "Jesus . . . shows that the presence of God's rule can also disrupt the structural violence done to persons."[63] The story exemplifies how "God's rule has subdued imperial domination."[64] This shows that empowerment also means the defeat of colonial oppression.

Jesus's words and deeds entail a redistribution of power at the political and religious levels.[65] Jesus offers "a conception of political power which promises to the powerless access to power in the *familia [D]ei*."[66] The same is true of religious power. In forgiving sins and rehabilitating sinners and social outcasts, Jesus bypasses the Temple and religious institutions.[67] Empowerment, in this sense, means a form of democratization of power, which is no longer held by few at the top, but flows down to the grassroots.

The reversals that the Kingdom brings include a challenge and a redefinition of power. Rick Talbott offers the example of Matthean communities, which "challenged kyriarchal marriage, divorce, and re-marriage that served to privilege men at the expense of women."[68] However, this was accomplished chiefly "by re-socializing how individuals in the communit(ies) exercised power in relationships."[69] Hence, empowerment means moving away from dominating and oppressive forms of power and suggesting alternative forms of powers that foster the flourishing of all.

Jesus offers alternative visions in the exercise of power. He clearly tells his followers "do not be called 'Rabbi.' You have but one teacher, and you are all brothers. Call no one on earth your father; you have but one Father in heaven. Do not be called 'Master'; you have but one master, the Messiah" (Mt 23:8–10). Elsewhere, he says in the context of power struggle among his disciples:

> Those who are recognized as rulers over the Gentiles lord it over them, and their great ones make their authority over them felt. But it shall not be so among you. Rather, whoever wishes to be great among you will be your servant; whoever wishes to be first among you will be the slave of all. (Mk 10:42–44)

These two biblical references from the Gospel of Matthew show a clear rejection of hierarchical and dominating forms of power. The first citation implies the mutuality and relationality of power (power with) since God is the ultimate provider of power. Both citations recognize the model of the Lord-Servant as the means to achieve the reality of shared power. The Lord-Servant paradigm is grounded in Second Isaiah's songs on the Servant (Is 42:1–9; 49:1–13; 50:4–11; 52:13–53:12). Paul Hanson warns that "the Servant does not offer a model of acquiescence to the oppressor, but empowerment."[70] He is the righteous One destined to make all righteous. In this respect, "righteousness is not a submissive quality. Righteousness is a power-sharing, community-restoring, society-constructing, world-healing, universe-building quality!"[71] Hanson is probably conscious of the criticism leveled against the serving-power paradigm, which tends to be disproportionately demanded of women, children, and marginalized groups.

Reinhald Feldmeier adds that "even the ideal of serving can be abused in a terrible way, for rulers are strongly inclined to legitimate themselves as "servants of the state," to act in the "correctly understood" interest of the others—and, in cases of doubt, even against the will of the others."[72] However, the category of service remains helpful when applied to leaders and those in authority. As highlighted earlier, for CST, the state is at the service of the common good. Jacques Maritain clearly writes that the state is at the service of the body politic, the whole political community.[73] This shows that the State is not the ultimate authority, and it puts a limit to the State's exercise of power. NT authors make it clear that service should be the key characteristic of community leaders called to foster the community's interest over theirs.[74]

Further, the human exercise of power should mirror divine power. It is noteworthy that in the gospels, God the King and/or the Almighty are not the dominant paradigms.[75] Jesus directs his followers to alternative models of power, beginning with their conception of God and of divine power. Indeed, "God is not a tyrant establishing rule through the power of domination, but through the sharing of power, through the empowerment of the lowly."[76] Divine power appears as a challenge to worldly powers that work generally to the benefit of the most powerful. "Divine power is shared power, power-with rather than power-over, patient power rather than power of imposition, persuasive power rather than power of coercion, luring rather than forceful power."[77] As a consequence, power should not be unilateral, but always generated in mutuality.[78]

Before moving to the next section, let me summarize the key points on empowerment garnered from this brief biblical survey. The goal of empowerment is to make people live flourishing lives. The empowerment of the oppressed and marginalized does not occur without conflict. Empowerment entails a democratization and redefinition of power. Shared and relational power (power with) generated in mutuality appears as the main paradigm. In addition, Jesus's activities provide tools to criticize dominant power (power over) when it becomes abusive and disempowering. Overall, the Bible provides us with a subtle criticism of power and a subversion of power through the example of Jesus Christ and God's actions.[79]

African Theologians and Empowerment

Here one needs to distinguish between the discussion on empowerment per se and a reconstruction of the image of African women. African female theologians draw from their cultures as well as from theological tradition. As for others, discussions on empowerment are closely related to those on power.

In this perspective, power is not first perceived as domination, but rather as the ability to perform and act. The patriarchal nature of African society prevents women from realizing their full potential. The use of the word "transformative" is important here. Hence, as Musa Dube writes, "transforming power . . . can only describe the intention to change all the known aspects of power to a new understanding, use and allocation of power that affirms the involvement of all members of a society."[80]

Power for Oduyoye is more than ability. Relying on her mother tongue, she sees power (*tumi* in Asante language) as "skill and know-how, and the strength to do something or to make something happen."[81] Her understanding seems to be close to Nussbaum's capabilities. In addition, "power also carries the connotation of the opportunity to act, as well as the space within which to act."[82] This is an important distinction. Power is exercised in society, not in a vacuum or in isolation. Empowerment cannot be considered outside of the specific space where it is taking place. It is at this level that difficult issues start for women. Oduyoye observes that "power is a concept least associated with women but one that rules women's lives in all its aspects."[83] In addition, when women have power, it is for "the well-being of the community."[84]

For Oduyoye, "transforming power" has a double meaning from the two NT words *exousia* and *dunamis*.[85] "First, it refers to that power which transforms, and second, to the notion of changing the meaning of the way power is conserved and applied."[86] Jesus's use of power helps people move from helplessness to full agency.

Going back to the question of space, the African context is a postcolonial space as argued earlier. When asked about abusive or patriarchal power, some rural women of the Sanga people in Eastern DR Congo called it colonialism.[87] I shall not return to the negative effects of colonialism on labor. I discussed it under the section on social sin (see chapter 9).

For Kabamba Kiboko, a Congolese female minister of the United Methodist Church, transforming power takes two forms: inner power and shared power.[88] Inner power refers to a power that is sui generis. From a

Christian perspective, this could refer to as Jesus's exercise of power. Jesus acted outside of any official approbation (Mk 11:27–33), but was empowered by the Spirit (Lk 4). Empowered women should act without seeking someone's approval. Furthermore, Jean-Marc Ela observes that the Bible emphasizes the notion of charism (the fact of being graced) as a result of being under the guidance of the Holy Spirit, which opens the possibility of ministries without the laying on of the hands.[89]

Kiboko affirms that without "the inner power that can transform [women's] lives and communities, [women] cannot hope to transform the outer power that oppresses."[90] The development of the inner power happens through the option of women for themselves and through an expanded agency. In that respect, one should differentiate a constrained agency from a nonexistent one and reject the construction of African women as "helpless victims" to "be redeemed by their Western counterparts."[91] Shared power is "a power that lifts up and strengthens others."[92] According to Kiboko, shared power is enhanced through the principle of participation. Shared power represents an alternative to dominating power. This makes people actors of their own destiny; by this, too, people are treated as adults. Associating people in the decision-making process is an example of this.

African theologians insist on empowerment as transforming power—like Kabeer—but underline the necessity of mutual (shared) power and the question of space. Empowerment is geared toward social change and an overhaul of power balance in society. What seems to be missing in the reflection of African theologians is the institutional approach to empowerment.

NOTES

1. Kabeer, "Gender Equality and Women's Empowerment," 13–14; Kabeer, "Resources, Agency, Achievements," 436–37.
2. Kabeer, "Gender Equality and Women's Empowerment," 13.
3. Ibid., 14.
4. Kabeer, "Resources, Agency, Achievements," 437; Kabeer, "Gender Equality and Women's Empowerment," 14.
5. Naila Kabeer, "Between Affiliation and Autonomy: Navigating Pathways of Women's Empowerment and Gender Justice in Rural Bangladesh," *Development and Change* 42, no. 2 (2011): 499.
6. Kabeer, "Gender Equality and Women's Empowerment," 14.
7. Kabeer, "Between Affiliation and Autonomy," 499.
8. Ibid.
9. Kabeer, "Resources, Agency, Achievements," 437.
10. Ibid., 438.
11. Ibid.

12. Ibid.

13. Kabeer, "Gender Equality and Women's Empowerment," 14.

14. Ibid., 15.

15. Ibid.

16. Kabeer, "Resources, Agency, Achievements," 437.

17. Kabeer, "Gender Equality and Women's Empowerment," 15.

18. Ibid.

19. Ibid.

20. Kabeer, "Resources, Agency, Achievements," 438.

21. Kabeer, "Gender Equality and Women's Empowerment," 15.

22. Kabeer, "Resources, Agency, Achievements," 448.

23. Ibid., 445.

24. Ibid., 452.

25. Indeed, "while changes in the consciousness and agency of individual women are an important starting point, it will do little on its own to undermine the systemic reproduction of inequality." See Kabeer, "Gender Equality and Women's Empowerment," 16; Kabeer, "Resources, Agency, Achievements," 457.

26. Kabeer, "Gender Equality and Women's Empowerment," 16.

27. Kabeer, "Resources, Agency, Achievements," 457.

28. See, for instance, the actions of women in rural Bangladesh in Kabeer, "Between Affiliation and Autonomy," 519–22.

29. Kabeer, "Resources, Agency, Achievements," 461.

30. Ibid.

31. Ibid.

32. Kabeer, "Gender Equality and Women's Empowerment," 15.

33. Ibid.

34. Martha Craven Nussbaum, *Creating Capabilities: The Human Development Approach* (Cambridge, MA: Belknap Press of Harvard University Press, 2011), 20.

35. Ibid., 21.

36. Martha C. Nussbaum, *Women and Human Development: The Capabilities Approach*, 13th print, The John Robert Seeley Lectures 3 (Cambridge: Cambridge Univ. Press, 2008), 84.

37. Nussbaum, *Creating Capabilities*, 21.

38. Ibid.

39. Nussbaum, *Women and Human Development*, 84–85.

40. Ibid., 72.

41. Ibid., 73.

42. Nussbaum, *Creating Capabilities*, 32.

43. For more see Ibid., 33–34.

44. Nussbaum, *Women and Human Development*, 75.

45. Nussbaum, *Creating Capabilities*, 39.

46. Ibid., 34.

47. Ibid.

48. Ibid.

49. Ibid.

50. Ibid.

51. Nussbaum, *Women and Human Development*, 285–86, 288.

52. Ibid., 285–86.

53. Rosalind Eyben and Rebecca Napier-Moore, "Choosing Words with Care? Shifting Meanings of Women's Empowerment in International Development," *Third World Quarterly* 30, no. 2 (2009): 289, doi:http://dx.doi.org/10.1080/01436590802681066. Some think that the phrase "women's empowerment" may be more confrontational because of apparent left-wing connotations, and could do a disservice to the cause advanced, and for strategic reasons prefer to speak about "gender equality."

54. William Schweiker and Michael Welker, "A New Paradigm of Theological and Biblical Inquiry," in *Power, Powerlessness, and the Divine: New Inquiries in Bible and Theology*, ed. Cynthia L. Rigby, Studies in Theological Education (Atlanta, GA: Scholars Press, 1997), 7.

55. Richard A. Horsley, *Jesus and the Powers: Conflict, Covenant, and the Hope of the Poor* (Minneapolis: Fortress Press, 2011), 1–2.

56. Ibid., 112.

57. Ibid.

58. Ibid., 114–16. Those alien spirits would receive names related to Europeans or to the European colonial enterprise.

59. Ibid., 126–28.

60. Ibid., 126–27.

61. Ibid., 117.

62. Ibid.

63. Pheme Perkins, "The Gospel of Mark: Introduction, Commentary, and Reflections," in *The New Interpreter's Bible: General Articles & Introduction, Commentary & Reflections for Each Book of the Bible Including the Apocryphal/ Deuterocanonical Books*, vol. VIII (Nashville: Abingdon Press, 1997), 584.

64. Ibid. As an illustration, the text provides the reader with a striking picture, "as soon as Jesus steps into this Gentile territory, a legion [symbolizes] prostates itself before him"; in addition, if a legion was made of 6,000 infantry, that term could also be used of battalion of 2,048 (a figure close to the number of pigs sent charging).

65. Gerd Theissen, "The Ambivalence of Power in Early Christianity," in *Power, Powerlessness, and the Divine: New Inquiries in Bible and Theology*, ed. Cynthia L. Rigby, Studies in Theological Education (Atlanta, GA: Scholars Press, 1997), 31.

66. Ibid., 27.

67. Ibid.

68. Note 19 in Rick Franklin Talbott, *Jesus, Paul, and Power: Rhetoric, Ritual, and Metaphor in Ancient Mediterranean Christianity* (Eugene, OR: Cascade Books, 2010), 73.

69. Ibid.

70. Paul D. Hanson, "Divine Power in Powerlessness: The Servant of the Lord in Second Isaiah," in *Power, Powerlessness, and the Divine: New Inquiries in Bible and Theology*, ed. Cynthia L. Rigby, Studies in Theological Education (Atlanta, GA: Scholars Press, 1997), 192.

71. Ibid., 192–93.

72. Reinhard Feldmeier, *Power, Service, Humility: A New Testament Ethic* (Waco, TX: Baylor University Press, 2014), 43.

73. Maritain, *Man and the State*, 13.

74. Feldmeier, *Power, Service, Humility*, 42, 45.

75. As Feldmeier asserts: "Jesus proclaims the kingly rule of God, but he calls God "Father," not "King." He emphasizes that God can do all things, but he does not speak of the "Almighty." Ibid., 30.

76. Hanson, "Divine Power in Powerlessness," 193.

77. Ibid., 197.

78. Catherine Keller, "Power Lines," in *Power, Powerlessness, and the Divine: New Inquiries in Bible and Theology*, ed. Cynthia L. Rigby, Studies in Theological Education (Atlanta, GA: Scholars Press, 1997), 72.

79. For fuller investigation on the issue of social justice, gender and the Bible see Yiu Sing Lúcás Chan, James F. Keenan, and Ronaldo Zacharias, eds., *The Bible and Catholic Theological Ethics*, Catholic Theological Ethics in the World Church Series (Maryknoll: Orbis Books, 2017).

80. Dube, "Introduction," 2001, 9.

81. Oduyoye, "Transforming Power," 223.

82. Ibid.

83. Ibid., 222.

84. Oduyoye, *Daughters of Anowa*, 29; Oduyoye, "Transforming Power," 223.

85. Oduyoye, "Transforming Power," 224.

86. Ibid.

87. Kabamba Kiboko, "Sharing Power: An Autobiographical View," in *Talitha Cum! Theologies of African Women*, ed. Nyambura J. Njoroge and Musa W. Dube (Cluster Publications, 2001), 219.

88. Ibid.

89. Ela, *Repenser la théologie africaine*, 321.

90. Kiboko, "Sharing Power: An Autobiographical View," 219.

91. Musa W. Dube Shomanah, *Postcolonial Feminist Interpretation of the Bible* (St. Louis, Mo: Chalice Press, 2000), 24.

92. Kiboko, "Sharing Power: An Autobiographical View," 219.

Chapter 11

Looking at Concrete Practices

How would the empowerment of working women be theorized and put into practice by Christian communities? The present chapter tries to answer this question by suggesting a non-exhaustive set of practices and by applying what has been said in the previous chapters. I have identified four possible ways: "resocializing" or socializing the feminine (STF), Church's conversion, storytelling, and partnering with other groups especially women associations. As I have indicated earlier, each area is an application of the key features of the GASE. STF and the Church's conversion address the need for social conversion, which takes place at the level of inner perceptions and representations as well as attitudes. STF responds to the first need while the Church's conversion substantiates the second need. Biblical storytelling illustrates the option for the (poor) working woman, especially the need for her to take control of her own story, to regain sense of herself and to break the silence. Partnering with other institutions embodies the communal approach where the Church, with the collaboration of others and the awareness of the social dynamics of power, tries to effect change at the institutional level.

I would like to make clear that I operate at the local level unless stated otherwise. However, even there the understanding of what Church means is very diverse. It can refer to the institutional Church made of various bishops' bodies, bishops' words and deeds and diocesan bodies, or to the level made of local parishes, small Christian communities, Christian movements, various institutions (schools, hospitals, social centers, NGOs) and simply individuals. Action can be taken by clergy, lay, or both; it can be formal or informal. In a church where everyone is endowed to some degree by God's Spirit, everyone has the duty to develop God's gifts (see the parable of talents/minas Mt 25:14–30; Lk 19:11–17).[1] This is why the impulse and initiative for change can come from any corner.

SOCIALIZATION OF THE FEMININE[2]

This is a first step toward social conversion. This targets individuals for structural purposes, changing society's perception of certain types of works. In previous chapters, I showed how activities predominantly performed by women—such as reproductive labor—tend to be overlooked or underappreciated. There is a strong link between the underestimation of caring labor and the way related economic activities are underpaid and socially undervalued. There was also a strong suggestion in the section on social conversion about the necessity of reassessing the role of reproductive labor. This current section suggests ways to achieve that.

STF "means that all society members, male and female, acknowledge and take responsibility for so-called feminine characteristics . . . and so-called feminine work."[3] It is based on the assumption that "the morality needed to sustain family and community life must also shape the nature and practices of the economy."[4]

Socialization is generally "the way in which individuals are assisted in becoming members of one or more social groups."[5] Socialization is a process, not something fixed once and for all. For instance, the introduction of a Western type of education system in Africa basically changed the methods by which people were being raised and prepared for adulthood. Socialization is not a process where the individual who is being socialized is passive.[6] It involves interaction between the individual being socialized and the rest of society with mutual influence. My focus here is at the level of individuals, with young members and with adults, which involve different dynamics. I also consider socialization as a process that impacts the society as a whole.

Furthermore, "socialization involves a variety of outcomes,"[7] in particular, the acquisitions of rules, roles, standards, and values. It is a lifelong process involving various agents of socialization that can be individuals or institutions.[8]

Given the complexity of socialization, it demands time and patience. Likewise, in STF, one may take the long view and expect social conversion not to happen at once. Church-led institutions and various Christian groups can be of a certain help to achieve this socialization of the feminine. For a start, the Church, at least, recognizes the importance of mothering and caring labor (see chapter 1). The issue lies in the fact that these are disproportionately assigned to women.

I will borrow the analysis from Mark O'Keefe's book on social sin to frame how the Church could concretely act in STF.[9] Society exercises its influence on people in two ways, from the outside and from the inside.[10] This should also be the case in STF.

Working from Outside

Social control and social stratification are the two main ways that society and social structures use to influence its members and protect themselves against nonconforming behavior.[11] Social control operates through the threat of violence, economic pressure, the commonly accepted morality, customs, and at a personal level, by the fear of ridicule and ostracism.[12] Social stratification consists of the fact that "each society has a system of ranking persons."[13] Social control involves a certain level of coercion, while social stratification points to hierarchy and subordination. We already saw how these work against women. Ultimately, social control and social stratification are about a certain understanding of power and of power relationships within a society.

In STF, the Church needs to uphold the values of the Kingdom with a subversion of the notion of power and a liberationist approach. More concretely, it should endeavor to deconstruct customs and accepted morals that lead to devaluation of women's work. It should attack assumptions that tend to ostracize working women and men who do not follow the social script. For instance, I showed in the second section of chapter 7 that men are increasingly involved in caring labor, especially childcare. However, many in society tend to ridicule men involved in laundry, cooking, or any other activities in their home. This type of attitude displays a biased understanding of gender as well as shows a lack of appreciation for the so-called feminine work.

Jobs are ranked according to criteria such as gender, race/ethnicity, financial considerations, religious worldview, and any other relevant criteria.[14] A popular saying in French goes: "*il n'y a pas de sôt métier, il n'y a que de sottes gens.*" It literally means: there is no stupid job, there are only stupid people. The Church should reject the hierarchization of jobs, which tends to disadvantage women-dominated works. Indeed, as St Paul says about Church offices —which can be applied *mutatis mutandis* to labor in general—using the allegory of the human body: "Even those members of the body which seem less important are in fact indispensable" (1 Co 12:22). A society can survive without stock exchange brokers, finance gurus, or engineers in computer science. However, it cannot survive without caring labor; people need to feed themselves, clean their bodies, and live in a clean environment. The challenge against hierarchization need not be made only through teaching but also through concrete acts, such as appreciating the works of cooks, janitors, homemakers, and any groundbreaking women in the Church through prizes or special events.

However, for the challenge against the distorted use of power in social stratification and social control to be more effective, two separate things need to be done. First, Church-led institutions must rid themselves of autocratic and authoritarian practices. Moreover, any sign of authoritarian exercise of power must be challenged. There should be more participative power, especially at the diocesan level, in the parish, small Christian communities, Christian groups, and associations. Collegiality and subsidiarity are two ways of promoting a more participative approach in church structures and institutions. Second, as long as women are stuck in subaltern positions, any activity associated with them will continue to be perceived as belonging to a lesser rank of important things. The Church needs to promote women to positions of leadership and avoid assigning women to mere representative leadership positions.

Working from Inside

This is a deeper level than the previous one. There are three possible ways of understanding how society works from the inside: role theory, the sociology of knowledge and the reference group.[15] I will only dwell on the first two. Institutions that want to work on change may inspire themselves from any of these approaches or adopt any one of them that are relevant to the context of a particular institution.

Role theory focuses on social roles and tries to understand how these are learned.[16] A role can be defined as "a typified response to a typified expectation."[17] Social roles are learned as part of socialization, and "role expectations play a major part in maintaining societal structures in their current state."[18] If a Christian institution or group decides to use this theory in STF, it is important to pay attention to the way gender affects role expectations. A distinction between gender-ascriptive roles and gender-bearing roles must be made.[19] "Gender-ascriptive roles necessarily imply persons of a particular gender."[20] For instance, "father" implies a male person, and "mother" refers to a female person. This distinction allows one to look at role expectations that depend on one's position in the family, and how gender affects it: what is expected of a parent or child, and how it is different for a father, mother, daughter or son. "Gender-bearing roles in principle need not be inhabited by a person of any gender but have empirically come to do so."[21] For instance, unpaid reproductive/caring labor is primarily associated with women. This distinction between gender-ascriptive and gender-bearing roles reveals that there is no connaturality between gender and labor and that ideas behind the so-called feminine jobs are socially constructed.

This level of analysis needs to be carried out by Christian academics who can pinpoint the different evolutions, but mostly suggest concrete strategies in reshaping ways in which people conceive gender roles. The academics need to team up with Christian institutions and groups to share their findings and devise concrete strategies that will affect actual people. For instance, in cultures where domestic chores disproportionately fall into the hand of the female child, gender-mixed activities should be encouraged among children. At a social level, there could be specific activities, informal discussions within small Christian communities, and campaigns of awareness in the mass media, with the specific intention to challenge the notion of reproductive labor as a women's ascribed activity. The radio as a popular communication medium can be used to animate discussions on gender social roles even in remote places of the world. Interactive shows and outdoor posters showing men performing the so-called women's work at home would also help. In the case of the latter, for instance, the picture of a man doing laundry could be accompanied with the caption: "he is doing this for money, why not doing this for love?"[22]

The sociology of knowledge approach looks at "knowledge as a social reality"[23]: its transmission, as a common possession, and in relationship with social structures and processes.[24] Values and attitudes are learned, and they influence self-image and self-perception.[25] Indeed, "a significant part of character formation is the internalization of societal myths, stories, symbols, and traditions."[26] This forms part of the "symbolic apparatus" that society gives us, and "with which we grasp the world and order and interpret our experience."[27] Within the Catholic tradition in particular, attention must be paid to the creed, the liturgy, the sacraments, the Bible, the catechesis, and other lived practices. The Bible plays a major role by providing myths, stories, symbols, and sayings that shape the lives of the faithful.

The sociology of knowledge also pays a particular attention to ideologies.[28] We saw how this distortion of reality disadvantages working women. In this particular case, the ideologies are sexism, patriarchy, kyriarchy, classism, ethnocentricism, and colonialism. A successful challenge of ideology requires an initial groundwork by Christian academics, which will then be proposed to Christian communities. It is important to see how ideologically tainted Christian teaching is, and to try to remedy it.

There must be a liberationist reading of the Bible. This entails the rejection of biased understandings that justify the domination of communities or segments of the population. For instance, Gn 3:16 and Eph 5:22ff is used to justify the domination of women in the household. Must not society be challenged? A balanced reading of the Scripture must be introduced to both laity and clergy, in catechesis, various Christian workshops, and in preaching. In addition, an inclusive theology of work inspired from CST should be propagated. The theology of labor as developed by CST is free from patriarchal and colonial ideologies, and rehabilitates manual labor. The theology of labor counters the way economists and secular institutions understand labor; they are quick to commercialize and tend to overvalue financial outcomes. Furthermore, this theology puts the workers' well-being at the center of its preoccupations. This theology of labor also rejects individualistic approach and adopts a communal approach that locates individuals within a community. The language must be accessible and the content made simpler for quick and easy comprehension by the Christian communities.

All these different ways by which society shapes people and institutions reveal the complexity of STF. They provide an understanding of the ways in which people and institutions could be influenced.

THE CHURCH'S CONVERSION

There are two distinct things to consider here: first, the Church should atone for its sins and second, it should move toward atonement.

Recognizing One's Sins against Working Women

Before acting in any capacity it is important for Christians at the individual and collective levels to acknowledge ways in which they have contributed or benefited from the sinful social environment that marginalizes and oppresses working women. This is a sort of cathartic moment destined to foster a humble posture from the Church. The focus is not the marginalized workers, but the Church as individuals and institution. There are no doubts about the positive effects associated with the acknowledgment of one's sin and demand for forgiveness, but my primary intent here is to probe the Church's attitude.[29] While the Church is the whole people of God, I put the burden of initiating the process on the institutional Church and on the leadership at the grassroots level. Since there is a lack of awareness on the issue on the part of Church official representatives, a third party (NGO, government institution, or any respected body) could present the terrible condition of Church workers and women workers in particular, which could trigger a positive reaction.

A couple of attitudes should be avoided. First, making cheap excuses and asking for blanket absolution. Second, making general and vague statements about wrongdoings. The level of responsibility may vary depending on the entity that confesses its sins. Given what has been said that certain forms of injustice can be so prevalent and imbedded in social institutions, it is obvious that people become insensitive to them. It is also important not to separate individual sins from social sin, but to put both in connection. There are some elements to consider.

First, it is important to recognize that sin is perpetrated against working women, who are human, that is, creatures made in God's image and likeness, and therefore are endowed with dignity. And by sinning against a fellow human being, Christians have also sinned against God, and failed to incarnate the ideals of the Kingdom.

Second, it is important to identify and name the particular sins as well as the persons/category of persons sinned against. At the individual level, people should recognize ways in which they have exploited, verbally abused and/or physically assaulted, committed injustice against working women, or did not intervene to prevent an injustice. This injustice can be cheap labor (low wages, long working hours, no social security), absence of wage/back pay, and sexual harassment. It is important to note that there is not always a clear-cut line between oppressors and oppressed and people, depending on the circumstances, may find themselves in any category. For instance, in rural areas of Cameroon's forested areas, farmers are oppressed by local policies as I showed in chapter 2, but in their turn, they take advantage of the local indigenous people (Baka). Moreover, men and women alike may be wrongdoers. At an institutional level, as I pointed out in chapter 9, the way Church institutions poorly treat their workers with the widespread practice of cheap labor. In addition to this practice, one can look at the pastoral teaching that rarely addresses the question of labor let alone that of working women (see chapter 1, section 3). If there are general statements condemning the abuse of human rights by local bishops, condemnations of unjust working conditions and the unjust treatment of working women are virtually absent. Added to this, there is the failure to act in the face of blatant injustice against this category of workers. This is a sin by omission, and it seems to be a predominant one.

Third, it is important to identify the persons/categories of persons against whom those sins are perpetrated. At an individual level, female domestic workers are taken advantage of because of the absence of a legal status of their employment in the vast majority of African countries. Their activity carries all the characteristics of cheap labor. At the institutional level, other categories such as market/street vendors, and day laborers need to be considered.

Repentance and Conversion

The recognition of sins must lead to repentance. This can be done formally through statements or rituals. Formal statements can be issued by local bishops or regional/national episcopal conferences. These can take inspiration from the various apologies issued by recent popes.[30] The letter of Pope Benedict XVI to the Catholics of Ireland following the child abuse sexual scandal is a good example of what is expected. There are recognition of the sin by the Church, of the factors leading into it, a humble posture, the inaction of bishops, the identification of clear categories of people among which the victims and the perpetrators, and the suggestion of concrete initiatives to prevent this situation to repeat itself in the future.[31]

The ritual can be inspired from the communal rite of reconciliation.[32] The latter proposes an examination of conscience, a communal asking for forgiveness, and a suggestion of collective commitment as a sign of penance and conversion. The examination of conscience to be grounded needs to be prepared by either a real-life story told by a witness or by listing concrete situations of violations of the dignity of working women.[33] As I pointed in the subsection on the preferential option for the poor woman (chapter 9), it is important to break the silence in regard to these situations. Such stories increase the awareness of the community as a whole. Individuals are invited to discern what concrete acts of forgiveness and friendship they need to perform as visible signs of their conversion.

The Church's repentance needs to include a pledge for change and for concrete commitment to social justice. The communal ritual for reconciliation offers the possibility of communal commitment, which is just the first step toward a new reality.[34] It is not enough here to correct wrongdoings—like paying living wages—it must include a real change of perspective as noted in the section on social conversion in chapter 3. True repentance, with the grace of God, calls to renewal.

Although the dogmatic constitution on the Church *Lumen Gentium* (LG) recognizes the presence of divine and human in the Church,[35] there is a tendency to downplay the significance of the human element, and how it makes the Church a worldly reality influenced by its environment. Hence, there is a tendency to act as if the Church is immune from abuses and social dysfunctions (racism, ethnocentrism, sexism, classism, abusive power, etc.) although these are not present in the Church.[36] The practical consequence of this is to think that the Church does not need to reform its practices and ways of dealing with people—especially those working within its institutions. In virtue of this, distinctions are made between *work for* and *work outside* the Church. Work within the Church is perceived as service, volunteer work, and nonprofit. It comes as no surprise that many people with authority in Church institutions perceive paying any sort of wage as a favor, with the idea that working for the Church should be free.

There is also a need to address the distorted social relationships that we call kyriarchy, which is embedded within the Church and the society. True repentance demands the transformation of unjust social relationships and dynamics.[37] The Church of Africa needs to address its postcolonial character thoroughly and not limit itself to rituals and theology. The relation of dependence generates an unhealthy pattern of relationships. The structures of organization and ministry still mirror those of European churches. There is a certain form of authoritarian leadership ad intra that shapes relationships between lay and clergy, and among lay people. Without a serious move toward a more collegial and participatory forms of leadership, any change in the way working women are dealt with will only be cosmetic. In a special way, the issue of sexism needs to be confronted. One clear area where this needs to happen is in the elaboration of teachings and pastoral priorities. It is true that synods offer the opportunities for a larger consultation of faithful from all corners. However, these happen to be the exception rather than the rule. Pastoral letters from individual bishops or bishops' conferences are issued with very little input from lay people and non-ordained religious. It is primarily the ordained clergy who design pastoral plans with little and/or no input from the laity.

BIBLICAL STORYTELLING

This subsection builds on the previous subsections on liberationist theology and the preferential option for the poor working woman. The issue at stake here is the question of Mveng's anthropological poverty and how to overcome it. I believe that the preferential option for the woman for herself is very important for two reasons: (1) to foster proper understanding of self-care and self-esteem and (2) to give voice to women's concerns and perspectives.

I consider the practice of biblical storytelling, as understood by Musa Dube,[38] to be important in shaping women's imagination and self-understanding and helping the process of self-discovery and self-recovery. Kabeer makes it clear that empowerment is rooted in women's sense of self-worth.[39] For Kiboko, without that inner power no change can occur.[40] Empowerment has cognitive dimensions, which means that the person grows in self-awareness and in recognition of her contribution to the community.[41] Storytelling is a narrative process involving biblical figures but told by women from their own perspectives and in their own terms. As Jean-Marc Ela points out, since orality dominates African societies, the spoken word is of paramount importance.[42] "Within this oral culture . . . important is the story, which mingles the real with the imaginary, and creates archetypal heroes who are both images and symbols."[43] Nussbaum warns that "storytelling is never neutral; the narrator always directs attention to some features of the world rather than others."[44]

This takes a specific meaning in a postcolonial context. By the fact that these stories are told in a context of oppression, storytelling should be a prophetic and a healing experience.

Biblical storytelling as conceived by Musa Dube allows for fluidity in retelling the story in terms of characters' composition, gender, the whole plot of the story, and so on.[45] Thus, storytelling is not simply the retelling of a biblical narrative, but a "process of constructing that narrative."[46] Since a distorted conception of humanity leads to women's marginalization, one needs the Word of God not only to confront this biased anthropology but also to suggest alternative visions. Storytelling involves "a transformation of the narrative of events from a narrative of loss, humiliation, and defeat to a narrative of recovery, redemption, and new resolve."[47] It allows women to regain their role as storytellers in African society, to appropriate the Word, and to use it for their own benefit. Hence, there is more to storytelling than merely narrating a story to feel good about oneself. It is about taking control of the narrative of one's life and of one's community. It is an attempt to reverse the anthropological poverty trend: alienated personality and lack of control over one's destiny.[48] As Malcolm and Ramsey observe, "narratives also enable the creation and re-creation of the Self as a character in her own, ongoing story."[49] The Bible is just one way of doing it.

I argued earlier for the need to break the silence or to positively make one's concerns and perspectives heard. Storytelling is one way of achieving that purpose.[50]

The Practice of Biblical Storytelling

Certain clarifications need to be made about the Bible and storytelling as an activity. One must be aware of the patriarchal and androcentric character of the Bible[51] as well as its use for Western imperialistic purposes.[52] The patriarchal and androcentric character can be seen, for instance, in the fact that God is primarily referred as the "God of Abraham, Isaac and Jacob" (Ex 3:6) and not the one of Sarah, Rebecca, and Rachel, or both put in pair; that family trees barely mention women; and that most of the important characters are male. Moreover, what stands out is the depiction of gender relationships that condone the domination of men over women (Gn 3:16; 1 Co 11:3; Eph 5:22ff; 1 Tim 2:12) and the ambivalent character of women's bodies and qualities (menstruations as a sign of impurity, Lev 15:19–30; 19:19).

The imperialist use of the Bible is linked to the collusion between the colonial enterprise and the evangelization in Africa. The Christian mission was an integral part of the westernization process: adoption of European names, cutting ties with one's community (called "heathen"), abandoning one's cultural practices (called "demonic"), and other factors. As a popular saying puts it, while the colonial administrators took care of the bodies of the Africans, the missionary took care of their souls. The Bible was used to tame the spirits of Africans and soften for the kill. The centrality of the Bible in carrying out this enterprise is undeniable. This is why, although the Bible has become part of the African ethos, it "will always be linked to and remembered for its role in facilitating European imperialism."[53]

However, the patriarchal and androcentric nature and imperialistic use of the Bible is not a reason to abandon it or to disqualify it, given the fact that it shapes the lives of millions in the African continent. It is an invitation to read it critically. As far as women are concerned, "the personally and politically reflected experience of oppression and liberation must become the criterion of appropriateness for biblical interpretation and evaluation of biblical authority claims."[54] In such perspective, the Bible is a prototype, which is an original model that "is not a binding timeless pattern or principle."[55] This grounds the Bible and the Christian community in history and makes the latter capable to respond to "new social needs and theological insights, as well as to allow and to extrapolate new social-ecclesial structures, while preserving the liberating biblical vision by engendering new structural formations that belong to this vision."[56] In addition, the African women reading the Bible need to do that as "postcolonial subjects," that is, as participants in the liberation struggle of their political communities and as seekers of liberating ways of interdependence.[57]

In addition, Kabeer makes it clear that the awareness that fosters the cognitive dimension of empowerment comes through training and not spontaneously.[58] Training does not refer to formal reflection, but rather to various activities, such as "on-going processes of learning, reflection, action, experience, observation and analysis"[59] that lead to increased awareness. Likewise, for biblical storytelling to be fruitful, and given what has been said above, there is a need for preparation.

Dube's biblical storytelling takes cues from African storytelling.[60] Storytelling is primarily a communal activity. It is not something done in isolation. In the story, the teller can call out the audience who can respond. The story is adapted according to the needs of the audience. In addition, there are interesting features in many African folktales: their gender-neutral character, and values and philosophies embodied by flat characters. The fact that animals are generally characters in African folktales allows for gender fluidity. This, in turn, influences the practice of biblical storytelling, which should include the following:[61]

- Retelling a story/stories as many times as possible, with different/new characters to meet the need of the audience or address a particular issue.
- Making the retelling of a biblical story as a participatory experience that includes listeners; take a fixed story to make it open-ended.
- Using the gender-neutral techniques of retelling biblical stories to counteract patriarchal and colonizing ideology.
- Reading as tricksters to subvert powerful and exploitative powers.

I view biblical storytelling as an activity carried from the grassroots instead of an academic exercise. In what follows, I will now move to present the figures of Tabitha and Lydia in the Acts of the Apostles as suggestions.

Tabitha and Lydia: Exegesis

Tabitha (also known as Dorcas) and Lydia are mentioned respectively in Acts 9:36–42 and 16:11–15. Tabitha is resuscitated by Peter while Lydia responds favorably to Paul's preaching and is baptized a Christian. Both figures are selected because they are working and independent women. There are other figures who could have been selected, but I chose these to show how concretely biblical storytelling can work. Tabitha and Lydia are striking figures because they are not mentioned as wives or mothers.[62] The Acts of the Apostles presents them as "working women who are not at all dependent on any man in their intimate circles."[63] In addition, "both are without a husband, male guardian, or lawyers."[64] Both women are praised in virtue of what they do for the Christian faith.[65] In the case of Tabitha, Teresa Calpino[66] observes that she "was not lauded for the typical female virtues of chastity, mother-hood, or domesticity. Her good works were not described as being directed toward her husband or children, but on behalf of others beyond family and relatives."[67] Both women were involved in trading. Tabitha was in the cloth industry while Lydia was selling purple goods (mostly clothes). This makes the evaluation of these women by the author of Acts more remarkable: "Although elite authors in the ancient world may have looked down upon those involved in the trades, Tabitha and Lydia are held up as honorable and respectable women."[68]

Given that she lives in Joppa and has an Aramaic name, Tabitha is from a Jewish background.[69] Since her name, Tabitha, was common among the slave population of the time, it is unclear if she was initially a slave before being freed or born in a family of former slaves.[70] In any case, her role as an "inde-pendent, female head of household who was also a business owner"[71] stands out. Tabitha is the only woman in the entire NT to receive formally the title of "disciple," although the use of the phrase "a certain female disciple" suggests that there may have been other women "disciples."[72] Nonetheless, "by nam-ing Tabitha a disciple, the narrator designates that she was someone who was an exemplary follower of"[73] Jesus Christ. This is confirmed by the fact that she performed "good deeds and acts of charity" (Acts 9:36b). Furthermore, the recipients of her good acts are unspecified, which suggests she may have helped both Christians and non-Christians.[74] She was involved in cloth industry, as the mention "the various garments Dorcas had made when she was still with them" (Acts 9:39) indicates. She appears to be a small business owner since women shop owners in the clothing industry in the first century in the Greco-Roman world also worked in their shops.[75] In general, "garment production was both labor and resource intensive."[76] The widows weeping in front of her dead body might have belonged to her business network or were recipients of her acts of charity.[77] Overall, "Tabitha used her home, her means, and the profits of her business in service to her community."[78]

Lydia is reportedly the first person converted in Europe by Paul and his companions. Her name and the lack of Aramaic equivalent tend to indicate her Gentile background.[79] Lydia used to gather at a praying space outside

Philippi with other women to worship the God of Israel.[80] Like Tabitha, she is a business owner and homeowner.[81] She is a seller of purple cloth that was destined for the nobility and the wealthy.[82] This does not necessarily mean that she was wealthy, but at least she had enough means to be self-reliant. If purple dye was of high quality, its production involved hard and dirty work.[83] Her city of origin was renowned for its textile industry.[84] Her sense of hospitality showcases her fine character.[85] The Risen Lord directly opens her heart, and she answers the call by having her household and herself baptized (Acts 16:14–15).[86] She is then emboldened and demands that the missionaries come and stay at her place as a confirmation of her righteous character (Acts 16:16).

Tabitha and Lydia: Storytelling

Here, I will attempt to illustrate how biblical storytelling could be done in the case of Tabitha and Lydia whose stories I blended into one. I take into account biblical exegesis, but I cast them as African working women facing various challenges. I am inspired by Musa Dube's treatment of the hemorrhage woman in Mk,[87] and Kabamba Kiboko's discussion of the Samaritan Woman's story.[88] Time is very elastic in this context where a single figure will cover 140 years of recent African history. I make use of African storytelling techniques. Overall, this requires a lot of imagination, but an imagination grounded into facts. Given the constraint of space, the stories will be short, and it assumes that there is an interaction between the narrator and her audience.

Narrator: Tabitha was born into a working-class family in a coastal city of the Gulf of Guinea. Some in her vicinity thought that she belonged to a lower-class family because of her name Tabitha. She learned hard work from a tender age and was initiated by her mother into the family business: cloth trading. She learned all the stories related to the industry working side by side with her mother. She learned that at one point the people with light skin who looked like ghosts arrived in their land and claimed authority over the people and everything in that land. Soon everything changed.

Narrator: Soon everything changed!
Audience: What?
Narrator: They introduced new crops for men only, soon everything changed!
Audience: What?
Narrator: They registered the land in men's name. Soon everything changed!
Audience: What?
Narrator: Men went to school so as to work in offices, women to become good wives and mothers. Soon everything changed!

They introduced new clothes made of fabric, which threatened the old industry since it required less time to manufacture and was cheaper. However, Tabitha's mother told her that women rose to the challenge. They adopted different solutions. Some continued to weave and dye cloth fabric like in the past. Others abandoned it and decided to use the new fabric to make cloths. Still others decide to salvage what they could from the past and combine it with the new. Tabitha's mother belonged to this category. This is why Tabitha would have to go to school to learn how to use a sewing machine, now that she knew how to weave and dye.

Tabitha went to school, run by people with light skin. They found her name funny, and could barely pronounce it properly. Even when they got the syllables right, a tone would be misplaced. So she decided to take the name Dorcas, which was the Greek equivalent of her name for her interaction with outsiders. After completing her formation, she joined the cooperative of businesswomen involved in cloth trading, and set up her own business.

Setting up a business was difficult in general, even more so for women. The narrator can stop here and ask the audience what possible difficulties women could encounter in the course of setting up a business.

She struggled, but managed to be successful; and after many years of hard work, she effectively owned her own business and her own home. However, very soon the competition grew stiffer. The people with light skin set up a big corporation of textile, which monopolized the production of textile goods from the cotton farms to the manufacturing of fabric. Tabitha was discouraged.

That was when she met Jesus. During her days in school, she heard some missionaries and Christians discussing about Jesus; she heard so many things, but she was not convinced. She felt inside her that Christianity was a ploy designed to strip Africans of their identity and culture. She decided that she wanted none of that although many of her friends and relatives decided to join the new religion. However, this time was different. Jesus was speaking directly to her. He might have said to her "fear not, for I am with you" always (Is 41:10), or "I have overcome the world" (Jn 16:33). She strongly felt that Jesus was standing by her side in her troubles. She found in him a new hope and a new energy and decided to get baptized along with her whole household. She found in the Church a source of new energy. She met people with whom she could relate and people who cared about her beyond her business abilities. She came to the help of the needy and more vulnerable of the Christian community and her neighborhood as well. The sick, the hungry, the homeless, orphans, widows, and strangers all found in her open arms and listening ears. She became also an inspiration for so many young women.

Sometime later, the people with light skin left, and the local people took back the control of their land, but the influence of the people with light skin never really left. Everyone thought that things would be different. However, the situation grew worse. The new leaders increased the taxes on small business owners, such as Tabitha, which threatened to put them out of business. The new leaders maintained the hegemony of the big textile corporation in the country. In addition, they opened the local market to second-hand clothing from Europe. Cheap clothes from China flooded the country. Locally, many workers were laid off, and this affected business income. These made things difficult for Tabitha, and eventually affected her health.

Audience: What happened next?
Narrator: Tabitha fell seriously ill.
Audience: What happened next?
Narrator: She died!
Narrator: The death hit the community like a storm. She was the pillar of the community and a source of comfort and inspiration for many. When everything was thought to be lost, the Apostle came, touched her and called her out "Tabitha, stand up," the Apostle said. Tabitha opened her eyes and saw the Apostle. He stretched out his hand to her, and she took it. She had come back from the dead. The Lord had brought her back to life. If she had been brought back to life, her struggling business, too, would come back to life. "I shall not die, but live" (Ps 11817), Tabitha said, for Jesus is standing by my side.

The narrator stops here to let people figure out for themselves possible endings to the story. At any time of the story, listeners can interrupt with a question or begin a possible debate.

PARTNERING WITH OTHER INSTITUTIONS

As important as biblical storytelling is in fostering cognitive empowerment and self-empowerment, it is not enough in itself for solving the problem of marginalization of the working woman. This is why it needs to be supplemented by this approach, that is, collaboration, which tries to address structural deficiencies to bring long-lasting and collective solutions to the issue of disempowerment of the working woman.

The Church is not the only institution in the society. She exists in a pluralistic society in which she cohabitates with other Christian religious denominations, non-Christian faithful as well as with secular institutions and political governments. If the Church wants to achieve a durable modification of the social environment in favor of working women, it needs to collaborate with other groups. The main target here should be to influence the "indirect employer." To bear fruit, the Church needs to learn from actors who operate on the ground. This requires her to be a listening Church that reads the signs of the times,[89] a Church that listens to the Holy Spirit (see Rev 2:7), and which remains "attentive to the goodness that Holy Spirit sows in the midst of human weakness."[90] In a special way, the struggle for justice and gender equality is "the working of the Holy Spirit for a clearer recognition of the dignity and the rights of women."[91] Since I already laid out the possible actions that the Church can take on at the institutional level (see the last section of chapter 9), I now concentrate on the Church's collaboration at the local and the global level. At the local level, I will look at the works of a concrete association such as *Mbonweh*, and how the Church can learn from such initiatives. At the global level, I will draw insights from the Church's involvement in the 2000 Jubilee Campaign for the cancellation of debt in favor of poor countries.

Reading the Signs of Times: The Case of Mbonweh Women's Development Association

The Church, as "historical reality," "has profited by the history and development of humanity."[92] Here, it needs to learn and profit from those organizations that already operate on the ground.[93] One of such is the Mbonweh Women's Development Association (MWDA, henceforth Mbonweh). Mbonweh, in one of the local languages of Cameroon, means unity. I have chosen this particular association for three reasons. First, its founder was a leader of the World Union of Catholic Women Organization, and used Catholic resources to advance her agenda.[94] Second, its membership, as it is obvious from its name, is entirely female, most of whom are rural farmers. Third, Mbonweh is specifically committed to empowering women. This association was founded in March 1988 by Mrs. Dorothy Atabong and 100 other women. It began in the South West region of Cameroon and, by 2007, was present in more than four regions of the country with 4,000 members from 30 socio-cultural groups made up of different Christian denominations.[95] By 1997, it was registered as a common initiative group (CIG)[96] and NGO.[97] Mbonweh is a "self-managed"[98] type of association that promotes gender equality and social justice, and targets, in a special way, women and youths of both male and female genders.[99] For the sake of my argument, I will only focus on their women-oriented activities. According to Mbonweh's vision, change cannot come unless women themselves become their own messengers through their active participation in the development process to achieve the needed change in their lives, families and society at large.[100]

To address this challenge directly, the women of Mbonweh decided to (1) set up consciousness-raising groups, (2) create opportunities for education and training, and (3) establish a revolving loan scheme.[101] These consciousness-raising groups exemplify what was suggested in chapter 9 concerning option of the poor woman for herself. These are "small and congenial gatherings" destined to encourage women to "overcome their limitations, express themselves and share their experiences, learn about their rights and raise their self-esteem."[102] What is at stake here is the "education of self, which is teaching and educating women to accept themselves," and to know that despite their minimal level or nonexistent formal education, they still have a valuable contribution to make to society.[103] This level also addresses the burning issues of domestic violence as well as healthcare.[104]

Creating opportunities for education and training addresses the needs of the members who for the most part are farmers and illiterate. This level promotes adult literacy, skill training in the management of income-generating activities, and training in better agricultural methods.[105] Concerning the latter, women are trained to produce "manure and insecticides using local material," cultivate "new crops in new areas," and are equipped with skills such as "seed multiplication, food preservation, food processing, and marketing."[106] Concerning business, women are taught, among other things, "budgeting, small business conception, finance management, small industry agricultural methods, marketing."[107] Those educational programs take the form of conferences, workshops, seminars, and short-courses.[108] These training sessions are participatory in nature to help boost women's self-confidence and self-esteem.[109] In some cases, the beneficiaries are trained to become instructors and facilitators so as to encourage them and to make them believe in themselves.[110]

The revolving loan scheme is there to help women put into practice the skills they have received in their formation.[111] At the beginning, Mbonweh used the savings of its members, which amounted to $940 at the end of its first year of existence.[112] The savings and shares of members—that have increased since—still make up the core on which the revolving loan scheme operates and to which aid from various donors is added.[113] Loans are given to individuals through group membership.[114] The particular sociocultural group affiliated to Mbonweh serves as collateral since the individual woman is not asked to provide any. In case of failure to reimburse the loan the sociocultural group has the responsibility to do so. The participatory nature of Mbonweh also plays here where loan beneficiaries are represented on the board of directors, and may act as field workers, facilitators, president, and so on.

Each sociocultural group affiliated to Mbonweh runs a project or activity tied to development. An important characteristic of Mbonweh is that projects are designed by the members themselves unlike what is reported in other groups or countries.[115] This allows the women involved to "own" the project and to work on something that fits their needs.

Overall Mbonweh presents instructive characteristics. First, it believes in effecting change through women's collective action. Indeed, "the underlying

Christian message [places] a strong emphasis on collective action, mutual assistance, fairness and democracy."[116] Mbonweh does not favor an individualistic approach, and perceives women within the context of their community. Second, the Christian roots inform the fight for social justice and gender equality, which should start from the household.[117] Third, its model of power is participatory, and involves the members in decision-making processes and in actual important decisions. Fourth, it understands that the economic marginalization of women is the result of a complex process not limited to economic reasons. In a way of addressing anthropological poverty, they promote the option of the woman for herself, which eventually fosters integral development. In fostering literacy and skills acquisition, the association tries to address some of the hindrances that prevent working women from achieving their full potential. Fifth, Mbonweh understands the importance of forming alliances and networks. It seeks to "build on women's networks to increase mutual support among women and to bring about change in society."[118] This is why Mbonweh has financial partners to boost its portfolio. It also works with the University of Buea in Cameroon and the Pan-African Institute for Development for training and workshops.[119] Mbonweh is also part of the Network of Eco-Farming Organizations of Africa that tackles the environmental challenges (rain-washed soil, declining soil fertility) that women farmers face.[120]

The way Mbonweh tries to empower women starts from restoring their agency and sense of themselves, or the power within. The association is also concerned with the know-how and women's skills or the power to. Then, the association seems to empower women through shared and relational power. Women are consulted, made participants, and empowered to train others, take responsibility or demonstrate their skills. Relational power is demonstrated by the democratic nature of the institution, and the emphasis on solidarity. It is only through this solidarity that effective change can be effected. Hence, the emphasis is on the power within (agency), the power to (ability), and power with (relationality). This assumes a holistic approach to the person who is not perceived as a monad, but as embedded in a human community. One can find implicitly some of the key principles of CST useful for working women that were listed in the first chapter: participation, dignity, and solidarity.

The impact of Mbonweh in the life of its members sometimes leads to intra-household conflict mostly with the husband.[121] This tension can be healthy if it brings about change in gender relations and renegotiations of roles within the household. For instance, this could be in terms of shared workload at home. Some of the criticisms that I leveled against certain of the women farmers' associations earlier (subsection 3.3 of chapter 2) may apply here (dependence on foreign money, no change in societal perceptions on gender, inability to address structural causes). Further, the vast majority of women involved in income-generating activities complained of increased workload.[122] Moreover, there is no visible strategy to confront the community leaders and institutions that could change attitudes vis-à-vis women's work and education. It is not clear how Mbonweh addresses the causes and tries to prevent the repetition of the marginalization of women workers. As Kabeer pointed out, change at the individual level is insufficient. There must also be a change at a structural level.[123] In STF, I pointed to ways in which some structural changes could be brought about at least at the societal level. Further, those who influence the labor market (state, corporations, international institutions, etc.) need to be confronted. This appears as a shortcoming of Mbonweh's approach.

The presence of Christian members and implicit elements of the Christian ethos in Mbonweh means that the Church is already present there. However, in virtue of solidarity and subsidiarity, one should not expect an NGO like Mbonweh to achieve everything by itself. The members of the association do not believe it, this is why they network with other organizations. The whole Church can be inspired by what such organizations do well in terms of conscientizing, training, and helping women in setting up businesses. Its participatory model of decision-making must be emulated. This type of model can be emulated by other Christian groups. Like Mbonweh, the Church knows its own limits and that it cannot do everything.

A concrete way of doing that is to allow organizations such as Mbonweh to interact with Christian communities. Mbonweh should not be given only a space for their meetings in parishes or other church institutions. They should work and team up with groups such as women's groups (for instance the Catholic Women Association), youth groups (the Christian Student Youth, for instance), and small Christian communities. Through workshops and trainings, such associations can raise awareness on the condition of women workers, and also teach skills to better equip the working Catholic women and youth.

Moreover, the experience of outreach ministries in other areas can illuminate how the experience of groups like Mbonweh could be appropriated within a Catholic community, and even address some of their shortcomings. I will focus here on the outreach ministry concerning the fight against AIDS in Africa. Given the scarcity of space, I will just mention few initiatives that will help drive home my point. I have chosen the Ecumenical HIV and AIDS Initiative in Africa (EHAIA) of the World Council of Churches, and the African Network of Religious living with AIDS (ANARELA) of the Ugandan Anglican priest Gideon Byamugisha. EHAIA has been successful by striving at making the Church competent on HIV/AIDS from within and without.[124] Inside the Church, the focus was on the "factors that increase vulnerability, such as stigma, denial, and discrimination," and the way to deal with those with "compassion, accountability, and intentionality."[125] In its mission to the outside world, there is a need for the enhancement of "theological and institutional capacity in socially relevant, inclusive, suitable collaborative ways"[126] in the fight against HIV/AIDS and with the aim of restoring hope and dignity. I am more interested with the former, because part of the latter will be in harmony with what I called STF, and with the next section that will deal with bringing change at an institutional level. To that effect, EHAIA "poured out resources into education and training to make churches welcoming and healing communities."[127]

The ANARELA, which later morphed into International Network of Religious Living with AIDS is the fruit of the experience of Byamugisha, an Anglican priest who decided to go public with his seropositive status.[128] ANARELA is a support network destined to fight against the isolation of AIDS patients born out of social rejection.[129] It uses Byamugisha's holistic model called Safer Practices, Access to Treatment, Voluntary counseling and testing, and Empowerment (SAVE) that addresses both prevention and treatment, AIDS patients sexually infected or not, and public policies.[130] To fight stigma and ostracism, ANARELA couples SAVE in the fight against social viruses that are grouped under the acronym SSDDIM (Stigma, Shame, Denial, Discrimination, Inaction, and Misaction).[131] ANARELA provides a platform for religious leaders living with AIDS to voice their problems and also those of forgotten people, to end a complicit silence of stigma, denial, and fear, and to provide hope in the face of the scourge.[132] As such, these leaders "exemplify and model resilience, courage, and hope in the face of HIV and AIDS."[133]

The example of EHAIA and ANARELA as outreach ministries can inspire the way to promote the empowerment of working women at the level of the local Catholic community. The first thing to do is to have a structure that deals specifically with the issue of women's labor. Such a structure must be at least national to make more impact. The local Justice and Peace Commissions can be put to the task, and a special committee depending on them can be appointed. This must come with a real investment in financial and material resources that will help support local communities and groups such as Mbonweh that promote the empowerment of working women. Second, it is important to pay attention to the factors that worsen the situation, and how the Church can start addressing those within its own structures. I have dealt extensively with those in chapters 2 and 3, I shall not come back to them. However, I can name a few here: patriarchy, colonialism, and distorted understandings of work. A concrete way of doing this is "mainstreaming" gender and postcolonial issues in the theological training of priests and pastoral agents.[134] Mainstreaming those issues can be done in the various groups and institutions. This will help raise the awareness of Catholics on the issue.

Third, it is important that bishops and priests are directly involved in this effort by propagating it in their homilies and public addresses, by involving themselves in the outreach campaigns, and by teaming up with working women. Fourth, as I noted earlier in STF, the Church must come up with alternative economic visions and a countercultural message.

Another important factor is to use mass media to inform the general public and the targeted women about the activities of these groups. I have in mind particularly the radio—community radios that are tailored to address the needs of local communities—that can reach people even in remote areas. The help of mass media in helping the work of justice is important. For instance, in the case of Mbonweh, roughly 13 percent of women interviewed in a 2007 survey had heard about the association through mass media.[135] The hierarchical Church has not failed to notice the importance of mass media in social life since Paul VI in *OA*, without failing to notice the risks associated with it.[136] John Paul II, in *Ecclesia in Africa*, recognized the importance of mass media as a means "of information and education, of guidance and inspiration," for individuals, families, and society at large.[137] Hence, it is important that the agents of evangelization learn and use the mass media.[138] In *Africae Munus,* Benedict XVI reiterated that "the Church needs to be increasingly present in the media so as to make them not only a tool for the spread of the Gospel but also for educating the African peoples to reconciliation in truth, and the promotion of justice and peace."[139] Churches should collaborate from the diocesan, national, regional to intercontinental level to achieve that goal.[140]

Improving the Indirect Employer: Lessons from the Jubilee 2000 Campaign

Other Church-led institutions can step up to address areas where organizations like Mbonweh fall short. Justice and Peace Commissions and Christian NGOs can help with advocacy to change laws and the whole economic environment. They can partner with other forces in the civil society to put pressure on the state to change discriminatory laws and to enforce egalitarian laws that are already there. One important area is the legal protection of working women, especially those in the informal economy such as farmers.

A concrete example of multilevel commitment of the Church as well as partnership with other groups is the Jubilee 2000 campaign for debt cancellation, which can provide a template to be used in the case of working women. That campaign saw the involvement of the Church from the grassroots to the top. Indeed, those involved were

individual Catholics, parish-based justice and peace groups, church personnel (especially missioners), religious orders and their social action offices, relief agencies, academics and universities, national episcopal conferences, the Vatican's justice and peace office, and Pope John Paul II.[141]

Building on the biblical notion of jubilee and the idea of debt relief attached to it,[142] as well as on CST,[143] the Church inspired a global coalition in favor of debt cancellation for poor countries. This explains why debt cancellation was thought as a matter of justice rather than charity. This work that climaxed in mid-1990s and early 2000s had started in the late 1970s with especially churches and NGOs working on the alleviation of the harmful consequences of debt.[144] The actions included issuing statements and engaging directly key policy-makers.[145] At an intermediary level, there was an effort to alert public opinions to increase pressure on key actors. A clear case of that is Carmen Rodriguez, the head of a parish charismatic group in Lima, Peru, who launched a petition calling for one-time debt cancellation that gathered more than 1.8 million signatures in Peru, and 17 million worldwide; the petition was eventually presented in June 1999 in Cologne, to members of the Group of 8 (G8), the most industrialized nations.[146]

The Jubilee 2000 or J2K campaign started by British groups led by Anglican and Catholic agencies in 1996, made the one-time cancellation of debt by the end of 2000 its primary goal.[147] It took its inspiration from the appeal made by Pope John Paul II in *Tertio Millenio Adveniente* that recommended a substantial reduction of debt and perhaps its outright cancellation.[148] J2K became a broad-based coalition[149] that was global and also local with approximately sixty-nine national J2K networks.[150] It targeted decision-makers as well as the general public, and used simple statistics (cost of cancellation for each citizen in rich countries, the number of children dying due to the debt, etc.) and historical references (comparing the debt's burden to the slave trade) to impress minds and create an urge for action.[151] Further, J2K put pressure on creditor countries and multilateral institutions by criticizing their efforts to push for further reforms.[152] This is why, although its activism led to the HIPC (High Impoverished Poor Country) initiative from the IMF, the debt relief legislation passed by the U.S. Congress in November 1999, the 1999 Cologne initiative, and the 2005 pledge by the G8 to cancel all the debt owed by poor countries, J2K still criticized the shortcomings of these initiatives.[153]

At the local level, J2K Zambia used statistics to show the real cost of the debt, and what toll it was taking on ordinary citizens in terms of health and education.[154] Further, the Zambian J2K campaigners focused on the Structural Adjustment Plans and their economic measures adopted by the Zambian government as the key problem.[155] Not only did the jubilee campaigners pushed for debt relief, but also for more involvement of the civil society with the government to monitor the allocation and management of debt relief funds from HIPC.[156]

It is worth noting that as important as debt cancellation is, the Church realized that without a change in the economic environment, a cancellation could not prevent the start of another cycle of indebtedness for a country. This is why the Church tackled some of the root causes of the problem: the imbalance in international trade, modifying banking regulations, and the high interest rate, among others.[157] The U.S. bishops suggested that the debt cancellation to be effected must be accompanied by other measures such as fostering the participation of civil society, ensuring economic reform policies, the inclusion of mechanisms of accountability and using the resources freed for the fight against poverty.[158] One could say that even though the debt cancellation did not reach all its goals, such as changing the economic environment or getting the whole debt completely wiped out, it definitely made the question of debt a critical issue in global policy.

The debt relief campaign provides an interesting example of how the Church could work for the empowerment of working women. First, it is important to identify a simple and a focal point, from which a variety of issues could be addressed.[159] The question of debt served to raise issues of the fight against poverty, imbalances in international trade, the unfair exchange rates, the reform of the banking system, corruption, and many other issues. In the case of working women, the issue of cheap labor can be brought forward in such a campaign. The question of cheap labor has many interrelated facets: low wages, absence of social benefits, absence of a contract, no legal recognition, and poor working conditions. These are concrete elements that can be assessed on the ground.

Second, find a theological grounding. J2K for debt cancellation was grounded on Leviticus 25 and Deuteronomy 15. In the case of cheap labor, the Exodus and *tsedakah* could provide two useful paradigms. The Exodus tells the story of exploited labor and how God sides with the exploited and enslaved Hebrews against the powerful pharaoh. Moses's repeated demand "let my people go" (Ex 5:1; 7:16.26) could provide a motivation. *Tsedakah*, which is translated as righteousness, combines distributive justice and charity.[160] *Tsedakah* "concerns active intervention in social affairs, taking an initiative to intervene effectively to rehabilitate society, to respond to social grievance, and to correct every humanity-diminishing activity."[161] A combination of both paradigms could prove helpful.

Third, empower all levels of Church and various Christian organizations to get involved, even at the individual level. Furthermore, it would be good that the pope formally supports the issue as John Paul II did on debt cancellation and Francis on climate change. Fourth, identify potential allies among religious denominations outside of the Church and in the civil society (trade unions, NGOs specialized in labor and gender, and any relevant group or movement), and create broad coalitions capable of influencing decision-makers.

Fifth, target public opinions as well as key decision-makers and actors. Public opinion is very important because political leaders and business people care about public perception. One must also distinguish the various levels of responsibility. Action should be global and local. Cheap labor that is experienced locally is caused by the deregulation of labor encouraged by neoliberal policies carried out by various international economic actors.

In this particular case, corporations and international legal agreements should come to the forefront. At the local level, the state needs to enforce existing laws and pass new laws for the protection of workers. The Church and some groups of the civil society can put a monitoring committee that will check how the state concretely enforces laws to protect workers. In addition, the state should give legal recognition to some informal activities: domestic workers, buyam sellam, street vendors, bartenders, hairdressers, and the like. The government cannot simultaneously collect tax from these people and not grant their legal status. To modify one of the reasons that led to the American Revolution "taxation without legal recognition is tyranny." In addition, there should be a push against sweatshops. Corporations that practice it should be exposed, and the state should act to improve the worker's conditions. Moreover, special attention must be paid to the practice of subcontracting or outsourcing. Generally, subcontractors employ people informally, and formal companies use outsourcing and subcontracting as a way of saving costs. Since this practice contributes to the precariousness of workers; one must document concrete cases, and expose corporations and subcontractors that exploit workers, especially women. Finally, the question of social benefits needs to be advanced and extended to all workers.[162]

NOTES

1. *Lumen Gentium* observes that the Holy Spirit, "distributes special graces among the faithful of every rank," see Vatican II Council, *Dogmatic Constitution on the Church* Lumen Gentium (Vatican City, 1964), 12, http://www.vatican.va/archive/hist_councils/ii_vatican_council/documents/vat-ii_const_19641121_lumen-gentium_en.html.

2. I borrow the phrase from Hinze, "Women, Families, and the Legacy of *Laborem Exercens*," 89.

3. Ibid.

4. Ibid.

5. Joan E. Grusec and Paul D. Hastings, "Preface," in *Handbook of Socialization: Theory and Research*, ed. Joan E. Grusec and Paul D. Hastings, Second Edition (New York/London: The Guilford Press, 2015), xi.

6. Ibid.

7. Ibid.

8. Ibid., xii.

9. O'Keefe, *About Social Sin*, 52–56.

10. Ibid., 51.

11. Ibid., 52.

12. Ibid.

13. Ibid.

14. Ibid.

15. Ibid., 53.

16. Ibid.

17. Ibid.

18. Ibid.

19. Ayesha M. Imam, "Engendering African Social Sciences: An Introductory Essay," in *Engendering African Social Sciences*, ed. Ayesha M. Imam, Amina Mama, and Fatou Sow, Codesria Book Series (Dakar, Senegal: Codesria, 1997), 3.

20. Ibid.

21. Ibid.

22. In countries like Cameroon, men own laundry services, and are hired to do the laundry in private homes.

23. O'Keefe, *About Social Sin*, 54.

24. Ibid.

25. Ibid.

26. Ibid.

27. Ibid., 54–55.

28. Ibid., 55. O'Keefe observes that "an ideology involves a systematic distortion of reality to serve those who benefit from this distortion."

29. For more on the positive psychological effects of forgiveness on the victims/oppressed see Eben Scheffler, "Reflecting on Jesus' Teaching on Forgiveness from a Positive Psychological Perspective," *HTS Teologiese Studies/Theological Studies* 70, no. 1 (2015): 1–10, doi:10.4102/hts.v70i.2982; Brandon J. Griffin, Caroline R. Lavelock, and Everett L. Worthington, Jr., "On Earth as It Is in Heaven: Healing through Forgiveness," *Journal of Psychology & Theology* 42, no. 3 (2014): 252–59.

30. Among others there are John Paul II, "Homily of the Holy Father 'Day of Pardon'" (Homily, Ash Wednesday Mass, Rome, March 12, 2000), http://w2.vatican.va/content/john-paul-ii/en/homilies/2000/documents/hf_jp-ii_hom_20000312_pardon.html; Benedict XVI, *Pastoral Letter to the Catholics of Ireland* (Vatican City: Libreria Editrice Vaticana, 2010), http://w2.vatican.va/content/benedict-xvi/en/letters/2010/documents/hf_ben-xvi_let_20100319_church-ireland.html; "Pope Expresses 'sorrows' for Abuse at Residential Schools," *Cbcnews*, April 29, 2009, http://www.cbc.ca/news/world/pope-expresses-sorrow-for-abuse-at-residential-schools-1.778019; Francis, "Meeting with Victims of Sexual Abuse, Address of the Holy Father" (speech, Apostolic Journey to Cuba, to the United States of America and Visit to the United Nations Headquarters (September 19–28, 2015), Philadelphia, PA, September 27, 2015), http://w2.vatican.va/content/francesco/en/speeches/2015/september/documents/papa-francesco_20150927_usa-vittime-abusi.html; Francis, "Participation at the Second World Meeting of Popular Movements, Address of the Holy Father" (speech, Apostolic Journey to Ecuador, Bolivia and Paraguay (July 5–13, 2015),

Santa Cruz de la Sierra (Bolivia), July 9, 2015), http://w2.vatican.va/content/france
sco/en/speeches/2015/july/documents/papa-francesco_20150709_bolivia-movimenti
-popolari.html.

31. Benedict XVI, *To the Catholics of Ireland*, 4, 6, 8–11, 14.

32. Pierre Jounel and Jean Evenou, *La célébration des sacrements* (Paris: Mame-Desclée, 2006), 830–45.

33. On the use of narratives in forgiveness and rebuilding of the victims' agency see Lois Malcolm and Janet Ramsey, "On Forgiveness and Healing: Narrative Therapy and the Gospel Story," *World & World* 30, no. 1 (2010): 23–32.

34. Jounel and Evenou, *La célébration des sacrements*, 835.

35. Vatican II Council, *Lumen Gentium*, 8.

36. An example of that can be found in the pastoral letter of the Cameroon's episcopal conference on corruption, where the effects of corruptions on various institutions and different categories of individuals are analyzed, but the Church is notably left out of the analysis; for more see Conférence Episcopale Nationale du Cameroun, "Lutter contre la corruption au Cameroun."

37. Rose Dowsett, "Reconciliation as Reconstruction of a Wounded and Unjust Society," in *Mission as Ministry of Reconciliation*, ed. Robert Schreiter and Knud Jørgensen, vol. 16, Regnum Edinburgh Centenary (Eugene, Oregon: Wipf & Stock Publishers, 2013), 106; Robert J. Schreiter, "A Practical Theology of Healing, Forgiveness, and Reconciliation," in *Peacebuilding: Catholic Theology, Ethics, and Praxis*, ed. Robert J. Schreiter, R. Scott Appleby, and Gerard F. Powers (Maryknoll, NY: Orbis Books, 2010), 372–73.

38. Musa W. Dube, "Introduction," in *Other Ways of Reading: African Women and the Bible*, ed. Musa W. Dube, Global Perspectives on Biblical Scholarship 2 (Atlanta; Geneva: Society of Biblical Literature-WCC Publications, 2001), 1–19.

39. Kabeer, "Gender Equality and Women's Empowerment," 15.

40. Kiboko, "Sharing Power: An Autobiographical View," 219.

41. Kabeer, "Between Affiliation and Autonomy," 511–13.

42. Ela, *My Faith as an African*, 36.

43. Ibid.

44. Nussbaum, *Creating Capabilities*, 15.

45. Dube, "Introduction," 2001, 4.

46. Schreiter, "A Practical Theology of Healing, Forgiveness, and Reconciliation," 382.

47. Ibid.

48. Mveng, *L'Afrique dans l'Eglise*, 210.

49. Malcolm and Ramsey, "On Forgiveness and Healing," 26.

50. For more on the issue reading the Bible among the marginalized or in a context of oppression see Jaime Vidaurrázaga, "Appropriating the Bible as 'Memory of the Poor,'" in *The Bible and Catholic Theological Ethics*, ed. Yiu Sing Lúcás Chan, James F. Keenan, and Ronaldo Zacharias, Catholic Theological Ethics in the World Church Series (Maryknoll, NY: Orbis Books, 2017), 183–92; Anthony Egan SJ, "Reading in a Revolution: Activist Catholics' Use of Scripture during the Last Decades of Apartheid, 1974–1994," in *The Bible and Catholic Theological Ethics*, ed. Yiu Sing Lúcás Chan, James F. Keenan, and Ronaldo Zacharias, Catholic

Theological Ethics in the World Church Series (Maryknoll, NY: Orbis Books, 2017), 193–204; Irmtraud Fischer, "Gender Issues in Biblical Ethics: On the Reception of Old Testament Texts for a Sexual Ethics in Gender-Democratic Societies," in *The Bible and Catholic Theological Ethics*, ed. Yiu Sing Lúcás Chan, James F. Keenan, and Ronaldo Zacharias, Catholic Theological Ethics in the World Church Series (Maryknoll, NY: Orbis Books, 2017), 251–61.

51. For more on this see, Elisabeth Schüssler Fiorenza, *In Memory of Her: A Feminist Theological Reconstruction of Christian Origins*, 10th anniversary ed. (New York: Crossroad, 1994).

52. Dube Shomanah, *Postcolonial Feminist Interpretation of the Bible*, 12–15.

53. Ibid., 3.

54. Schüssler Fiorenza, *In Memory of Her*, 32.

55. Ibid., 33.

56. Ibid., 34.

57. Dube Shomanah, *Postcolonial Feminist Interpretation of the Bible*, 19–20.

58. Kabeer, "Between Affiliation and Autonomy," 511.

59. Ibid.

60. From here onward see Dube, "Introduction," 2001, 3–4.

61. Ibid., 4.

62. Teresa J. Calpino, *Women, Work and Leadership in Acts*, Wissenschaftliche Untersuchungen Zum Neuen Testament. 2. Reihe 361 (Tübingen: Mohr Siebeck, 2014), 2.

63. Ibid.

64. Calpino, *Women, Work and Leadership in Acts*.

65. Ibid., 2.

66. Theresa Calpino is a New Testament professor from Loyola University of Chicago.

67. Calpino, *Women, Work and Leadership in Acts*, 166.

68. Ibid., 229.

69. Lucinda Brown, "Tabitha," ed. Carol Meyers, *Women in Scripture: A Dictionary of Named and Unnamed Women in the Hebrew Bible, The Apocryphal/ Deuterocanonical Books, and the New Testament* (Boston, NY: Houghton Mifflin Company, 2000), 159.

70. Ibid., 160; Calpino, *Women, Work and Leadership in Acts*, 152–53.

71. Calpino, *Women, Work and Leadership in Acts*, 141.

72. Brown, "Tabitha," 159; Calpino, *Women, Work and Leadership in Acts*, 150.

73. Calpino, *Women, Work and Leadership in Acts*, 151.

74. Ibid., 157.

75. Ibid., 142.

76. Ibid., 147. Teresa Calpino adds: "Transporting goods over land was expensive and dangerous. Besides the agricultural labor needed to provide the raw materials, labor was also required to prepare, spin, dye, and produce the materials and garments that eventually were sold in the market. Women provided the bulk of this industry" (Ibid.).

77. Ibid., 165–67.

78. Ibid., 142.

79. Ibid., 185.

80. Ibid., 194.

81. Robert W. Wall, "The Acts of the Apostles," in *The New Interpreter's Bible: General Articles & Introduction, Commentary & Reflections for Each Book of the Bible Including the Apocryphal/Deuterocanonical Books*, vol. X (Nashville: Abingdon Press, 1997), 231.

82. Calpino, *Women, Work and Leadership in Acts*, 180; Wall, "The Acts of the Apostles," 232.

83. Ivoni Richter Reimer, "Acts of the Apostles: Looking Forward and Looking Back," in *Feminist Biblical Interpretation: A Compendium of Critical Commentary on the Books of the Bible and Related Literature*, ed. Luise Schottrof and Marie-Theres Wacker, trans. Lisa E. Dahill et al. (Grand Rapids, Mich: William B. Eerdmans Publishing Company, 2012), 692.

84. Wall, "The Acts of the Apostles," 231–32.

85. Ibid., 235.

86. Calpino, *Women, Work and Leadership in Acts*, 224.

87. Musa W. Dube, "Fifty Years of Bleeding: A Storytelling Feminist Reading of Mark 5:24-43," in *Other Ways of Reading: African Women and the Bible*, ed. Musa W. Dube, Global Perspectives on Biblical Scholarship 2 (Atlanta/Geneva: Society of Biblical Literature-WCC Publications, 2001), 50–60. Dube transforms the twelve years of bleeding of the woman into Africa's fifty years of struggle in postcolonial times, where Africa is turned into a woman.

88. Kiboko, "Sharing Power: An Autobiographical View." Kiboko offers a vision born of interaction with illiterate rural women from eastern DRCongo.

89. Vatican II Council, *Gaudium et Spes*, 4.

90. Francis, *Amoris Leatitia*, 308.

91. Ibid., 54.

92. Vatican II Council, *Gaudium et Spes*, 44.

93. Ibid., 40.

94. "History of Mbonweh Women's Development Association" (Global Hand, 2010), 3, https://www.globalhand.org/system/assets/94d5f3555cdc68192284d241 101f8f6f89976332/original/History_to_Croosroads.pdf.

95. Ida Tonge Akwo, "The Role of Non Governmental Organisations in Fostering Women's Economic Empowerment and Development in Cameroon: The Case Study of The Mbonweh Women's Development Association" (Master Thesis, University of Cape Town, 2007), 68.

96. According to Cameroonian law, "Common initiative groups are organizations of an economic and social nature set up voluntarily by individuals having common interests and working together as a group" see

National Assembly of Cameroon, "Relating to Co-Operative Societies and Common Initiative Groups," Law N. 92/006 § (1992), sec. 49, http://www.ilo.org/i mages/empent/static/coop/policy/pdf/camero.pdf.

97. "History of Mbonweh Women's Development Association," 3.

98. Linda Mayoux, "Tackling the Down Side: Social Capital, Women's Empowerment and Micro-Finance in Cameroon," *Development and Change* 32, no. 3 (2001): 442.

99. Akwo, "Fostering Women's Economic Empowerment and Development in Cameroon," 69.

100. Ibid., 68–69.

101. "History of Mbonweh Women's Development Association," 2.

102. Akwo, "Fostering Women's Economic Empowerment and Development in Cameroon," 2.

103. Ibid., 71.

104. "History of Mbonweh Women's Development Association," 5.

105. Ibid., 2.

106. Ibid., 5.

107. Ibid.

108. Ibid.

109. Akwo, "Fostering Women's Economic Empowerment and Development in Cameroon," 71–72.

110. Ibid., 72.

111. "History of Mbonweh Women's Development Association," 2.

112. Ibid.

113. Akwo, "Fostering Women's Economic Empowerment and Development in Cameroon," 67. Among these, there are CEBEMO (Catholic Organization for joint Financing of Development Project/Netherlands) that has become since 1995 Bilance after a merger with another Catholic Dutch organization; Associated Country Women of the World (ACWW, a UK-based NGO that supports women associations in rural and urban areas in the developing world), and Cameroon Gatsby Trust (provides microfinance to women's groups).

114. From here onward see Ibid., 73–74, 99–100.

115. Ibid., 100.

116. Mayoux, "Tackling the Down Side," 454.

117. Ibid.

118. Ibid.

119. "History of Mbonweh Women's Development Association," 4.

120. Ibid.

121. Akwo, "Fostering Women's Economic Empowerment and Development in Cameroon," 101–2. The fact that women find themselves in control of resources outside of the husband's power is not always seen positively by the latter.

122. Ibid., 102.

123. Kabeer, "Gender Equality and Women's Empowerment," 16.

124. Teresia Hinga, "Africa's Transformative Responses to the Gender Global HIV and AIDS Syndemic," in *HIV & AIDS in Africa: Christian Reflection, Public Health, Social Transformation*, ed. Jacquineau Azetsop (Maryknoll, NY: Orbis Books, 2016), 228. Teresia Hinga calls these "inner" and "outer" competence.

125. Ibid.

126. Ibid.

127. Elias Kifon Bongmba, "HIV and AIDS and Stigma," in *HIV & AIDS in Africa: Christian Reflection, Public Health, Social Transformation*, ed. Jacquineau Azetsop (Maryknoll, N.Y: Orbis Books, 2016), 270.

128. Hinga, "Responses to the Gender Global HIV and AIDS Syndemic," 235–36.

129. Ibid., 236.

130. Ibid.

131. From here onward see Ibid.

132. Bongmba, "HIV and AIDS and Stigma," 270.

133. Hinga, "Responses to the Gender Global HIV and AIDS Syndemic," 236.

134. I borrow the idea of mainstreaming in theological training from Ibid., 229.

135. Akwo, "Fostering Women's Economic Empowerment and Development in Cameroon," 82.

136. Paul VI, *On the Occasion of the Eightieth Anniversary of the Encyclical "Rerum Novarum" Apostolic Letter Octogesima Adveniens* (Libreria Editrice Vaticana, 1971), 20, http://w2.vatican.va/content/paul-vi/en/apost_letters/documents /hf_p-vi_apl_19710514_octogesima-adveniens.html; He acknowledges "their influence on the transformation of mentalities of knowledge, of organizations and of society itself." John Paul II, *On the Church in Africa and Its Evangelizing Mission, Post-Synodal Apostolic Exhortation Ecclesia in Africa* (Yaoundé, Cameroon: Libreria Editrice Vaticana, 1995), 51, 71, 76, http://www.vatican.va/holy_father/john_paul_ii/ apost_exhortations/documents/hf_jp-ii_exh_14091995_ecclesia-in-africa_en.html.

137. John Paul II, *Ecclesia in Africa*, 71.

138. Ibid.

139. Benedict XVI, *Africae Munus*, 145.

140. John Paul II, *Ecclesia in Africa*, 126.

141. Elizabeth A. Donnelly, "Making the Case for Jubilee: The Catholic Church and the Poor-Country Debt Movement," *Ethics & International Affairs* 21, no. S1 (November 2007): 189, doi:10.1111/j.1747-7093.2007.00090.x.

142. William Bole, "Forgiving Their Debts," *America Magazine*, March 25, 2000, https://www.americamagazine.org/issue/281/article/forgiving-their-debts.

143. Donnelly, "Making the Case for Jubilee," 192.

144. Ibid., 191.

145. Ibid., 196, 209–10. Elizabeth Donnelly specifically thinks of two statements, one issued by the Pontifical Commission of Justice and Peace in 1987 and the other by U.S. Conference of bishops in 1989 that have had an impact on international institutions such as the International Monetary Fund (IMF) and the World Bank as well as other banking institutions and rich country.

146. Ibid., 190.

147. Ibid., 207–8.

148. Ibid.

149. J2K was led by Christian Aid U.K., the Vatican, Oxfam, the European Network on Debt and Development, a Washington-based coalition of church and anti-poverty groups, Catholic national episcopal conferences, and relief agencies. See Ibid., 190.

150. Ibid., 207.

151. Ibid., 208.

152. Ibid.

153. Ibid., 211–12; Bole, "Forgiving Their Debts."

154. Donnelly, "Making the Case for Jubilee," 205.

155. Ibid.

156. Ibid., 206.

157. Ibid., 203.

158. Ibid., 210.

159. I owe this idea to Dr. Martin Luther King, Jr who pointed out that the failure of the civil rights movement in Albany, Ga, was due to a general protest against segregation rather than against a distinct facet of it. See Martin Luther King, *The Autobiography of Martin Luther King, Jr*, ed. Clayborne Carson (New York; Boston, MA: Intellectual Properties Management in association with Warner Books, 1998), 168.

160. Jonathan Sacks, *The Dignity of Difference, How to Avoid the Clash of Civilizations*, revised edition (London; New Dehli; New York; Sydney: Bloomsbury, 2014), 113.

161. Donahue, *Seek Justice That You May Live*, 10.

162. Workers benefiting of work-related insurance are 38 percent in the public sector, 36 percent in the private sector, and less than 5 percent in the informal sector; see Institut National de Statistiques du Cameroun, *Annuaire Statistique Du Cameroun 2014*.

Conclusion to Part IV

This final part explored the concrete practices of empowering working women. Chapter 10 focused on empowerment. Empowerment enables the ability to make life-strategic choices. The ability to make choices is assessed through three interrelated notions, namely, *agency*, *resources*, and *achievements*. Agency and resources are tools for capabilities, and achievements are functioning capabilities. The notion of capabilities shows clearly the importance of the social context for the sound exercise of one's ability to choose and to act. Hence, empowerment needs to be connected to disempowerment. Empowerment is closely related to what Paul VI called integral human development. It is a process that entails progressive transformation of society and the person.

The idea of empowerment is closely tied to that of power. For Christians, Jesus of Nazareth offers the paradigm concerning the exercise of power in a way that it uplifts the lowly and downtrodden. As such, the Bible redefines and subverts the notion of power as the world understands it. There cannot be real empowerment without a criticism and reevaluation of the common notion of power. What emerges from the reevaluation of power are the notions of transformative power, mutual power, and grace. These need to be added to the conception of "power to" (agency) and "power with" (relational power) present in social science literature and, most importantly, in the way power is practiced.

As we have also seen in chapter 11, four Church-inspired practices can contribute to the empowerment of working women. The first practice concerns socializing the feminine, which means that the so-called, socially determined feminine jobs have to become masculine tasks as well. It is ultimately about the way to affect society's core values and attitudes concerning labor. To achieve this, society should be influenced internally and externally.

Externally, the Church, animated by the Kingdom's values, should reject in words and in deeds practices and customs that demean the values of working women. The hierarchization of jobs needs to be rejected. In order that this be successful, Christian institutions should repudiate authoritarian and autocratic forms of leadership, and promote women to positions of leadership. At the internal level, one must look at the symbolic apparatus and the fact that gender roles are socially constructed. Attention must be given to ideologies that pervert gender relations. For the Church, a balanced reading the Bible must be introduced and promoted to challenge the negative portrayal of women. A theology of labor inspired from CST and free from patriarchal and colonial prejudices must be promoted.

The second thing the expected from the Church that could turn the situation of working women around is to ask for forgiveness and make amends for the sins committed against working women. The way of repentance and conversion restores the credibility of the Church in her fight for social justice in favor of working women. This practice is not limited to the Church hierarchy but involves the whole Christian community and the various Christian-led institutions.

The third thing is biblical storytelling. A story of the Bible is re-narrated by women to fit their own particular interest. This uses, among others, African storytelling techniques, and it is interactive. It allows for fluidity where the story can be transformed at will. I chose the story of Tabitha and Lydia as example, by adapting it to the experience of twentieth-century African women who have to face various challenges in their businesses.

The fourth and final point collaboration: the Church needs to partner with other institutions to promote the empowerment of women. The example of the Mbonweh's Women Development Association of Cameroon shows what type of work and how much associations do in favor of women. This involves conscientization, education and skills acquisition, and creation of income-generating activity. Given the presence of Christians in its membership, Mbonweh can be considered as an example of the Church's intervention. However, associations like Mbonweh fall short in tackling the structural causes of women's marginalization. Examples such as AIDS outreach ministry can inspire on how to help structures like Mbonweh in its exemplary strides within the Church. Mass media can also be used to give a visibility to the action of the Church in favor of these women. Other Christian entities such as Justice and Peace Commission can help through their advocacy. The Jubilee 2000 campaign on debt cancellation provides a template on how to act to bring about favorable institutional changes. This requires a multilevel organization that is capable of remaining focused and assiduous toward its goals.

General Conclusion

The aim of this book has been to construct an African-gendered social ethics to address the issue of disempowered African working women as well as their empowerment in Africa. This work brought in dialogue CST, African theology, Feminist/women's theology, and social sciences. My scope was working women from working and poor classes in Sub-Saharan Africa, with a special focus on Cameroon.

The first part of this book (chapters 1–4) presented the strengths and weaknesses of CST in its handling of the question of the empowerment of women workers. I looked at CST's teaching at the levels of the papal magisterium and African bishops' declarations, with special attention on the African synods. I also addressed CST's limits at the end of the chapter.

Chapter 1 showed that CST provides a sound grounding for a gendered African social ethics (GASE). First, it addresses contemporary social issues and challenges from a Christian faith perspective. Second, it offers important principles such as human dignity and human rights, solidarity, common good, participation, and the social nature of the human person. Third, its holistic understanding of the human person correlates with its comprehensive view of the economy.

As far as labor and the economy are concerned, post-conciliar CST highlights two key visions, namely, integral development and the primacy of labor over capital. The notion of integral development sees the well-being of the person as holistic (involving social, economic, cultural, and spiritual dimensions). Authentic development is grounded in the *imago Dei* and love of God and of neighbor, and has to be extended to the nonhuman world. It is also the enhancement of the individual capacity to respond to her personal vocation. The primacy of labor over capital is a reminder that the good of human beings and human communities should be the guiding factors of a sound economy.

In that respect, decent work, just wage, and the indirect employer (institutional background, actors, and factors influencing labor market and policies) play an important role.

Still in relationship with labor and the economy, there are other elements such as the acknowledgment of the importance of work and economic life for individuals, the association of the pursuit of social justice with the proclamation of the gospel, the preferential option for the poor, the call to the Church to be a credible witness, and the awareness of social sin. CST is also important for GASE because it is prophetic. For instance, the African bishops routinely denounce the terrible conditions of workers and the unbalanced trade relations at the expense of Africa. CST offers, in this particular case, a regional and contextual perspective to labor and economic issues.

However, CST on its own is not enough to address the marginalization of working women because of various reasons. First, gender receives scant attention in CST, and is rarely at the center of these documents. One needs to look outside the usual CST documents to find in other magisterial documents such as *Familiaris Consortio*, *Mulieris Dignitatem* and the *Letter to Women*, elements concerning working women. The arguments circle around the rejection of discrimination against women, the recognition of women's right to work outside of the household, right to assume public responsibilities, and a strong emphasis of women's family roles.

Second, CST's theology of labor needs a balanced biblical theology and a critical theory of biblical interpretation. Third, the other limits of CST are: western and patriarchal view of the role of women in the family, and the inadequacy of the concept of "development" (controversial history, problematic affirmation of the primacy of the sovereign nation-state in a context of economic globalization and the multiplication of global actors, and the lack of concern for gender). Fourth, there is a failure in papal discourse to use social analysis to ground reflections on women in sociohistorical context. Fifth, in the case of the African bishops, they fail to take concrete initiatives to translate their concerns about (working) women into pastoral outreach.

The subsequent parts of the book not only addressed the perceived limits of CST concerning women's work but also build on the foundations laid down by CST's principles.

The second part (chapters 5–7) addresses CST's lack of sociohistorical reflections on women by providing a social analysis of the condition of working women. The GASE needs social analysis, which provides a nuanced and comprehensive view of a particular phenomenon. That social analysis leans on the work of social sciences, which provide a systematic assessment of the phenomenon. In the particular case of labor, the main social science used is economics, and I reflected on neoclassical economics, which is the dominant trend and the one used by international institutions whose reports and reflections I use in my description of women's work.

Going back to the question of women and labor, one learns a lot from social sciences. Working women are disadvantaged by occupational segregation, which puts them in jobs and positions less rewarding and prestigious than those of men. Occupational segregation is rooted in gender bias and stereotypes that people have about women. Occupational segregation impacts the informal sector and (unpaid) reproductive labor. The informal economy is the sector where the majority of working women in the "Third World" countries are employed. Not only that this sector is characterized by cheap labor, but also women are often found in the most vulnerable positions of the informal sector as the subsection on Cameroon showed. In this country, most of the workforce is in agriculture, and the vast majority of women are self-employed or family-contributing workers, which are the most vulnerable positions. Concerning nonagricultural jobs in Cameroon, women are stuck in the less advantageous jobs with little prospect of promotion (domestic workers, hairdressers, bartenders, petty traders, street vendors, etc.).

Reproductive labor is also negatively affected by occupational segregation. Reproductive labor, which refers to household work, has been recently considered as work by the International Labor Organization. Unpaid reproductive labor disproportionately falls into the hands of women. It tends to be culturally exalted but economically underappreciated.

In addition to occupational segregation, there is also the issue of the unfriendly environment. An example of this in Sub-Saharan Africa is the way customary law negatively affects women in land tenure. Women are prevented from inheriting native land in many cultures. This curtails the right of rural women to own land and exercise decision-making power on how to manage the land on which they farm. Another consequence is the inability to get financial loans, since they cannot offer any collateral.

Nonetheless, as valuable as social sciences are, GASE built on CST must be aware of their limitations. In the case of neoclassical economics these are (1) a restricted view of labor that excludes most of women's labor; (2) an individual and atomistic understanding of the person and a disembedded economy that both isolate from the influence of the other social spheres; (3) the supra-historical approach to the distribution of the various social resources results in a lack of a critical appraisal of its own assumptions (taking the distribution of various resources as a given or the claim of a value-free science for instance). For these reasons, many of their solutions have failed to change the social environment. The usual solutions have been granting access to paid jobs, educating women, and passing gender-friendly legislations. The wage gap, segregation in field studies, and other disparities still remain in spite of these solutions. The reality is that the disempowerment of working women remains is so because the proposed solutions are too individualistic in their scope and fail to address the oppressive social power dynamics. Some of these are gender stereotypes and biases like the suspicion in African societies against financially independent and autonomous women.

Part II, in the end, shows that the use of social sciences is important, but not sufficient for the realization of GASE. One needs to include aspects overlooked in economic analysis like the pervasiveness of gender discrimination, and move away from an individualistic outlook. A fair ethical analysis must place the worker within the broader communities and look for solutions that will positively affect society and not only the individual worker.

Part III (chapters 8–9) suggests elements that form the backbone of a GASE and which, at the same time, supplement CST and boost social ethical analysis. Four elements constitute the core of GASE: African liberation theology (which provides the general orientation), the preferential option for the poor (for working woman), social sin, and the communal orientation.

At this theoretical level, there are two levels of analysis, namely, critical and constructive analysis. On the critical side, African liberation theology brings awareness of the history of oppression of Africa and the painful experiences of the people, which provide the starting point for theological reflection. In that respect, Mveng's anthropological poverty captures Africa's context of oppression since it describes the state of dehumanization, depersonalization, deprivation, and precariousness of Africans as individuals and communities. Anthropological poverty is carried out in postcolonial Africa in a neoliberal economy that perpetuates the exploitation of workers (Ela) or in a sociopolitical environment and in cultures that sideline women (Oduyoye). African liberation theologians call out the Church for its role in the oppression of Africans and workers in particular. They pinpoint the postcolonial character of the Church.

The other aspect of the critical analysis is the realization that the disempowerment of working women is a social sin. In this step, it is important to identify and name the structures of oppression that lead to women's oppression. In the case of labor, kyriarchy and colonialism appear as the most important structures. Kyriarchy (the rule of the lord/master) is exercised by the ruling male elite. It perpetrates and engenders other forms of women's oppression. Colonialism has established economic patterns in Africa that negatively affect working women until this day. These consequences are the lack of voice of locals in the decision-making process, the outward orientation of the economy, and cheap labor.

The last aspect of the critical analysis is to grasp how social structures of oppression interact and intersect in working women's lives. Intersectionality is a critical analytical tool to that effect. Intersectionality stresses the fact that oppression is multilayered and cumulative, and individuals experience this complexity. The various identities of the individual (gender, race, class, location, level of education, dis/ability, etc.) crisscross so as to exacerbate her marginalization. Intersectionality helps identify the power dynamics at play in the marginalization of women.

The constructive side is the second step of a GASE. It suggests a way forward to bolster hope. At the level of African liberation theology, it starts with the notion of liberation, which is holistic and encompasses all aspects of human experience. From this perspective, salvation is not otherworldly, but must be experienced here and now (Ela). Redemption is a holistic concept that takes into account all the facets of human experience (Oduyoye). The other point is the image of God relevant to such a task. God is a liberating God, who stands by the poor and defends them, and so does Jesus Christ. The cross in particular reveals God from the perspective of the poor and the oppressed. For the Church to remain credible, it must follow the footsteps of Jesus and stand by the oppressed.

The next element of a constructive approach is the option of the poor working woman for herself. This means an option for herself and option for others. The option for herself means to regain a sense of oneself and self-appreciation about oneself. The option for others puts her in solidarity with those who suffer and are marginalized. Thus, the option for the poor, far from being a paternalistic project, helps the poor to become subjects and artisans of their humanity. This option pushes the Church to readjust its practices and outreach ministries.

The third element of a constructive approach is social conversion. Social sin points to the need for conversion and transformation to bring lasting change to the condition of working women. Social conversion provides the answer. There are four things that could lead to social conversion: the Kingdom of God, alternative paradigms of economics and labor, breaking the silence, and the integration of caring labor. The first two provide the conceptual framework. The Kingdom of God furnishes the eschatological and epistemological horizon, which is to be pursued: a world where all relationships of domination, oppression, and unjust social structures are abolished and where justice and peace reign. The Kingdom is the antithesis of kyriarchy or any sinful structures, and as such demands conversion—radical transformation—for one to enter into it. Alternative views of the economy and labor aim to move beyond the neoliberal model since the latter treats labor as a commodity and fosters an individualistic and atomistic vision of society. The principles of CST should inspire an alternative vision of the economy, centered on the human person as worker and on the local human community.

The last two aspects of social conversion indicate initiatives that need to be taken so as to affect individuals and the social context. Breaking the silence gives working women a voice. It makes visible their oppression and jump-starts their healing process. The integration of caring/reproductive labor is a sign of a holistic economy, which acknowledges its importance. A holistic economy allows for a renewed understanding of caring labor and the fact that it should be a shared responsibility, not something that disproportionately falls into the hands of women

The fourth and last element of the constructive analysis is the institutional approach. It is the level of social policy engagement, and its goal is to influence the indirect employer. The institutional approach is rooted in the CST's institutional, relational, and solidaristic understandings of the common good. The institutional understanding of the common good insists on the importance of the social context in providing proper conditions for individuals or communities to flourish. The institutional approach targets States, international agencies, legal agreements, and non-State actors who can influence the local and global economy.

Part IV showed the practical side of GASE by offering a set of (non-exhaustive) practices that could help transform the social environment and ultimately improve the condition of working women. However, since empowerment is the focus of this book, it was important to clarify the meaning of the notion since CST does not use the term. Looking at the social sciences, political philosophy, and theology, some patterns seem clear. First, empowerment is closely related to the notion of power. This is why the scholars (Kabeer, Nussbaum, and others) try to deconstruct and redefine power from the standpoint of the (oppressed) women. Domination and hierarchical forms of power ("power over") are rejected in favor of more mutual and relational forms of power ("power with"), and power as ability ("power to," "power within"). Second, empowerment is only relevant within a given social context. The capabilities (agency, resources, and achievements for Kabeer, and substantial freedoms for Nussbaum) only make sense in a social environment. Third, empowerment is geared toward social change and more inclusion. Hence, empowerment must be viewed as transforming and shared power. Transforming power entails not only social change and a reallocation of power that is inclusive but also helping people move from helplessness to full agency. Shared power is enhanced through the principle of participation. All this is predicated on the fact that the empowerment of the individual woman is tied to collective empowerment and social change.

Furthermore, I then move to four empowering practices: socializing the feminine, the Church's conversion, biblical storytelling, and partnership with other institutions. Each of these practices addresses a particular concern. Socializing the feminine targets the core values, convictions, and attitudes behind society's attitude to women's work and women workers, and suggests alternative ones. This leans on social conversion and particularly gives flesh to the ideal of the Kingdom, imagining an alternative economy and the integration of caring/reproductive labor into a holistic economy. The role of the Church here is to simultaneously look outside and inside its own practice and structures. By looking outside its walls, the Church should help to deconstruct customs and accepted social morals that lead to the devaluation of women's work, and reject the hierarchization of jobs. Looking at the inside, the Church should pay attention to its own practices. It means getting rid of autocratic and authoritarian tendencies within its own structures and affiliated institutions, and promoting women to position of leadership. In addition, attention must be paid to the creed, liturgy, sacraments, Bible readings, catechesis and other lived practices and the way ideologies (sexism, patriarchy, kyriarchy, colonialism, classism, ethnocentrism/racism, etc.) can affect them. The role of Christian academics in deconstructing but also reflecting on transforming practices is key to enlightening local Christian communities.

The second practice, Church's conversion, touches on the issue of the credibility of the Church highlighted by CST as well as African liberation theologians. It is also an echo of the section on social sin, which also affects the Church. This is a prerequisite before the Christian community can side with the working women. It involves recognizing the sins of the Church and the need for changing vision and attitudes. The repentance is started to formal rituals and statements from Church leadership. It leads to a conversion that seeks the transformation of unjust social relationships and dynamics within the Church and in society.

The third practice, biblical storytelling, addresses the level of individuals and particular communities. It substantiates the sections on the option of the poor woman for herself and breaking of silence. It is exclusively an "ad intra" moment and inward-orientated initiative centered on the main actors: working women. This practice is important in shaping women's imagination and self-understanding, and it facilitates the process of self-discovery and self-recovery. Empowerment is rooted in women's sense of self-worth. Biblical storytelling involves telling the story but from the women's perspectives. This entails the fluid reconstruction of the plot, characters and so on, so as to defile and continue to raise awareness on the androcentric and postcolonial character of the Bible. The stories of Tabitha and Lydia in the Acts of the Apostles were used to illustrate this point. In the retelling of the story I blend Tabitha and Lydia and transform them into twentieth-century African women and tried to imagine retelling the story in an African setting, recasting the story in all the troubles the continent underwent since the arrival of the colonizers in the late 1800s.

The final practice, the collaboration of the Church with other institutions, exemplifies how the institutional approach could be carried out. One should distinguish here between the actions at the local and the global levels. At the local level, it is important for the Church to learn from local institutions and initiatives already in place to improve the condition of working women. Hence, the example of Mbonweh, a Cameroonian NGO entirely made of women (most of whom are Christian and rural farmers); which promotes gender equality and social justice. Not only that the Church can learn from their actions and modus operandi, but also Church institutions and groups should team up with such groups. Still, at the local level, it is vital to set up a special structure that will address the issue of working women, and to use mass media to promote that cause.

The global level is important, because of its capacity to act at a structural level. Taking a cue from the 2000 Jubilee campaign for debt cancellation, the effectiveness of action at the global level depends on the following elements: the choice of a single focal point, finding theological grounding, empowering all levels of the Church to be involved, and the involvement of public opinion and decision-makers.

At the end of this book, I see some paths worth exploring in the future. There is an invitation to the Catholic Church to offer a better analysis of women's work and better concerted action than what has been done until now. One issue that could be explored in future works is how to achieve gender mainstreaming in Church structures. There is also the issue of exploring how concretely the interactions between Christian academics (theologians, philosophers, social scientists, etc.) and local Christian communities/church-run institutions could work together to effect change.

Bibliography

Abéga, Séverin Cécile. *Les violences sexuelles et l'État au Cameroun. Les terrains du siècle.* Paris: Karthala, 2007.

African Union. Protocol to the African Charter on Human and People's Rights on the Rights of Women in Africa (2003). http://www.achpr.org/files/instruments/women-protocol/achpr_instr_proto_women_eng.pdf.

Agheneza, Z. "Why Development Projects Fail in Cameroon: Evidence from Ngie in the NW Province of Cameroon." *International Journal of Rural Management* 5, no. 1 (April 1, 2009): 73–90. doi:10.1177/097300520900500104.

Akwo, Ida Tonge. "The Role of Non Governmental Organisations in Fostering Women's Economic Empowerment and Development in Cameroon: The Case Study of The Mbonweh Women's Development Association." Master Thesis, University of Cape Town, 2007.

Alston, Philip, and Ryan Goodman. *International Human Rights: Text and Materials.* Oxford: Oxford University Press, 2013.

Aquino, Maria Pilar. "The Feminist Option for the Poor and Oppressed in the Context of Globalization." In *The Option for the Poor in Christian Theology*, edited by Daniel G. Groody, 191–215. Notre Dame, IN: University of Notre Dame Press, 2007.

Arabome, Anne. "When a Sleeping Woman Wakes...A Conversation with Pope Francis in *Evangelii Gaudium* about the Feminization of Poverty." In *The Church We Want: African Catholics Look to Vatican III*, edited by Agbonkhianmeghe E. Orobator, 55–64. Maryknoll, NY: Orbis Books, 2016.

———. "'Woman, You Are Set Free!' Women and Discipleship in the Church." In *Reconciliation, Justice, and Peace: The Second African Synod*, edited by Agbonkhianmeghe E. Orobator, 119–30. Maryknoll, NY: Orbis Books, 2011.

Ardener, Shirley. "The Comparative Study of Rotating Credit Associations." *The Journal of the Royal Anthropological Institute of Great Britain and Ireland* 94, no. 2 (December 1964): 201–29.

Assie-Lumumba, N'Dri Thérèse. "Educating Africa's Girls and Women: A Conceptual and Historical Analysis of Gender and Inequality." In *Engendering African Social Sciences*, edited by Ayesha Imam, Amina Mama, and Fatou Sow, 297–316. Codesria Book Series. Dakar, Senegal: Codesria, 1997.

Assogba, Yao. *Jean-Marc Ela: le sociologue et théologien africain en boubou: entretiens*. Collection Etudes africaines. Paris: L'Harmattan, 1999.

Baker, John, Kathleen Lynch, Sara Cantillon, and Judy Walsh. *Equality: From Theory to Action*. Houndmills, Basingstoke, Hampshire; New York: Palgrave Macmillan, 2004.

Barbier, J. C., ed. *Femmes du Cameroun: mères pacifiques, femmes rebelles*. Hommes et sociétés. Bondy [France] : Paris: Orstom ; Karthala, 1985.

Barker, Drucilla K., and Susan Feiner. *Liberating Economics: Feminist Perspectives on Families, Work, and Globalization*. Ann Arbor: The University of Michigan Press, 2004.

Barrera, Albino, O. P. "What Does Catholic Social Thought Recommend for the Economy? The Economic Common Good as a Path for True Prosperity." In *The True Wealth of Nations: Catholic Social Thought and Economic Life*, edited by Daniel K. Finn, 13–36. Oxford: Oxford University Press, 2010.

Beattie, Tina. "Maternal Well-Being in Sub-Saharan Africa: From Silent Suffering to Human Flourishing." In *The Church We Want: African Catholics Look to Vatican III*, edited by Agbonkhianmeghe E. Orobator, 175–88. Maryknoll, NY: Orbis Books, 2016.

Benedict XVI. *On Christian Love, Encyclical Letter* Deus Caritas Est. Rome: Libreria Editrice Vaticana, 2005. http://w2.vatican.va/content/benedict-xvi/en/encyclicals/documents/hf_ben-xvi_enc_20051225_deus-caritas-est.html.

———. *On Integral Human Development in Charity and Truth, Encyclical* Caritas in Veritate. Rome: Libreria Editrice Vaticana, 2009. http://w2.vatican.va/content/benedict-xvi/en/encyclicals/documents/hf_ben-xvi_enc_20090629_caritas-in-veritate.html.

———. *On the Church in Africa in Service to Reconciliation, Justice and Peace, Post-Synodal Apostolic Exhortation* Africae Munus. Ouidah, Benin: Libreria Editrice Vaticana, 2011. http://www.vatican.va/holy_father/benedict_xvi/apost_exhortations/documents/hf_ben-xvi_exh_20111119_africae-munus_en.html.

———. *Pastoral Letter to the Catholics of Ireland*. Vatican City: Libreria Editrice Vaticana, 2010. http://w2.vatican.va/content/benedict-xvi/en/letters/2010/documents/hf_ben-xvi_let_20100319_church-ireland.html.

Benne, Robert. "The Preferential Option for the Poor and American Public Policy." In *The Preferential Option for the Poor*, edited by Richard John Neuhaus, 53–71. Encounter Series. Grand Rapids, MI: William B. Eerdmans Publishing Company, 1988.

Beretta, Simona. "What Do We Know about the Economic Situation of Women, and What Does It Mean for a Just Economy?" In *The True Wealth of Nations: Catholic Social Thought and Economic Life*, edited by Daniel K. Finn, 227–65. Oxford: Oxford University Press, 2010.

Bigombe Logo, Patrice, and Elise-Henriette Bikie. "Women and Land in Cameroon: Questioning Women's Land Status and Claims for Change." In *Women and Land in Africa: Culture, Religion and Realizing Women's Rights*, edited by L. Muthoni Wanyeki, 31–66. London; New York; Cape Town: Zed Books Lt-David Philip Publishers, 2003.

Bilge, Sirma. "Le blanchiment de l'intersectionnalité." *Recherches féministes* 28, no. 2 (2015): 9–32.

Blosser, Philip. "Ethics." Edited by Michael L. Coulter, Stephen M. Krason, Richard S. Myers, and Joseph A. Varacalli. *Encyclopedia of Catholic Social Thought, Social Science, and Social Policy*. Lanham, MD; Toronto; Plymouth: The Scarecrow Press, 2007.

Bobga, Harmony. "Discrimination in Women's Property and Inheritance Rights in Cameroon: The Role of Human Rights NGOs in Promoting Gender Sensitive Land Reforms." In *Issues in Women's Land Rights in Cameroon*, edited by Lotsmart N. Fonjong, 135–56. Bamenda: Langaa Research & Publishing CIG, 2012.

Boff, Leonardo, and Clodovis Boff. *Salvation and Liberation*. Translated by Robert R. Barr. Maryknoll, NY: Orbis Books, 1984.

Bole, William. "Forgiving Their Debts." *America Magazine*, March 25, 2000. https://www.americamagazine.org/issue/281/article/forgiving-their-debts.

Bongmba, Elias Kifon. "HIV and AIDS and Stigma." In *HIV & AIDS in Africa: Christian Reflection, Public Health, Social Transformation*, edited by Jacquineau Azetsop, 264–74. Maryknoll, NY: Orbis Books, 2016.

Boswell, Jonathan, Francis P. McHugh, and Johan Verstraeten, eds *Catholic Social Thought: Twilight or Renaissance?* Bibliotheca Ephemeridum Theologicarum Lovaniensium 157. Leuven: University Press : Uitgeverij Peeters, 2000.

Brink, Rogier van den, and Jean-Paul Chavas. "The Microeconomics of an Indigenous African Institution: The Rotating Savings and Credit Association." *Economic Development and Cultural Change* 45, no. 4 (July 1997): 745–72.

Brown, Lucinda. "Tabitha." Edited by Carol Meyers. *Women in Scripture: A Dictionary of Named and Unnamed Women in the Hebrew Bible, The Apocryphal/ Deuterocanonical Books, and the New Testament*. Boston, MA; New York: Houghton Mifflin Company, 2000.

Burn, Shawn Meghan. *Women across Cultures: A Global Perspective*. 3rd ed. New York: McGraw-Hill, 2011.

Cahill, Lisa Sowle. "Commentary on *Familiaris Consortio* (Apostolic Exhortation on the Family)." In *Modern Catholic Social Teaching, Commentaries & Interpretations*, edited by Kenneth R. Himes O.f.M., Lisa Sowle Cahill, Charles E. Curran, David Hollenbach S.J., and Thomas A. Shannon, 363–88. Washington, DC: Georgetown University Press, 2005.

———. "The Common Good and Development," 1–38. KU Leuven, 2007.

Calpino, Teresa J. *Women, Work and Leadership in Acts*. Wissenschaftliche Untersuchungen Zum Neuen Testament. 2. Reihe 361. Tübingen: Mohr Siebeck, 2014.

Campillo, Fabiola. "Unpaid Household Labor: A Conceptual Approach." In *Macro-Economics: Making Gender Matter; Concepts, Policies and Institutional Change in Developing Countries*, edited by Martha Gutiérrez, 106–21. London; New York: Zed Books, 2003.

CENCO. "Changeons nos coeurs, Appel à un engagement réel pour la reconstruction, Message des évêques du Congo (RDC)." *La Documentation Catholique*, no. 2399 (April 6, 2008): 342–46.

CERAO. "Démocratie et promotion humaine, Lettre pastorale de la Conférence épiscopale régionale de l'Afrique de l'Ouest francophone (CERAO)." *La Documentation Catholique*, no. 2128 (December 17, 1995): 1084–92.

Chan, Yiu Sing Lúcás, James F. Keenan, and Ronaldo Zacharias, eds. *The Bible and Catholic Theological Ethics*. Catholic Theological Ethics in the World Church Series. Maryknoll: Orbis Books, 2017.

Cheza, Maurice, ed. "Les 64 propositions." In *Le Synode Africain: Histoire et textes*, 239–68. Paris: Karthala, 1996.

Cheza, Maurice, Henri Derroitte, and René Luneau, eds. *Les évêques d'Afrique parlent, 1969–1991: documents pour le Synode africain*. Les Dossiers de la Documentation Catholique. Paris: Centurion, 1992.

Clark, Meghan J. *The Vision of Catholic Social Thought: The Virtue of Solidarity and the Praxis of Human Rights*. Minneapolis, MN: Fortress Press, 2014.

Coleman, John A., S.J. "The Future of Catholic Social Thought." In *Modern Catholic Social Teaching: Commentaries & Interpretations*, edited by Kenneth R. Himes O.f.M., Lisa Sowle Cahill, David Hollenbach S.J., and Thomas A. Shannon, 522–44. Washington, DC: Georgetown University Press, 2005.

Conférence Episcopale du Cameroun, ed. *L'enseignement social des évêques du Cameroun 1955–2005: lettres pastorales et messages, communiqués et déclarations, approche analytique*. Yaoundé: AMA-CENC, 2005.

Conférence Episcopale du Congo. "A qui profite la manne du pétrole? Déclaration de la Conférence épiscopale du Congo-Brazzavile." *La Documentation Catholique*, no. 2278 (October 20, 2002): 885–88.

———. "Le rôle incontournable de la femme dans la société congolaise, Message des évêques du Congo-Brazzavile." *La Documentation Catholique*, no. 2278 (October 20, 2002): 894–96.

Conférence Episcopale du Tchad. "L'an 2000, une ère nouvelle pour une vie nouvelle, Message de Noël." *La Documentation Catholique*, no. 2220 (February 20, 2000): 179–83.

———. "Tout est possible quand le droit remplace la force, message de la conférence épiscopale du Tchad." *La Documentation Catholique*, no. 2087 (February 6, 1994): 133–35.

Conférence Episcopale du Togo. "Pour un esprit et un comportement nouveaux, lettre pastorale." *La Documentation Catholique*, no. 2117 (June 4, 1995): 557–62.

Conférence Episcopale Nationale du Cameroun. "Lutter contre la corruption au Cameroun: lettre pastorale des évêques du Cameroun." *La Documentation Catholique*, no. 2236 (November 19, 2000): 987–96.

Congregation for the Doctrine of the Faith. "Letter to the Bishops of the Catholic Church on the Collaboration of Men and Women in the Church and in the World." *Libreria Editrice Vaticana*, May 31, 2004. http://www.vatican.va/roman_curia/c

ongregations/cfaith/documents/rc_con_cfaith_doc_20040731_collaboration_en.h
tml.

Copeland, M. Shawn. "Poor Is the Color of God." In *The Option for the Poor in Christian Theology*, edited by Daniel G. Groody, 216–27. Notre Dame, IN: University of Notre Dame Press, 2007.

Copet-Rougier, Elisabeth. "Contrôle masculin, exclusivité féminine dans une société patrilinéaire." In *Femmes du Cameroun: Mères pacifiques, femmes rebelles*, edited by Jean-Claude Barbier, 153–91. Bondy [France]: Paris: Orstom ; Karthala, 1985.

Coquery-Vidrovitch, Catherine. *Les Africaines histoire des femmes d'Afrique subsaharienne du XIXe au XXe siècle*. Paris: la Découverte, 2013.

Craig, Campbell. "The Resurgent Idea of World Government." In *The Politics of Global Governance: International Organizations in an Interdependent World*, edited by Paul F. Diehl and Brian Frederking, Fourth ed., 397–407. Boulder; London: Lynne Rienner Publishers, 2010.

Creswell, John W. *Qualitative Inquiry and Research Design: Choosing among Five Approaches*. 3rd ed. Los Angeles: SAGE Publications, 2013.

Curran, Charles E., Kenneth R. Himes O.f.M., and Thomas A. Shannon. "Commentary on *Sollicitudo Rei Socialis* (On Social Concern)." In *Modern Catholic Social Teaching: Commentaries & Interpretations*, edited by Kenneth R. Himes O.f.M., Lisa Sowle Cahill, Charles E. Curran, David Hollenbach S.J., and Thomas A. Shannon, 415–35. Washington, DC: Georgetown University Press, 2005.

De Jonghe, Dr. E. "Participation in Historical Perspective." In *Principles of Catholic Social Teaching*, edited by David A. Boileau, 149–63. Marquette Studies in Theology 14. Milwaukee: Marquette University Press, 1998.

Deck, Allan Figueroa, S.J. "Commentary on *Populorum Progressio* (On the Development of Peoples)." In *Modern Catholic Social Teaching: Commentaries & Interpretations*, edited by Kenneth R. Himes O.f.M., Lisa Sowle Cahill, Charles E. Curran, David Hollenbach S.J., and Thomas A. Shannon, 292–314. Washington, DC: Georgetown University Press, 2005.

Deneulin, Séverine. "Amartya Sen's Capability Approach to Development and *Gaudium et Spes*: On Political Participation and Structural Solidarity." Edited by Cheryl Handel and Kathleen Shields. *Journal of Catholic Social Thought* 3, no. 2 (2006): 355–72. doi:10.5840/jcathsoc20063228.

Dermience, Alice. *La "question féminine" et l'Église catholique: approches biblique, historique et théologique*. Dieux, hommes et religions, no 11. Bruxelles ; Oxford: P. Lang, 2008.

Diehl, Paul F., and Brian Frederking. "Introduction." In *The Politics of Global Governance: International Organizations in an Interdependent World*, edited by Paul F. Diehl and Brian Frederking, Fourth ed., 1–9. Boulder; London: Lynne Rienner Publishers, 2010.

Donahue, John R. *Seek Justice That You May Live: Reflections and Resources on the Bible and Social Justice*. New York: Paulist Press, 2014.

Donahue, John R., S.J. "The Bible and Catholic Social Teaching: Will This Engagement Lead to Marriage?" In *Modern Catholic Social Teaching: Commentaries & Interpretations*, edited by Kenneth R. Himes O.f.M., Lisa Sowle Cahill, Charles E.

Curran, David Hollenbach S.J., and Thomas A. Shannon, 9–40. Washington, DC: Georgetown University Press, 2005.

Donnelly, Elizabeth A. "Making the Case for Jubilee: The Catholic Church and the Poor-Country Debt Movement." *Ethics & International Affairs* 21, no. S1 (November 2007): 189–218. doi:10.1111/j.1747-7093.2007.00090.x.

Dowsett, Rose. "Reconciliation as Reconstruction of a Wounded and Unjust Society." In *Mission as Ministry of Reconciliation*, edited by Robert Schreiter and Knud Jørgensen, 16:100–111. Regnum Edinburgh Centenary. Eugene, OR: Wipf & Stock Publishers, 2013.

Dube, Musa W. "Fifty Years of Bleeding: A Storytelling Feminist Reading of Mark 5:24-43." In *Other Ways of Reading: African Women and the Bible*, edited by Musa W. Dube, 50–60. Global Perspectives on Biblical Scholarship 2. Atlanta/Geneva: Society of Biblical Literature -WCC Publications, 2001.

———. "Introduction." In *Other Ways of Reading: African Women and the Bible*, edited by Musa W. Dube, 1–19. Global Perspectives on Biblical Scholarship 2. Atlanta; Geneva: Society of Biblical Literature -WCC Publications, 2001.

Dube, Musa Wenkosi. "Introduction: 'Little Girl, Get Up!'" In *Talitha Cumi!: Theologies of African Women*, edited by Nyambura J. Njoroge and Musa W. Dube, 3–24. Pietermatritzburg: Cluster Publications, 2001.

Dube Shomanah, Musa W. *Postcolonial Feminist Interpretation of the Bible*. St. Louis, MO: Chalice Press, 2000.

Egan, Anthony, S.J. "Reading in a Revolution: Activist Catholics' Use of Scripture during the Last Decades of Apartheid, 1974–1994." In *The Bible and Catholic Theological Ethics*, edited by Yiu Sing Lúcás Chan, James F. Keenan, and Ronaldo Zacharias, 193–204. Catholic Theological Ethics in the World Church Series. Maryknoll, NY: Orbis Books, 2017.

Ela, Jean-Marc. *Afrique, l'irruption des pauvres: société contre ingérence, pouvoir et argent*. Paris: L'Harmattan, 1994.

———. *Fécondité et migrations africaines: les nouveaux enjeux*. Etudes africaines. Paris: L'Harmattan, 2006.

———. *La plume et la pioche: réflexion sur l'enseignement et la société dans le développement de l'Afrique noire*. Yaoundé: Éditions Clé, 2011.

———. *Le cri de l'homme africain: questions aux chrétiens et aux Églises d'Afrique*. Paris: L'Harmattan, 1980.

———. *My Faith as an African*. Translated by John Pairman Brown and Susan Perry. Maryknoll, NY: London: Orbis Books ; G. Chapman, 1988.

———. *Repenser la théologie africaine: le Dieu qui libère*. Chrétiens en liberté. Questions disputées. Paris: Editions Karthala, 2003.

———. *Travail et entreprise en Afrique: les fondements sociaux de la réussite économique*. Hommes et sociétés. Paris: Karthala, 2006.

Elizondo, Virgilio. "Culture, the Option for the Poor, and Liberation." In *The Option for the Poor in Christian Theology*, edited by Daniel G. Groody, 157–68. Notre Dame, IN: University of Notre Dame Press, 2007.

Elsbernd, Mary, O.S.F. "What Ever Happened to *Octogesima Adveniens*?" *Theological Studies* 56 (1995): 39–60.

Elson, Diane. "Gender Analysis and Economics in the Context of Africa." In *Engendering African Social Sciences*, edited by Ayesha Imam, Amina Mama, and Fatou Sow, 153–89. Codesria Book Series. Dakar, Senegal: Codesria, 1997.

Estor, Marita. "Women's Work Is Never at an End: Paid and Unpaid Labour." In *Women, Work and Poverty*, edited by Elisabeth Schüssler Fiorenza and Anne E. Carr, 3–9. Concilium 194. Edinburgh: T. & T. Clark, 1987.

Evêques de Centrafrique. "La population centrafricaine paie le prix fort, Message des évêques de Centrafrique." *La Documentation Catholique*, no. 2285 (February 2, 2003): 159–60.

———. "Tenir bon face à la crise, Message des évêques de Centrafrique aux fidèles et aux hommes de bonne volonté." *La Documentation Catholique*, no. 2244 (March 18, 2001): 291–92.

Evêques du Congo. "Eglise-Famille et développement, Message des évêques du Congo aux chrétiens et aux hommes de bonne volonté." *La Documentation Catholique*, no. 2121 (August 6, 1995): 761–63.

Evêques du Rwanda. "Résoudre le problème de l' "ethnisme," Message des évêques du Rwanda pour la fin du grand Jubilé et le centenaire de l'évangélisation du pays." *La Documentation Catholique*, no. 2246 (April 15, 2001): 391–96.

Evêques du Sénégal. "Bâtir ensemble un Sénégal de justice et de paix, lettre pastorale." *La Documentation Catholique*, no. 2107 (January 1, 1995): 41–46.

———. "Quel Sénégal pour le troisième millénaire? Lettre pastorale." *La Documentation Catholique*, no. 2247 (May 6, 2001): 431–40.

Evêques du Zaïre. "Le chrétien et le développement de la nation, exhortation pastorale des évêques du Zaïre." *La Documentation Catholique*, no. 1992 (October 15, 1989): 885–913.

Eyben, Rosalind, and Rebecca Napier-Moore. "Choosing Words with Care? Shifting Meanings of Women's Empowerment in International Development." *Third World Quarterly* 30, no. 2 (2009): 285–30. doi:http://dx.doi.org/10.1080/0143659080 2681066.

Fearon, James D. "Bargaining, Enforcement, and International Cooperation." *International Organization* 52, no. 2 (1998): 269–305.

Feldmeier, Reinhard. *Power, Service, Humility: A New Testament Ethic*. Waco, TX: Baylor University Press, 2014.

Field, David N. "On (Re)Centering the Margins: A Euro-African Perspective on the Option for the Poor." In *Opting for the Margins: Postmodernity and Liberation in Christian Theology*, edited by Joerg Rieger, 45–69. Reflection and Theory in the Study of Religion. Oxford ; New York: Oxford University Press, 2003.

Finn, Daniel. "Human Work in Catholic Social Thought." *American Journal of Economics and Sociology* 71, no. 4 (December 2012): 874–85.

———. "John Paul II and the Moral Ecology of Markets." *Theological Studies*, no. 59 (1998): 662–79.

Fischer, Irmtraud. "Gender Issues in Biblical Ethics: On the Reception of Old Testament Texts for a Sexual Ethics in Gender-Democratic Societies." In *The Bible and Catholic Theological Ethics*, edited by Yiu Sing Lúcás Chan, James F. Keenan, and Ronaldo Zacharias, 251–61. Catholic Theological Ethics in the World Church Series. Maryknoll, NY: Orbis Books, 2017.

Fonjong, L., Lawrence Fombe, and Irene Sama-Lang. "The Paradox of Gender Discrimination in Land Ownership and Women's Contribution to Poverty Reduction in Anglophone Cameroon." *GeoJournal* 78, no. 3 (June 2013): 575–89. doi:10.1007/s10708-012-9452-z.

Fonjong, Lotsmart N. "Challenges and Coping Strategies of Women Food Crops Entrepreneurs in Fako Division, Cameroon." *Journal of International Women's Studies* 5, no. 5 (2004): 1–17.

———. "Equal Rights but Unequal Power over Land: Rethinking the Process of Engendering Land Ownership and Management in Cameroon." In *Issues in Women's Land Rights in Cameroon*, edited by Lotsmart N. Fonjong, 19–41. Bamenda: Langaa Research & Publishing CIG, 2012.

———, ed. *Issues in Women's Land Rights in Cameroon*. Mankon, Bamenda: Langaa Research & Publishing CIG, 2012.

Francis. "Meeting with Victims of Sexual Abuse, Address of the Holy Father." Speech presented at the Apostolic Journey to Cuba, to the United States of America and Visit to the United Nations Headquarters (19–28 September 2015), Philadelphia, PA, September 27, 2015. http://w2.vatican.va/content/francesco/en /speeches/2015/september/documents/papa-francesco_20150927_usa-vittime-abu si.html.

———. *On Care of Our Common Home, Encyclical Letter.* Laudato Si. Rome: Libreria Editrice Vaticana, 2015. http://w2.vatican.va/content/francesco/en/enc yclicals/documents/papa-francesco_20150524_enciclica-laudato-si.html.

———. *On Love in the Family, Post-Synodal Apostolic Exhortation* Amoris Laetitia. Rome: Libreria Editrice Vaticana, 2016. https://w2.vatican.va/content/dam/france sco/pdf/apost_exhortations/documents/papa-francesco_esortazione-ap_20160319 _amoris-laetitia_en.pdf.

———. *On the Proclamation of the Gospel in Today's World, Apostolic Exhortation* Evangelii Gaudium. Rome: Libreria Editrice Vaticana, 2013. http://w2.vatican.va /content/francesco/en/apost_exhortations/documents/papa-francesco_esortazione -ap_20131124_evangelii-gaudium.html.

———. "Participation at the Second World Meeting of Popular Movements, Address of the Holy Father." Speech presented at the Apostolic Journey to Ecuador, Bolivia and Paraguay (5–13 July 2015), Santa Cruz de la Sierra (Bolivia), July 9, 2015. http://w2.vatican.va/content/francesco/en/speeches/2015/july/documents/ papa-francesco_20150709_bolivia-movimenti-popolari.html.

Gebara, Yvone. "Option for the Poor as an Option for the Poor Woman." In *Women, Work and Poverty*, edited by Elisabeth Schüssler Fiorenza and Anne E. Carr, 110–17. Concilium 194. Edinburgh: T & T Clark, 1987.

Graham, Elaine. "Gender." Edited by Lisa Isherwood and Dorothea McEwan. *An A to Z of Feminist Theology.* Sheffield: Sheffield Academic Press, 1996.

Green, December. *Gender Violence in Africa: African Women's Responses.* 1st ed. New York: St. Martin's Press, 1999.

Griffin, Brandon J., Caroline R. Lavelock, and Everett L. Worthington, Jr. "On Earth as It Is in Heaven: Healing through Forgiveness." *Journal of Psychology & Theology* 42, no. 3 (2014): 252–59.

Grusec, Joan E., and Paul D. Hastings. "Preface." In *Handbook of Socialization: Theory and Research*, edited by Joan E. Grusec and Paul D. Hastings, second edition, xi–xiii. New York/London: The Guilford Press, 2015.

Gudorf, Christine E. "Commentary on *Octogesima Adveniens* (A Call to Action on the Eightieth Anniversary of *Rerum Novarum*)." In *Modern Catholic Social Teaching: Commentaries and Interpretations*, edited by Kenneth R. Himes O.f.M., Lisa Sowle Cahill, Charles E. Curran, David Hollenbach S.J., and Thomas A. Shannon, 315–32. Washington, DC: Georgetown University Press, 2005.

―――. "Encountering the Other: The Modern Papacy on Women." In *Feminist Ethics and the Catholic Moral Tradition*, edited by Charles E. Curran, Margaret A. Farley, and Richard A. McCormick, 66–89. Readings in Moral Theology, No.9. New York/Mahwah, NJ: Paulist Press, 1996.

―――. "Western Religion and the Patriarchal Family." In *Feminist Ethics and the Catholic Moral Tradition*, edited by Charles E. Curran, Margaret A. Farley, and Richard A. McCormick, 251–77. Readings in Moral Theology, No.9. New York/Mahwah, NJ: Paulist Press, 1996.

Gutiérrez, Gustavo. *A Theology of Liberation: History, Politics, and Salvation.* Maryknoll, N.Y: Orbis Books, 1988.

―――. "Memory and Prophecy." In *The Option for the Poor in Christian Theology*, edited by Daniel G. Groody, 17–38. Notre Dame, IN: University of Notre Dame Press, 2007.

Hanson, Paul D. "Divine Power in Powerlessness: The Servant of the Lord in Second Isaiah." In *Power, Powerlessness, and the Divine: New Inquiries in Bible and Theology*, edited by Cynthia L. Rigby, 179–98. Studies in Theological Education. Atlanta, GA: Scholars Press, 1997.

Henriot, Peter J., Edward P. DeBerri, and Michael J. Schultheis. *Catholic Social Teaching: Our Best Kept Secret.* Centenary ed. Maryknoll, NY; Washington, DC: Orbis Books ; Center of Concern, 1992.

Hilkert, Mary Catherine. "The Poor in the Context of Globalization: A Feminist Vision." In *The Option for the Poor in Christian Theology*, edited by Daniel G. Groody, 228–35. Notre Dame, IN: University of Notre Dame Press, 2007.

Himes, Kenneth R., O.f.M. "Commentary on *Justitia in Mundo* (Justice in the World)." In *Modern Catholic Social Teaching: Commentaries & Interpretations*, edited by Kenneth R. Himes O.f.M., Lisa Sowle Cahill, Charles E. Curran, David Hollenbach S.J., and Thomas A. Shannon, 333–62. Washington, DC: Georgetown University Press, 2005.

Hinga, Teresia. "Africa's Transformative Responses to the Gender Global HIV and AIDS Syndemic." In *HIV & AIDS in Africa: Christian Reflection, Public Health, Social Transformation*, edited by Jacquineau Azetsop, 226–39. Maryknoll, NY: Orbis Books, 2016.

Hinga, Teresia M. "The Dialogical Imperative: Listening to Concerned and Engaged African Women." In *Prophetic Witness: Catholic Women's Strategies for*

Reform, edited by Colleen M. Griffith, 83–96. The Boston College Church in the 21st Century. New York: A Herder & Herder Book, The Crossroad Publishing Company, 2009.

Hinze, Christine Firer. "Bridge Discourse on Wage Justice: Roman Catholic and Feminist Perspectives on the Family Living Wage." In *Feminist Ethics and the Catholic Moral Tradition*, edited by Charles E. Curran, Margaret A. Farley, and Richard A. McCormick, 511–40. Readings in Moral Theology 9. New York/Mahwah, NJ: Paulist Press, 1996.

———. *Glass Ceilings and Dirt Floors: Women, Work, and the Global Economy.* 2014 Madeleva Lecture in Spirituality. New York: Paulist Press, 2015.

———. "Women, Families, and the Legacy of *Laborem Exercens*: An Unfinished Agenda." *Journal of Catholic Social Thought* 6, no. 1 (2009): 63–92.

"History of Mbonweh Women's Development Association." Global Hand, 2010. https://www.globalhand.org/system/assets/94d5f3555cdc68192284d241101f8 f6f89976332/original/History_to_Croosroads.pdf.

Hittinger, Russel F. "Toward an Adequate Anthropology: Social Aspects of Imago Dei in Catholic Theology." In *Imago Dei: Human Dignity in Ecumenical Perspective*, edited by Thomas Albert Howard, 39–78. Washington, DC: Catholic University of America Press, 2013. www.jstor-org/stable/j.ctt3fgphw.1.

Hollenbach, David. *The Common Good and Christian Ethics*. New Studies in Christian Ethics 22. Cambridge; New York: Cambridge University Press, 2002.

———. "The Common Good as Participation in Community: A Theological/Ethical Reflection on Some Empirical Issues," 1–33. University of Southern California: Center for Advanced Catholic Studies, 2014.

Horsley, Richard A. *Jesus and the Powers: Conflict, Covenant, and the Hope of the Poor*. Minneapolis, MN: Fortress Press, 2011.

Imam, Ayesha M. "Engendering African Social Sciences: An Introductory Essay." In *Engendering African Social Sciences*, edited by Ayesha M. Imam, Amina Mama, and Fatou Sow, 1–30. Codesria Book Series. Dakar, Senegal: Codesria, 1997.

Imam, Ayesha, Amina Mama, Fatou Sow, and Codesria, eds. *Engendering African Social Sciences*. Codesria Book Series. Dakar, Senegal: Codesria, 1997.

IMBISA. "Justice et paix en Afrique australe, lettre pastorale." *La Documentation Catholique*, no. 1980 (March 19, 1989): 298–307.

Ingeborg, Gabriel. "Where Difference Matters: Social Ethics in the Contemporary World." *Journal of Ecumenical Studies* 48, no. 97–106 (Winter 2013): 97–106.

Institut National de Statistique du Cameroun. *Annuaire statistique du Cameroun 2014*. Yaoundé: Institut National de Statistique, 2016. http://www.stat.cm/downloads/2016/annuaire2016/.

———. *Annuaire statistique du Cameroun: recueil de séries d'informations statistiques sur les activités économiques, sociales, politiques et culturelles du pays jusqu'en 2013*. Yaoundé, Cameroon: Institut National de Statistique, 2013. http://www.stat.cm/downloads/annuaire/2013/Annuaire_statistique_2013.pdf.

———. *Annuaire statistique du Cameroun, recueil des séries d'informations statistiques sur les activités économiques, sociales, politiques et culturelles du pays*

jusqu'en 2010. Cameroon: Institut National de Statistique, 2012. http://www.stat
.cm/downloads/annuaire/2012/Annuaire-2012-complet.pdf.

———. *Quatrième enquête camerounaise auprès des ménages (ECAM 4): Tendances, profil et déterminants de la pauvreté au Cameroun entre 2001–2014*. Yaoundé: Institut National de Statistique, 2015. http://www.stat.cm/downloads/2016/Rappor t_tendances_profil_determiants_pauvrete_2001_2014.pdf.

International Labor Office, ed. *Global Employment Trends for Women: [2012]*. Geneva: ILO, 2012.

International Labour Office. *Women at Work: Trends 2016*. Geneva: ILO, 2016.

John Paul II. "Homily of the Holy Father 'Day of Pardon.'" Homily presented at the Ash Wednesday Mass, Rome, March 12, 2000. http://w2.vatican.va/content/john-p aul-ii/en/homilies/2000/documents/hf_jp-ii_hom_20000312_pardon.html.

———. "Letter to Women." *Libreria Editrice Vaticana*, June 29, 1995. https://w2 .vatican.va/content/john-paul-ii/en/letters/1995/documents/hf_jp-ii_let_29061995 _women.html.

———. *On Human Work, Encyclical Laborem Exercens*. Rome: Libreria Editrice Vaticana, 1981. http://w2.vatican.va/content/john-paul-ii/en/encyclicals/document s/hf_jp-ii_enc_14091981_laborem-exercens.html.

———. *On Reconciliation and Penance in the Mission of the Church Today, Post-Synodal Apostolic Exhortation Reconciliatio et Paenitentia*. Rome: Libreria Editrice Vaticana, 1984. http://w2.vatican.va/content/john-paul-ii/en/apost_exho rtations/documents/hf_jp-ii_exh_02121984_reconciliatio-et-paenitentia.html.

———. *On the Church in Africa and Its Evangelizing Mission, Post-Synodal Apostolic Exhortation Ecclesia in Africa*. Yaoundé, Cameroon: Libreria Editrice Vaticana, 1995. http://www.vatican.va/holy_father/john_paul_ii/apost_exhorta tions/documents/hf_jp-ii_exh_14091995_ecclesia-in-africa_en.html.

———. *On the Dignity and Vocation of Women on the Occasion of the Marian Year, Apostolic Letter Mulieris Dignitatem*. Rome: Libreria Editrice Vaticana, 1988. http://www.vatican.va/holy_father/john_paul_ii/apost_letters/documents/hf_jp-ii_ apl_15081988_mulieris-dignitatem_en.html.

———. *On the Hundreth Anniversary of Rerum Novarum, Encyclical Centesimus Annus*. Rome: Libreria Editrice Vaticana, 1991. http://w2.vatican.va/content/john -paul-ii/en/encyclicals/documents/hf_jp-ii_enc_01051991_centesimus-annus.html.

———. *On the Role of the Christian Family in the Modern World, Apostolic Exhortation Familiaris Consortio*. Rome: Libreria Editrice Vaticana, 1981. http:// www.vatican.va/holy_father/john_paul_ii/apost_exhortations/documents/hf_jp-ii_ exh_19811122_familiaris-consortio_en.html.

———. *The Social Concern of the Church, Encyclical Sollicitudo Rei Socialis*. Rome: Libreria Editrice Vaticana, 1987. http://w2.vatican.va/content/john-paul -ii/en/encyclicals/documents/hf_jp-ii_enc_30121987_sollicitudo-rei-socialis.html.

John XXIII. *On Christianity and Social Progress, Encyclical Mater et Magistra*. Rome: Libreria Editrice Vaticana, 1961. http://w2.vatican.va/content/john-xxiii/en /encyclicals/documents/hf_j-xxiii_enc_15051961_mater.html.

———. *On Establishing Universal Peace in Truth, Justice, Charity, and Liberty, Encyclical Pacem in Terris*. Rome: Libreria Editrice Vaticana, 1963. http://w2.

vatican.va/content/john-xxiii/en/encyclicals/documents/hf_j-xxiii_enc_11041963
_pacem.html.

Johnson, Elizabeth A. *She Who Is: The Mystery of God in Feminist Theological Discourse*. 10th anniversary ed. New York: Crossroad, 2002.

Jounel, Pierre, and Jean Evenou. *La célébration des sacrements*. Paris: Mame-Desclée, 2006.

Kabeer, Naila. "Between Affiliation and Autonomy: Navigating Pathways of Women's Empowerment and Gender Justice in Rural Bangladesh." *Development and Change* 42, no. 2 (2011): 499–528.

———. "Gender Equality and Women's Empowerment: A Critical Analysis of the Third Millenium Development Goal." *Gender and Development*, Millenium Development Goals, 13, no. 1 (March 2005): 13–24.

———. "Resources, Agency, Achievements: Reflections on the Measurement of Women's Empowerment." *Institute of Social Studies* 30 (1999): 435–64.

Kah, Henry Kam. "Husbands in Wives' Shoes: Changing Social Roles in Child Care among Cameroon's Urban Residents." *Africa Development* XXXVII, no. 3 (2012): 101–14.

Kanyoro, R.A. Musimbi. "Engendered Communal Theology: African Women's Contribution to Theology in the 21st Century." In *Talitha Cum! Theologies of African Women*, edited by Nyambura J. Njoroge and Musa W. Dube, 158–80. Pietermaritzburg: Cluster Publications, 2001.

Kasper, Walter. "The Position of Woman as a Problem of Theological Anthropology." In *The Church and Women: A Compendium*, edited by Helmut Moll, 51–64. San Francisco: Ignatius Press, 1988.

Kaulemu, David. "Building Solidarity for Social Transformation through the Church's Social Teaching." In *Catholic Social Teaching in Global Perspective*, edited by Daniel McDonald, 36–80. Gregorian University Studies in Catholic Social Teaching. Maryknoll, NY: Orbis Books, 2010.

———. "Catholic Social Teaching at a Crossroad." In *Theological Ethics Past, Present, and Future: The Trento Conference*, edited by James F. Keenan, 176–84. Catholic Theological Ethics in the World Church Series. Maryknoll, NY: Orbis Books, 2011.

———. "The African Synod for Those of Us Who Stayed at Home." In *Reconciliation, Justice, and Peace: The Second African Synod*, edited by Agbonkhianmeghe E. Orobator, 143–54. Maryknoll, NY: Orbis Books, 2011.

Keller, Catherine. "Power Lines." In *Power, Powerlessness, and the Divine: New Inquiries in Bible and Theology*, edited by Cynthia L. Rigby, 57–77. Studies in Theological Education. Atlanta, GA: Scholars Press, 1997.

Kiboko, Kabamba. "Sharing Power: An Autobiographical View." In *Talitha Cum! Theologies of African Women*, edited by Nyambura J. Njoroge and Musa W. Dube, 207–21. Cluster Publications, 2001.

King, Martin Luther. *The Autobiography of Martin Luther King, Jr.* Edited by Clayborne Carson. New York; Boston, MA: Intellectual Properties Management in association with Warner Books, 1998.

Komon, Jean-Paul. "La civilisation matérielle des relations sociales: Genre, organisations paysannes et sociétés rurales." In *La biographie sociale du sexe: Genre, société et politique au Cameroun*, edited by Luc Sindjoun, 197–229. La bibliothèque du Codesria. Dakar; Paris: Codesria; Karthala, 2000.

Lamoureux, Patricia A. "Commentary on *Laborem Exercens* (on Human Work)." In *Modern Catholic Social Teaching, Commentaries & Interpretations*, edited by Kenneth R. Himes O.f.M., Lisa Sowle Cahill, Charles E. Curran, David Hollenbach S.J., and Thomas A. Shannon, 389–414. Washington, DC: Georgetown University Press, 2005.

Lastarria-Cornhiel, Susana. "Impact of Privatization on Gender and Property Rights in Africa." *World Development* 25, no. 8 (April 1997): 1317–33.

Lau, Ephrem Else. "Women Religious and Lay Women as Workers in the Church." In *Women, Work and Poverty*, edited by Elisabeth Schüssler Fiorenza and Anne Carr, translated by Margaret Kohl, 79–84. Concilium 194. Edinburgh: T. & T. Clark, 1987.

Lykke, Nina. *Feminist Studies: A Guide to Intersectional Theory, Methodology and Writing*. Routledge Advances in Feminist Studies and Intersectionality 1. New York: Routledge, 2010.

Magesa, Laurenti. *African Religion: The Moral Traditions of Abundant Life*. Maryknoll, NY: Orbis Books, 1997.

Malcolm, Lois, and Janet Ramsey. "On Forgiveness and Healing: Narrative Therapy and the Gospel Story." *World & World* 30, no. 1 (2010): 23–32.

Maritain, Jacques. *Man and the State*. Chicago, IL: The University of Chicago Press, 1951.

———. *The Person and the Common Good*. Translated by John J. Fitzgerald. New York: Charles Scribner's Sons, 1947.

Massaro, Thomas. *Living Justice: Catholic Social Teaching in Action*. Third Classroom Edition. Lanham, MD: Rowman & Littlefield, 2015.

Mayoux, Linda. "Tackling the Down Side: Social Capital, Women's Empowerment and Micro-Finance in Cameroon." *Development and Change* 32, no. 3 (2001): 435–64.

Mbembé, Achille. *On the Postcolony*. Studies on the History of Society and Culture 41. Berkeley: University of California Press, 2001.

McCrudden, Christopher. "Human Dignity and Judicial Interpretation of Human Rights." *European Journal of International Law* 19, no. 4 (September 1, 2008): 655–724. doi:10.1093/ejil/chn043.

———, ed. *Understanding Human Dignity*. First edition. Proceedings of the British Academy 192. Oxford: Published for the British Academy by Oxford University Press, 2013.

McDonald, Daniel, ed. *Catholic Social Teaching in Global Perspective*. Gregorian University Studies in Catholic Social Teaching. Maryknoll, NY: Orbis Books, 2010.

Menthong, Hélène-Laure. "Les cadres masculins de l'expérience féminine: les représentations collectives des garçons sur les filles et leurs trajectoires scolaires." In *La biographie sociale du sexe: Genre, société et politique au Cameroun*, edited by Luc Sindjoun, 79–153. La bibliothèque du Codesria. Paris; Dakar: Karthala; CODESRIA, 2000.

Mhone, Guy. "Gender Bias in Economics and the Search for a Gender-Sensitive Approach." In *Engendering African Social Sciences*, edited by Ayesha Imam, Amina Mama, and Fatou Sow, 117–52. Dakar, Senegal: Codesria, 1997.

Ministère de la Promotion de la Femme et de la Famille. "Femmes et Hommes au Cameroun en 2012: une analyse situationelle de progrès en matière de genre." Yaoundé, Cameroon, March 2012. http://www.statistics-cameroon.org/downloads/ JIF/MINPROFF_Femmes_Hommes_Cameroun_28_02_2012.pdf.

Mveng, Engelbert. "African Liberation Theology." In *Theologies of the Third World: Convergences and Divergences*, edited by Leonardo Boff and Virgil Elizondo, translated by Barrie Mackay, 17–34. Concilium 199. Edinburgh: T. & T. Clark, 1988.

———. *L'Afrique dans l'Eglise: paroles d'un croyant*. Paris: L'Harmattan, 1985.

Mveng, Engelbert, and B. L. Lipawing. *Théologie, libération et cultures africaines: dialogue sur l'anthropologie négro-africaine*. Essai. Yaoundé [Cameroun] : Paris: C.L.E. ; Présence africaine, 1996.

Nallari, Raj, and Breda Griffith. *Gender and Macroeconomic Policy*. Washington, DC: World Bank, 2011.

Nana-Fabu, Stella. "An Analysis of the Economic Status of Women in Cameroon." *Journal of International Women's Studies* 8, no. 1 (November 2006): 153–67.

Nanche, Billa Robert. "Gender Difference and Poverty in the City of Douala." *Journal of International Women's Studies* 15, no. 2 (July 2014): 227–40.

Nasimiyu-Wasike, A. "The Missing Voices of Women." In *Catholic Theological Ethics Past, Present and Future: The Trento Conference*, edited by James F. Keenan, 107–15. Maryknoll, NY: Orbis Books, 2011.

National Assembly of Cameroon. Relating to Co-operative Societies and Common Initiative Groups, Law N. 92/006 § (1992). http://www.ilo.org/images/empent/st atic/coop/policy/pdf/camero.pdf.

Ngassa, Vera N. "Exploring Women's Rights within the Cameroonian Legal System: Where Do Customary Practices of Bride-Price Fit In?" In *Issues in Women's Land Rights in Cameroon*, edited by Lotsmart N. Fonjong, 65–86. Bamenda: Langaa Research & Publishing CIG, 2012.

———. "Women's Inheritance Rights in the North West and South West Regions of Cameroon." In *Issues in Women's Land Rights in Cameroon*, edited by Lotsmart N. Fonjong, 43–64. Bamenda: Langaa Research & Publishing CIG, 2012.

Ngome, Ivo, and Dick Foeken. "'My Garden Is a Great Help': Gender and Urban Gardening in Buea, Cameroon." *GeoJournal* 77, no. 1 (February 2012): 103–18. doi:10.1007/s10708-010-9389-z.

Nickoloff, James B., ed. *Gustavo Gutierrez: Essential Writings*. The Making of Modern Theology, Nineteenth and Twentieth-Century Texts 8. Minneapolis, MN: Fortress Press, 1996.

Njoh, Ambe J. "Gender-Biased Transportation Planning in Sub-Saharan Africa with Special Reference to Cameroon." *Journal of Asian and African Studies* 34, no. 2 (May 1999): 216.

Njoku, Uzochukwu Jude. *Examining the Foundations of Solidarity in the Social Encyclicals of John Paul II*. European University Studies. Series XXIII, Theology, v. 819. Frankfurt am Main ; New York: Peter Lang, 2006.

Njoroge, Nyambura J., and Musa W. Dube Shomanah, eds. *Talitha Cum!: Theologies of African Women*. Pietermaritzburg: Cluster Publications, 2001.

N'sangou, Arouna. "La contribution des buy'em sell'em au développement." In *Femmes du Cameroun: Mères pacifiques, femmes rebelles*, edited by Jean-Claude Barbier, 385–92. Bondy [France] : Paris: Orstom ; Karthala, 1985.

Nussbaum, Martha C. *Women and Human Development: The Capabilities Approach*. 13th print. The John Robert Seeley Lectures 3. Cambridge: Cambridge University of Press, 2008.

Nussbaum, Martha Craven. *Creating Capabilities: The Human Development Approach*. Cambridge, MA: Belknap Press of Harvard University Press, 2011.

O'Brien, John. *Theology and the Option for the Poor*. Theology and Life Series, v. 22. Collegeville, MN: Liturgical Press, 1992.

Odozor, Paulinus I., C.S.Sp. "Theology at the Service of the Church and Human Development." In *Committed in Solidarity: Sist Silver Jubilee Acts*, edited by Gabriel Mendy, 95–118. Enugu, Nigeria: Kingsley Publishers, 2015.

———. "Truly Africa, and Wealthy! What Africa Can Learn from Catholic Social Teaching about Sustainable Economic Prosperity." In *The True Wealth of Nations: Catholic Social Thought and Economic Life*, edited by Daniel K. Finn, 267–87. Oxford ; New York: Oxford University Press, 2010.

Oduyoye, Mercy Amba. *Beads and Strands: Reflections of an African Woman on Christianity in Africa*. Theology in Africa Series. Maryknoll, NY: Orbis Books, 2004.

———. "Christian Feminism and African Culture: The 'Hearth' of the Matter." In *The Future of Liberation Theology: Essays in Honor of Gustavo Gutiérrez*, edited by Marc H. Ellis and Otto Maduro, 441–49. Maryknoll, NY: Orbis Books, 1989.

———. *Daughters of Anowa: African Women and Patriarchy*. Maryknoll, NY: Orbis Books, 1995.

———. *Hearing and Knowing, Theological Reflections on Christianity in Africa*. Eugene, Oregon: Wipf & Stock Publishers, 2009.

———. *Introducing African Women's Theology*. Introductions in Feminist Theology 6. Cleveland, OH: Pilgrim Press, 2001.

———. "Jesus Christ." In *Hope Abundant, Third World and Indigenous Women's Theology*, edited by Kwok Pui-lan, 167–85. Maryknoll, NY: Orbis Books, 2010.

———. "Spirituality of Resistance and Reconstruction." In *Women Resisting Violence: Spirituality for Life*, edited by Mary John Mananzan, Mercy Amba Oduyoye, Elsa Tamez, J. Shannon Clarkson, Mary C. Grey, and Letty M. Russel, 161–71. Maryknoll, NY: Orbis Books, 1996.

———. "Transforming Power: Paradigms from the Novels of Buchi Emecheta." In *Talitha Cum!: Theologies of African Women*, edited by Nyambura J. Njoroge and Musa W. Dube, 222–43. Pietermatritzburg, South Africa: Cluster Publications, 2001.

Oduyoye, Mercy Amba, and Rachel Angogo Kanyoro, eds. *The Will to Arise: Women, Tradition, and the Church in Africa*. Maryknoll: Orbis Books, 1992.

O'Keefe, Mark. *What Are They Saying about Social Sin?* New York: Paulist Press, 1990.

Orobator, Agbonkhianmeghe E. "*Caritas in Veritate* and Africa's Burden of (under) Development." *Theological Studies* 71 (2010): 320–34.

O'Toole, Laura L., Jessica R. Schiffman, and Margie L. Kiter Edwards. "Preface: Conceptualizing Gender Violence." In *Gender Violence: Interdisciplinary Perspectives*, edited by Laura L. O'Toole, Jessica R. Schiffman, and Margie L. Kiter Edwards, second edition., xi–xiv. New York/London: New York University Press, 2007.

Park, Andrew Sung. *Triune Atonement: Christ's Healing for Sinners, Victims, and the Whole Creation*. 1st ed. Louisville, KY: Westminster John Knox Press, 2009.

Paul VI. *On the Development of Peoples, Encyclical* Populorum Progressio. Rome: Libreria Editrice Vaticana, 1967. http://w2.vatican.va/content/paul-vi/en/encyc licals/documents/hf_p-vi_enc_26031967_populorum.html.

———. *On the Occasion of the Eightieth Anniversary of the Encyclical "Rerum Novarum" Apostolic Letter* Octogesima Adveniens. Libreria Editrice Vaticana, 1971. http://w2.vatican.va/content/paul-vi/en/apost_letters/documents/hf_p-vi_apl _19710514_octogesima-adveniens.html.

Pearse, Rebecca, and Raewyn Connell. "Gender Norms and the Economy: Insights from Social Research." *Feminist Economics* 22, no. 1 (January 2, 2016): 30–53. doi :10.1080/13545701.2015.1078485.

Perkins, Pheme. "The Gospel of Mark: Introduction, Commentary, and Reflections." In *The New Interpreter's Bible: General Articles & Introduction, Commentary & Reflections for Each Book of the Bible Including the Apocryphal/Deuterocanonical Books*, VIII:507–733. Nashville: Abingdon Press, 1997.

Pianigiani, Gaia. "Italy's 'fertility Day' Call to Make Babies Arouses Anger, Not Ardor." *The New York Times*, September 13, 2016, online edition, sec. top stories.

"Pope Expresses 'sorrows' for Abuse at Residential Schools." *Cbcnews*, April 29, 2009. http://www.cbc.ca/news/world/pope-expresses-sorrow-for-abuse-at-reside ntial-schools-1.778019.

Pope, Stephen J. *The Evolution of Altruism and the Ordering of Love*. Moral Traditions & Moral Arguments Series. Washington, DC: Georgetown University Press, 1994.

Radford Ruether, Rosemary. "*Imago Dei*, Christian Tradition and Feminist Hermeneutics." In *Image of God and Gender Models in Judaeo-Christian Tradition*, edited by Kari Elisabeth Børresen, 258–81. Oslo: Solum Forlag, 1991.

Ramsay, Nancy J. "Intersectionality: A Model for Addressing the Complexity of Oppression and Privilege." *Pastoral Psychology* 63, no. 4 (August 2014): 453–69. doi:10.1007/s11089-013-0570-4.

Rauschenbusch, Walter. *A Theology for the Social Gospel*. Library of Theological Ethics. Louisville, KY: Westminster John Knox Press, 1997.

Reinders, Johannes S. "*Imago Dei* as a Basic Concept in Christian Ethics." In *Holy Scriptures in Judaism, Christianity and Islam: Hermeneutics, Values and Society*, edited by Hendrik M. Vroom and Jerald D. Gort, 12:187–204. Currents of Encounter: Studies on the Contact Between Christianity and Other Religions, Beliefs, and Cultures. Amsterdan-Atlanta, GA: RODOPI, 1997.

Richardson, John T., CM, ed. *Readings in Catholic Social Teaching: Selected Documents of the Universal Church 1891–2011.* Eugene, OR: Wipf & Stock Publishers, 2015.

Richter Reimer, Ivoni. "Acts of the Apostles: Looking Forward and Looking Back." In *Feminist Biblical Interpretation: A Compendium of Critical Commentary on the Books of the Bible and Related Literature,* edited by Luise Schottrof and Marie-Theres Wacker, translated by Lisa E. Dahill, Everett R. Kalin, Nancy Lukens, Linda M. Maloney, Barbara Rumscheidt, Martin Rumscheidt, and Tina Steinter, 680–97. Grand Rapids, MI: William B. Eerdmans Publishing Company, 2012.

Riley, Stephen, and Gerhard Bos. "Human Dignity." *Internet Encyclopedia of Philosophy: A Peer-Reviewed Academic Resource.* Accessed December 13, 2016. http://www.iep.utm.edu/hum-dign/.

Rodriguez, Jenny K., Evangelina Holvino, Joyce K. Fletcher, and Stella M. Nkomo. "The Theory and Praxis of Intersectionality in Work and Organisations: Where Do We Go From Here?" *Gender, Work & Organization* 23, no. 3 (May 2016): 201–22. doi:10.1111/gwao.12131.

Sacks, Jonathan. *The Dignity of Difference, How to Avoid the Clash of Civilizations.* Revised edition. London; New Dehli; New York; Sydney: Bloomsbury, 2014.

Sardón-Filipini, Mabel. "Domestic Service in Latin America." In *Women, Work and Poverty,* edited by Elisabeth Schüssler Fiorenza and Anne E. Carr, 51–55. Concilium 194. Edinburgh: T. & T. Clark, 1987.

Scheffler, Eben. "Reflecting on Jesus' Teaching on Forgiveness from a Positive Psychological Perspective." *HTS Teologiese Studies/Theological Studies* 70, no. 1 (2015): 1–10. doi:10.4102/hts.v70i.2982.

Schiltuis-Stokvis, Annekee. "Women as Workers in the Church Seen from the Ecumenical Point of View." In *Women, Work and Poverty,* edited by Elisabeth Schüssler Fiorenza and Anne Carr, translated by David Smith, 85–90. Concilium 194. Edinburgh, Scotland: T. & T. Clark, 1987.

Schreiter, Robert J. "A Practical Theology of Healing, Forgiveness, and Reconciliation." In *Peacebuilding: Catholic Theology, Ethics, and Praxis,* edited by Robert J. Schreiter, R. Scott Appleby, and Gerard F. Powers, 366–97. Maryknoll, NY: Orbis Books, 2010.

Schüssler Fiorenza, Elisabeth. *In Memory of Her: A Feminist Theological Reconstruction of Christian Origins.* 10th anniversary ed. New York: Crossroad, 1994.

———. "Introduction: Feminist Liberation Theology as Critical Sophialogy." In *The Power of Naming: A Concilium Reader in Feminist Liberation Theology,* edited by Elisabeth Schüssler Fiorenza, xiii–xxxix. Concilium. Maryknoll, NY: London, England: Orbis Books; SCM Press, 1996.

Schweiker, William, and Michael Welker. "A New Paradigm of Theological and Biblical Inquiry." In *Power, Powerlessness, and the Divine: New Inquiries in Bible and Theology,* edited by Cynthia L. Rigby, 3–20. Studies in Theological Education. Atlanta, GA: Scholars Press, 1997.

Sikod, Fondo. "Gender Division of Labour and Women's Decision-Making Power in Rural Households in Cameroon." *Africa Development* XXXII, no. 3 (2007): 58–71.

Sindjoun, Luc, and Mathias Eric Owona Nguini. "Egalité oblige! Sens et puissance dans les politiques de la femme et les régimes de genre." In *La biographie sociale du sexe: genre, société et politique au Cameroun*, edited by Luc Sindjoun, 13–77. La bibliothèque du Codesria. Paris : Dakar: Codesria; Karthala, 2000.

St Thomas Aquinas. *Summa Theologiae IIa-IIae*. Translated by Fathers of the English Dominican Province. Online. Kevin Knight, 2008. http://www.newadvent.org/summa/2.htm.

Standing, Guy. *The Precariat: The New Dangerous Class*. London; New York, NY: Bloomsbury, 2014.

Stiltner, Brian. *Religion and the Common Good: Catholic Contributions to Building Community in a Liberal Society*. Lanham, MD: Rowman & Littlefield, 1999.

Synod of Bishops. "Justice in the World." The Holy See, 1971. http://www.shc.edu/theolibrary/resources/synodjw.htm.

Synode des évêques pour l'Afrique. "Les 57 propositions pour l'Afrique, document du synode des évêques." *La Documentation Catholique*, no. 2434 (November 15, 2009): 1035–55.

Talbott, Rick Franklin. *Jesus, Paul, and Power: Rhetoric, Ritual, and Metaphor in Ancient Mediterranean Christianity*. Eugene, OR: Cascade Books, 2010.

Tamez, Elsa. "Poverty, the Poor, and the Option for the Poor: A Biblical Perspective." In *The Option for the Poor in Christian Theology*, edited by Daniel G. Groody, 41–54. Notre Dame, IN: University of Notre Dame Press, 2007.

Tantoh Farnyu, William, and Emmanuel Yenshu Vubo. "Gender and Rural Economy in the Wimbum Society, Cameroon: Perceptions, Practices and the Land Question." In *Gender Relations in Cameroon: Multidisciplinary Perspectives*, edited by Emmanuel Yenshu Vubo, 77–92. Mankon, Bamenda: Langaa Research & Publishing CIG, 2012.

Tarimo, Aquiline. "Ethnic Identities and the Common Good: Considerations on the Social Drama of Africa." *Revista Portuguesa de Filosofia* 65, no. 1/4 (2009): 577–92.

The Universal Declaration of Human Rights (1948). http://www.un.org/en/documents/udhr/.

Theissen, Gerd. "The Ambivalence of Power in Early Christianity." In *Power, Powerlessness, and the Divine: New Inquiries in Bible and Theology*, edited by Cynthia L. Rigby, 21–36. Studies in Theological Education. Atlanta, GA: Scholars Press, 1997.

United Nations. *Convention on the Eliminations of All Forms of Discrimination against Women (1979)*. http://www.un.org/womenwatch/daw/cedaw/text/econvention.htm.

———. *The World's Women 2015: Trends and Statistics*. New York: United Nations, Department of Economic and Social Affairs, Statistics Division, 2015.

———, ed. *Transforming Economies, Realizing Rights*. Progress of the World's Women 2015–2016. New York: UN Women, 2015.

Uti, Ngozi Frances. "Come, Let Us Talk This Over: On the Condition of Women Religious in the Church." In *Reconciliation, Justice, and Peace: The Second African Synod*, edited by Agbonkhianmeghe E. Orobator, 131–42. Maryknoll, NY: Orbis Books, 2011.

Vatican II Council. *Dogmatic Constitution on the Church Lumen Gentium.* Vatican City, 1964. http://www.vatican.va/archive/hist_councils/ii_vatican_council/do cuments/vat-ii_const_19641121_lumen-gentium_en.html.

———. *On the Church in the Modern World, Pastoral Constitution* Gaudium et Spes, 1965. http://www.vatican.va/archive/hist_councils/ii_vatican_council/do cuments/vat-ii_cons_19651207_gaudium-et-spes_en.html.

Vidaurrazága, Jaime. "Appropriating the Bible as 'Memory of the Poor.'" In *The Bible and Catholic Theological Ethics*, edited by Yiu Sing Lúcás Chan, James F. Keenan, and Ronaldo Zacharias, 183–92. Catholic Theological Ethics in the World Church Series. Maryknoll, NY: Orbis Books, 2017.

Wall, Robert W. "The Acts of the Apostles." In *The New Interpreter's Bible: General Articles & Introduction, Commentary & Reflections for Each Book of the Bible Including the Apocryphal/Deuterocanonical Books*, X:1–367. Nashville: Abingdon Press, 1997.

Walzer, Michael. *Spheres of Justice: A Defense of Pluralism and Equality.* New York: Basic Books, 1983.

Woodman, R. Gordon. "A Survey of Customary Laws in Africa in Search of Lessons for the Future." In *The Future of African Customary Law*, edited by Jeanmarie Fenrich, Paolo Galizzi, and Tracy E. Higgins, 9–30. Cambridge; New York; Cape Town; Madrid; Melbourne: Cambridge University Press, 2011.

Index

access, 36, 100, 193, 226; to basic
infrastructure, 51; to credit, 49, 121,
132, 165, 198; to dignified work,
22; to education, 101, 116, 146; to
equipment and means of production,
49, 195; formal employment,
97; to land, 51, 119, 121, 132; to
money, 131; to paid work, 6, 82,
101–2, 113, 131, 243; to positions of
responsibility, 41, 96; to power, 200;
to public functions, 40; to resources,
21, 195–96; to transportation, 121,
132; to work outside the home, 63,
198
Africa, 1, 3, 19, 31, 47, 50–52, 54,
67–68, 73, 80, 86, 98, 123–24, 133,
135–36, 138–44, 146–47, 149–50,
164, 168–69, 172–74, 199, 208, 216,
224–25, 227, 234n87, 241–42, 244;
Catholic Church in, 2; Central, 124;
the church in, 65, 74n32, 149, 190;
the church of, 69, 149, 214; colonial
and neocolonial, 143, 146; Eastern,
124; North, 14n3; oppression of, 7,
244; postcolonial, 103, 135, 137,
146, 169–70, 187, 244; poverty in,
141; poverty of, 137; precolonial,
154n136; raw materials of, 50;
South, 14n3; Sub-Saharan, 5, 67,

80, 93–94, 97–103, 115, 242; West,
ix, 124; women in, 73, 125, 138,
147, 169; women workers in, 133;
working women in, 1, 6
Africae munus, 50, 52, 227
African, 3, 5, 7, 50–52, 54, 72, 133,
135–37, 139–44, 150, 164, 170,
177–78, 198–99, 216, 219–20,
224–25, 244, 247; African women.
See women; African women
theology, 2; American, 172; bishops,
13–14, 31, 47–50, 52, 68, 71, 80,
241–42; Catholic bishops, 6, 13–14;
Christianity, 61, 144, 190; Christians,
50, 141, 143; Church, 141, 144–45;
communities, 123, 159; context,
2, 31, 82, 135, 146, 150, 170, 187,
202; continent, 187, 216; countries,
6, 14, 47, 52–53, 95, 147, 165, 213;
culture, 67, 138, 148, 150, 154n136,
164, 183n120; economies, 139;
élites, 139; environment, 7, 123;
ethos, 138, 216; folktales, 217;
gendered social ethics. *See* social
ethics; gendered. *See* gendered;
independence, 140; independent
churches, 143; liberation theology.
See liberation theology; nations, 48,
51, 67, 72, 123; people, 7, 136, 199,

informal, 7, 98–99, 103, 112, 115, 117, 119–20, 131–32, 140, 170, 197; justice in, 37, 80; justice, 62; legal status of, 213; low-paying, 112; nonagricultural informal, 112, 117; nonagricultural self, 98; opportunities, 104–5; relationship, 37; and reproductive labor, 63; security, 89; self, 25, 97–98, 176; vulnerable, 99–100, 111–12; wage, 98–99, 146; of women, 125

empower, 9, 148, 160, 171, 197, 203, 224

empowered, 224; women, 124, 203

empowering, 62, 81, 173, 178, 239, 246, 248; downtrodden, 148; goal, 190; myths, 148; people, 20; project, 125; women, 222

empowerment, 4, 6–9, 21, 32, 49, 61, 99, 133, 189–90, 193, 197–99, 201–2, 215, 226, 229, 239, 241, 246–47; achievements, 195–96; agency, 194; cognitive dimensions of, 215, 217, 221; collective, 198, 246; communal approach, 157; as defeat of colonial oppression, 200; definition, 4, 194; of the female worker, 13, 79, 133, 241; goal of, 201; of the individual woman, 198; institutional approach to, 203; and integral human development, 198; liberationist view of, 198; of local actors, 169; of the lowly, 201; policies, 195; as a process, 195; social dimensions of, 193; task of the whole society, 9; women, 137, 171, 190–91, 196–98, 205n54, 224, 240; of workers, 13, 35, 40, 47, 61, 80; of the working woman, 5–6, 8–9, 40, 188–89, 207, 226, 229

engender, 163, 171, 217, 244; cultural hermeneutics, 128

equality, 19–21, 23, 27n23, 35, 41, 52, 68, 70, 137, 173–75; aspiration to, 21; basic human, 61; basic, 20,

79; between husband and wife, 21; between men and women, 40, 65; between sexes, 123; of condition, 20, 70, 193; difference discourse, 48; dignity and. *See* dignity; egalitarian, 20; essential, 21, 40–41; fundamental, 21; gender. *See* gender; human dignity and. *See* human dignity; of men and women, 66, 71; and mutuality, 165; participation and, 36; undifferentiated, 71; of women, 66

ethical, 69, 146, 171, 244; framework, 133; value, 33

ethics, 5, 187; African gendered social. *See* gendered, social ethics; African theological. *See* African; biblical, 149; definition, 5; feminist, 2, 14. *See also* feminist; gendered African social. *See* gender; gendered. *See* gendered; social. *See* social ethics; of women's work, 1

Familiaris consortio, 1, 13, 40, 242

family, 1, 4, 34–35, 40–41, 49, 54–55, 63, 66–69, 71, 75n37, 75n45, 81, 84, 87–88, 100–101, 104, 115, 117, 119, 121, 124–25, 131, 146, 170–71, 210, 218–19; care, 43n42; contributing workers. *See* worker; contribution of women to, 50, 52; family and society, 41; farms, 98; in-law, 55; life, 18, 21, 49, 52, 146; lower-class, 219; related issues, 51; role of women in, 14, 35, 63, 66, 242; sustenance, 98, 208; trees, 216; wage, 34; women and, 89; women working for their, 115, 120; work, 66; working-class, 219

female, 2–5, 8, 13, 18, 41, 62, 79, 95–96, 103, 112–13, 117–19, 121–22, 124, 127, 163n31, 132, 138, 163, 190, 198, 202, 208, 210–11, 213, 218, 222; anthropology, 163; child, 211; disciple, 218; domestic workers,